African Americans in the Post-Emancipation South

The Outsiders' View

Alton Hornsby, Jr.

UNIVERSITY PRESS OF AMERICA,® INC.
Lanham • Boulder • New York • Toronto • Plymouth, UK

Copyright © 2010 by
University Press of America,® Inc.
4501 Forbes Boulevard
Suite 200
Lanham, Maryland 20706
UPA Acquisitions Department (301) 459-3366

Estover Road
Plymouth PL6 7PY
United Kingdom

Library of Congress Control Number: 2010922647
ISBN: 978-0-7618-5105-9 (paperback : alk. paper)
eISBN: 978-0-7618-5106-6

To the memory of Edward F. (Ed) Sweat and Benjamin (Ben) Wall,
historians of the South

Contents

Preface

Historians and other scholars often use first-hand accounts, including oral interviews and written contemporary observations, as sources for their studies of the past. While such sources have their limitations because of the fallibility of memory and the intrusion of exaggerations and embellishments into personal recollections, they remain valuable, especially when used in conjunction with other documents, in helping us to approximate the past. This study uses these types of sources to attain glimpses of African American life in the post-emancipation South.

This study is conducted longitudinally from the 1860s through the New Deal. A broad cross section of foreign travelers as well as northern visitors are used. We have sought to have racial and gender balances. But the outsiders are largely European and Euro-American and almost entirely middle and upper class. The work is constructed in the context of contemporary anthropology, ethnography, psychology and sociology. It is based largely on travel books and articles and essays in periodicals and scholarly journals. In the endnotes, I provide a brief biographical sketch of the authors following their first mention in the text.

The contents allow a reconstruction of African American life and labor in the major aspects of black culture—religion, education, politics, criminal justice, employment and entrepreneurship, social life and status—of the times. Interspersed with the narrative are historical analyses of the events and assessments of the outsiders' views as compared with scholarly treatments of the subjects. The study ends with an epilogue which synthesizes the outsiders' observations and assesses their overall validity for increasing our understandings of the lives of blacks in the post-emancipation South.

Acknowledgments

I am very grateful for invaluable assistance given by several persons in the preparation of this study. They include Ms. Donna Johnson for the French translations and Robert L. Williams for the Spanish translations; the late professor Barnes F. Lathrop of the history department at the University of Texas at Austin and professor Robert A. Divine of that same department.; librarians of the Main Library of the University of Texas at Austin and the Robert W. Woodruff Atlanta University Center Library; professors Cason Hill and Delores Stephens of Morehouse College, who proofread portions of the manuscript; my student assistant Augustus Wood III; Belinda Brown, Nyla Dixon, and Bettye Spicer who typed several drafts of the manuscript; and my family, stalwart supporters throughout.

Introduction

It has been generally assumed, often without adequate verification, that the typical southern white in the post-emancipation era looked upon the African American as a distinct creature, lying somewhere between beast and man, as a creature to be hated and pitied or, most often, to be feared. Assigned general characteristics have included immorality and piousness; laziness and unindustrious; excessive joviality and constant despair; treachery and loyalty; and ignorance and avidity for education.[1]

Many commentators on American race relations have contended that southern whites and southern blacks have seen each other so closely and for so long that their mutual view has been dimmed, leading to the misconceptions and misunderstandings which have darkened, and often bloodied, southern history. Conversely, many have claimed that "outsiders" have a different, less biased picture of the situation. What validity these assertions have, if any, will be more evident after an examination of the impressions which "outsiders" or non-southerners have attained through visiting the South.[2]

Though outsiders can be expected to possess a certain amount of detachment, they too are inevitably open to various influences, from the contemporary historical setting, from prevailing scientific or pseudo-scientific opinions about race, from their own social, economic, and political positions at home, and to the representative or unrepresentative character of the particular persons, places, and reading matter encountered on their travels. The mere fact they are "outsiders," sometimes guests, may limit the candor of the remarks made to them, or render them reluctant to pursue some lines of questioning.[3]

In its greater aspect the present study seeks to enlarge the understanding of the life of southern African Americans by describing and interpreting eyewitness accounts thereof. The endeavor will be to determine whether or not, according to "outsiders'" observations, the material progress of blacks from period to period was as rapid and significant as is sometimes claimed or as retarded as others contend. The findings may also be expected to add to the perception of the African American's role in American culture. The beginning date is 1877, at the formal end of military Reconstruction in the South, and the examination extends to the eve of the Great Depression and The New Deal. The South is construed to include all of the states that were slaveholding in 1860 plus Washington D.C. Non-southerners will generally be taken to mean persons who lived outside the South until they were adults or persons native to the South who became northern residents prior to adulthood and prior to 1877.[4]

The observers who figure in these pages are almost equally divided between natives of the United States and of foreign countries, a great majority of the foreigners being Western Europeans. Attention has been focused on what the outsiders saw and upon what they heard from African Americans. Though, perforce, their views on race relations have been noticed, the primary interest here has been on their general impressions of the group and their accounts of the everyday life of blacks--their labor, education, religion, political affairs, and social activities and attitudes.

In order to make an intelligent evaluation of outside impressions of southern blacks, it is important to bear in mind not only the more significant forces and events which influenced African American life at the time but also the contemporary opinion in the world at large, especially as represented by scientific or pseudo-scientific learning, with respect to the African American's physical and social character.

The lives of southern blacks, as Americans, were affected by national and international events and movements, but, because they were black the effects upon them were quite distinct from the effects upon the general populace. In the period 1877–1900 the newly reunited United States was reaping fully the fruits of an industrial and technical revolution and setting its feet upon the world stage. For African Americans, however, this period was what Professor Rayford Logan and others have called "The Nadir." The Republican Party had abandoned them to the "benevolent" hands of former enslavers and their descendants. Segregation, discrimination, anti-black violence, and economic exploitation were increasing. It is true that Booker T. Washington, in his "Atlanta Compromise" address at the Cotton States International Exposition in 1895 pointed to significant signs of economic and social progress. But others like Henry McNeal Turner and John Hope could see only more lynchings, more exploitation, and discrimination.[5]

Between 1870 and 1900, the black population in the United States almost doubled, while the white population more than doubled. In 1870 nearly four and one-half million of the 4,880,009 African Americans were residents of the late slave states and of Washington, D.C.; in 1900, 7,823,786 of 8,833,994 lived in those places. To observe the southern African American during these decades was tantamount to seeing the African American. In the South the black population was about half the size of the white.[6]

From the time of his famous address at Atlanta in 1895, Booker T. Washington was the most widely hailed African American in the United States. By the early 1900s presidents had called at his door, and by the time he died in 1915 he had dined with presidents and princes. He and his so-called 'Tuskegee Machine" largely determined the African American's response to the issues of the day. In many respects, it was "the Age of Booker T Washington."

The Washington era in black history coincided with the reformist Progressive era in the nation at large. To Washington and his adherents it seemed that the African American shared the social and economic improvements wrought by Progressive reformers and politicians. Several scholars give some credence to this view, while others assert that Progressivism completely ignored the African American. W. E. B. Du Bois and other blacks of his school of thought, probably influenced by the Statesboro, Georgia lynchings, the Atlanta, Georgia and Brownsville, Texas riots, were convinced that the "age of recovery" was not at hand. Booker T. Washington might be at his zenith, but the mass of blacks were still at their nadir.[7]

The "Atlanta Compromise" address, universally hailed by Washington's proponents, and even many critics, as a gem of public oratory, set the stage for the long, often bitter, conflict between the "Tuskegee Machine," or Washington school, and the Du Bois School over black goals and policies in economics, political power, and educational development. The best type of training to implement Washington's policy would be the agricultural and industrial education emphasized at Hampton and Tuskegee Institutes.

W.E.B. Du Bois, who dubbed Washington's address a "Compromise," and the cliques of black intellectuals spread from Harlem to Washington, Nashville, and Atlanta clamored for racial equality in all aspects of American life, and for power at the highest political levels. Because they would need more than farmers and blacksmiths to accomplish their goals, they steadfastly demanded academic-classical training.[8]

The outcome of the debate between these two schools, and the progress, if any, made by African Americans in this period, were to be seen at the South; in 1910, eighty-nine percent of all African Americans remained there, and by 1920, when the effects of the first great wave of black migration to the North were being felt, 85.2 percent of all blacks were still in the region.

The American participation in World War I sets the stage for the last period of this study. More than 200,000 blacks, many of whom were southerners, served in Europe during the First World War. Most were in labor battalions that unloaded ships and sent supplies to the front, but more than 10,000 were in the Ninety-third Infantry Division, largely black, which saw combat duty. The war produced its share of black heroes, recipients of the *Croix de guerre* and Distinguished Service Medals and Crosses, and its share of black wounded and dead.[9]

The spilling of black blood in the pursuit of democracy did not, however, have the favorable results many had anticipated. Even during the war, white soldiers, particularly in France, circulated rumors among Europeans to the effect that blacks were sexual maniacs who endangered the safety of all Caucasian women. At home, African American soldiers from Camp Logan, Texas, were harassed by the Houston police. A full-fledged race riot resulted, seventeen whites were killed, thirteen blacks were hanged, and forty-one blacks sentenced to life imprisonment. At Spartanburg, South Carolina, a probable similar outbreak was prevented only by sending the black troops stationed there to Europe.

Once the war was over, hopes for racial reconciliation based upon military service were severely disappointed. During the first post-war year newspapers North and South reported rumors of plots, revolts, and insurrections by "French-woman ruined" African American veterans. The first great wave of African American migration to the North, which had accompanied the war, helped also to inflame northern white public opinion. The result was "the greatest period of interracial strife the nation had ever witnessed." Most of the violence took place during the summer of 1919, beginning with a racial incident at Longview, Texas, in July. By October, twenty-five cities and towns, North and South, had seen bloodshed, mostly black blood, in what James Weldon Johnson called "The Red Summer."

As the Springfield, Brownsville, and Atlanta riots a decade earlier had led to the formation of the National Association for the Advancement of Colored People, the "Red Summer" sparked the establishment of the South's first successful interracial civil-rights group—the Commission on Interracial Cooperation, organized by prominent southerners at Atlanta in 1919. It set out to still the "deadly menace" of race antagonism, and to assist blacks to improve their economic, political, social, and physical conditions. But whatever progress this and similar groups might make was handicapped by the recession of 1919–1920, and practically wiped out by the Great Depression which began in 1929. The disposition of many blacks to turn, in despair, to Marcus Garvey-type black nationalism and pseudo-religious cults strongly suggests that even the roaring twenties did not roar for them.[10]

The presumptions about blacks which outsiders brought with them to the South were unlikely, as far as they were based upon learned studies of the African American's physical and mental traits prior to World War I, to have advanced much beyond the views of the seventeenth and eighteenth centuries. Anthropologists, ethnologists, and psychologists, writing between 1890 and 1914, generally concluded that physically and mentally the African American was more animal than man.[11]

Among the better known works current in the nineties was *Races and Peoples* (1890) by Daniel G. Brinton, a noted University of Pennsylvania ethnologist. Brinton believed there were distinct racial traits, including different jaws, teeth, skin color, and "special senses." His studies showed the "projection of the maxillaries, or upper and lower jaws, beyond the line of the face" to be "much more observable in the black than in the white race" and "more pronounced in the old than in the young." Such a condition was "considered to correspond to a stronger development of the merely animal instincts." The African's skin color was largely the product of "a congenital disproportion of lungs to liver" which caused the retention of carbonic oxide in the lungs, and hence "an increased tendency to pigmentary deposit of the skin." In a musical sense the "native African" excelled the "native American," though the difference was not greater than that between European nations.[12] Brinton's general conclusion respecting African American and Euro-American was that:

> the adult who retains the more numerous fetal, infantile or simian traits, is unquestionably inferior to him whose development has progressed beyond them, nearer to the ideal form of the species, as revealed by a study of the symmetry of the parts of the body, and their relation to the erect stature. Measured by these criteria, the European or white race stands at the head of the list, the African or Negro at its foot.[13]

Francis Galton, sometimes called the founder of the science of eugenics, "studied the relative capacity of the black and the white races by dividing each race into sixteen defined grades of ability, eight above and eight below its racial average, and considered that the intervals separating the grades were equal throughout. He surveyed eminent men of each race, and concluded that the ablest black ranked two grades below the ablest white". Then, "by an application of the 'Law of deviation from an average' he held that blacks as a race have two degrees of ability less than Europeans." Even though the number of "half-wits" among blacks was very large, the African race was "by no means wholly deficient in men capable of becoming good factors, thriving merchants, and otherwise considerably raised above the average of whites." The social disabilities placed upon blacks in America, Galton admitted, made any comparison of their achievements and those of whites difficult.[14]

In discussing "human faculty as determined by race," anthropologist Franz Boas concluded that there were physical differences between races making it probable that there might be differences in faculty. The face of the African he found larger in proportion to the skull than that of the American Indian or the Caucasian. There was, Boas said, "no denying that this feature - - - represents a type slightly nearer the animal than the European type." Despite this, Boas conceded that there was no evidence that the African and other "lower" races could not attain the level of civilization represented by the bulk of the whites.[15]

Gustave LeBon, another of the early modern psychologists, classified blacks as one of "the primitive and inferior peoples." From measurements of the volume of several thousand skulls, he found differences in the relative size of the brains of races. Though the differences were not very considerable, the "primitive and inferior" races, such as the African, "had a relative incapacity to reason or associate, to compare and draw conclusions. . . . to observe and reflect, to exercise foresight, to persist in a given line of activity, to hold to a distant rather that a present end." Unfortunately these traits "are practically ineradicable and they determine the achievement of races."[16]

Anthropologist N. B. Taylor, basing his conclusions on the testimony of "European teachers," noted that at the age of twelve, children of the "lower races," mainly African, fell behind those of the "ruling race," Caucasian. This confirmed what "anatomy teaches of the less developed brain in the . . . African than in the European."[17]

The famed psychologist, G. Stanley Hall, writing in 1905, asserted that no two races in history differed so much in both physical and psychic traits as the Caucasian and the African. "The color of the skin and the crookedness of the hair" were only the outward signs of many far deeper differences, including cranial and thoracic capacity, glands and secretions, "vita sexualis," food, temperament, character, emotional traits, and disease. In addition, because the black child ceased development at about age twelve, the "virtues and defects of the Negro through life remain largely those of puberty."[18]

One of the few scholars in the early twentieth century to deny significant differences in African and Caucasian brain weights and ape-like qualities to the African was F. P. Hall. In 1909 he stated that the brain weight of "eminent men" was 100 grams above that of the general run of men, and that the average white man has a brain 100 grams heavier than that of the average black. But the frontal lobe as compared with the rest of the brain had the same relative weight in both races, and in both sexes. He found also that the configuration of black and white brains was the same. Thus Hall concluded that "with the present crude methods the statement that the Negro brain approaches the fetal or simian brain more than does the white is entirely unwarranted."[19] Edward L. Thorndike also urged caution in making racial generalizations.

He cited the need for "more actual measurements of race differences, and of intelligence in interpreting them."[20]

In 1913 Joseph Bardin, a little-known psychologist, writing for a larger audience, rejected the cautions of Thorndike and the conclusions of Hall. He agreed that there must be a connection between mental differences and physical differences since both evolved together. It had, he said, become increasingly evident that blacks and whites differed physically; therefore it followed that there were corresponding neural differences, "as marked . . . as are the external physical signs of race, such as skin, hair texture and facial angle." Those attempting to "modify" the African's mind while yet keeping him "a physical Negro" were undertaking the impossible. The African could never measure up to the "ideas and political philosophies" of Caucasians.[21]

In as far as learned estimates of black racial traits were concerned, the post-war era saw the beginning of demonstrations "that the facts of human heredity were not as simple as had been portrayed by some eugenicists and that environmental and cultural factors played a much greater part in man's development than earlier eugenicists were willing to admit."[22]

It is clear, then, that the intelligent observers of the post-World War One period brought with them beliefs or expectations which were being influenced by knowledge quite different from the weight of nineteenth century learning, which had concluded that the African was an inferior being, closer to beast than to man.

NOTES

1. Excellent analyses of southern attitudes toward blacks can be found, among other places, in Gunnar Myrdal, *An American Dilemma: The Negro Problem and Modern Democracy* (2 vols. New York: Harper and Brothers Publishers, 1944). I, 42–50, 50–60, 83–113, 380–397; II, 640–689, 768–781; John Dollard, *Caste and Class in A Southern Town* (3rd ed., New York; Doubleday and Co., 1957), 315–390, *passim*; Frank Tannenbaum, *Darker Phases of the South* (New York: G. P. Putnam's Sons, 1924). 165–167, Floyd Hunter, *Community Power Structures: A Study of Decision Makers* (Chapel Hill: The University of North Carolina Press, 1953), 144–147, 151–159, 221–226; George Fredrickson, *The Black Image in the White Mind* (Middleton, CT: Wesleyan University Press, 1987).

2. This reasoning was partially responsible for the Carnegie Foundation's selection of Gunnar Myrdal, Swedish economist and sociologist, to lead the study which culminated in the publication of *An American Dilemma*.

3. For a good discussion of the question of observer bias see Dollard, *Caste and Class in a Southern Town*, 32–40.

4. The states are Alabama, Arkansas, Delaware, Florida, Georgia, Kentucky, Louisiana, Mississippi, Missouri, North Carolina, South Carolina, Tennessee, Texas and Virginia.

5. See Rayford W. Logan, *The Negro in American Life and Thought: The Nadir, 1877–1901* (New York: The Dial Press, Ind., 1954), ix-x, 11; Charles W. McKinney, Jr. and Rhonda Jones, "Jim Crowed-Emancipation Betrayed: African Americans Confront the Veil," in Alton Hornsby, Jr., ed. *A Companion to African American History* (Malden, MA: Blackwell, 2005, 2008), 271–282. Please also note their extensive bibliography.

6. U.S. Bureau of the Census, Negro Population, 1790–1915 (Washington: Government Printing Office, 1918), 43.

7. For differing views on the relationship between Progressives and African Americans, see Ray Stannard Baker, *Following the Color Line: American Negro Citizenship in the Progressive Era*, New York: Harper and Row, 1908; Jack Temple Kirby, *Darkness at the Dawning; Race and Reform in the Progressive South* (Philadelphia; Lippincott, 1972); C. Vann Woodward, "Progressivism—For Whites Only," in *Origins of the New South, 1877–1913*. Baton Rouge: Louisiana State University Press, 1951. For an excellent synthesis of these views, see Jimmie Franklin," Blacks and the Progressive Movement: Emergence of a New Synthesis." http://www.oah. org/pubs/magazine/progressive/franklin.html

8. See U.S. Bureau of the Census, *Negroes in the United States*, 1920–32 (Washington: Government Printing Office, 1935), 3.

9. For a good general discussion of the role of African Americans in the First World War; See Hayward "Woody" Farrar, "The Black Soldier in Two World Wars," in Alton Hornsby, Jr., ed., *A Companion to African American History*, 349–363. Please also note his extensive bibliography.

10. Tindall, *The Emergence of the New South*, 151–156. See also the reports on Negro migration to the North in U.S. Bureau of the Census, *Negroes in the United States*, 1920–32, p. 3; For "the Red Summer" and lynching, see Philip Dray, *At the Hands of Persons Unknown: The Lynching of Black America*, New York: Random House, 2002; William Trutle, Jr., *Race Riot: Chicago in the Red Summer of 1919*; Jon Voogd, *Race Riots and Resistance: Chicago and the Red Summer of 1919*, New York: Peter Lang, 2008; Robert Whitaker, *On the Laps of Gods: The Red Summer of 1919 and the Struggle for Justice that Remade a Nation*, New York: Crown Publishing Group, 1919.

11. Adequate summaries of learned views prior to 1890 on the African American's physical, mental and social traits can be found, among other places, conveniently in Brinton, *Races and Peoples*, in John C. Greene, *The Death of Adam: Evolution and Its Impact on Western Thought* (New York: Mentor Books, 1961), and in Mark Hughlin Haller, *American Eugenics: Heredity and Social Thought, 1870–1930* (Ann Arbor: University Microfilms, Inc., 1959). For the period 1890 to the First World War see, in addition to Haller, Ferguson, *Archives of Psychology* V. no. 36, Works which bring the subject down to recent times include Oscar Handlin, *Race and Nationality in American Life* (Boston: Little, Brown and Co., 1957), Haller, Eugenics (New Brunswick: Rutgers University Press, 1963, and Thomas F. Gossett, Race: *The History of*

an Idea in America (Dallas: Southern Methodist University Press, 1963: Schocken Paperback, 1966); See also the extensive bibliography in Jeffrey Elton Anderson, "Ethnicity, Nationality, and Race in Colonial America," in Alton Hornsby, Jr., ed., *A Companion to African American History*, 89–104.

12. Daniel G. Brinton, *Races and Peoples: Lectures on the Science of Ethnography* (New York: N.D.C. Hodges, Publisher, 1890), 24–30, 36, 48.

13. Quoted in George Oscar Ferguson, Jr., "The Psychology of the Negro: An Experimental Study," Archives of Psychology, Vol. (1916) , No. 36, p. 8.

14. Francis Galton, "The Comparative Worth of Different Races, "Library of the World's *Best Literature*, ed., Charles Dudley Warner (New York: J. A. Hill and Co., 1896), XV, 6177–6184.

15. Franz Boas, "Human Faculty as Determined by Race, "American Association for the Advancement of Science, Forty-Third Annual Meeting, *Proceedings* (Brooklyn, New York, 1894), 311–327.

16. Gustave LeBon, The *Psychology of Peoples* (2nd ed., New York: G. E. Stechert and Co., 1912), 233–236.

17. Quoted in Ferguson, *Archives of Psychology*, Vol. 36, pp. 4.

18. G. Stanley Hall, "The Negro in Africa and America," *Pedagogical Seminary*, XII (1905), 358–362.

19. F. P. Hall, "Anatomical Characters of the Human Brain," American Journal of Anatomy, IX (1909), 20.

20. Quoted in Ferguson, *Archives of Psychology*, Vol. 36, pp. 8–9.

21. J. Bardin, "The Psychological Factor in Southern Race Problems," *Popular Science Monthly*, LXXXIII (1913), 374.

22. Haller, *American Eugenics*, 6.

Chapter One

Appearances

For many of the persons who visited the South following Reconstruction the very sight of the African was a source of amazement. Except in the very large cities, blacks had been a very small element in the European population. The same was largely true, as the census reports show, for the northern United States until the twentieth century.

Examining African Americans at Norfolk very carefully, Mary Allan-Olney, an Englishwoman found that they were "rarely as black as they were painted." They gave the appearance rather of "having been much burnt by the sun and then rubbed with soot." As a rule, they were "bandy-legged," and walked like parrots with their toes turned in. She was surprised to discover that the palms of their hands and the soles of their feet and their heels were not black at all, but a "dirty colour, somewhat resembling that of a London brick." Feet were flat and "enormously large," with spreading toes. On the other hand the blacks' hands were well shaped and inclined to be small. They constantly grinned and rolled their eyes in a way that made the sensitive lady's "blood curdle." Their skin shone as if polished and their hair was like wool. Many of the black women managed to achieve "fine, statuesque forms and a splendid carriage." Their method was not secret: they went barefoot in summer, never wore "stays," and carried everything on their heads.[1]

The physical appearances of a few Virginia blacks encountered by Arthur Granville Bradley, English author and traveler, was striking though seemingly not representative. One was a man barely five feet, who "had a head upon him the size of a Missouri pumpkin." He wore upon his "dark seamed face a perennial frown." Bradley felt that his "front view was hideous," but "his reverse side was much the funniest in the whole county." Another Virginia black had a "bad stammer, with terrific facial contortions," a condition that Bradley thought rare among the African race. The stammer in this case gave a "quizzical appearance," which added to the black's "round, smooth, beardless," and oily black face made laughter "irresistible" for the onlooker.[2]

Three-fourths of the African-American school children seen in Virginia by William Saunders, an English journalist and politician were more or less white. Indeed, "many are quite fair, and some have red or golden hair, which would prevent them from being regarded as mulattoes in any place where their parentage was unknown."[3]

Beauty was found among the mulattoes and quadroons of Louisiana by the noted traveler George Augustus Sala, on a second visit to the South in 1879–1880. He saw mulattoes and quadroons, very handsome individuals, sitting in the state legislature at New Orleans. He could not say the same for the "full-blooded" Africans.[4]

"Fair complexioned" mulattoes drew the attention also of Sir George Campbell, a Scot, whose *White and Black* became one of the most widely used travel books about the South. After long service in India, this British M. P. visited the United States in 1878 specifically to observe the African American and to compare his condition with that of the Indian.[5] Remaining through part of 1879, he toured Georgia, North Carolina, South Carolina and Virginia. Campbell saw "some extremely fair children—sometimes fairer than the average of white children—among the ebony, woolly-headed Negroes." One mulatto, in particular, "who would have been very fair for a European, was placed among the blacks, many of whom are very black and hideous." These latter blacks led him to reflect that he "hardly knew before what an ugly race some of the blacks are."[6]

The allusion to hideous blacks by Campbell is mild in comparison with the statements of Charles Boissevain, a Dutch journalist. To him the blacks were wild and savage in appearance, no different from their forefathers "on the shores of the Congo."[7]

African American deckworkers on a cargo boat sailing south from St. Louis, men who were black and flat-nosed but proud, presented a picturesque sight that Ernst Von Hesse-Wartegg thought all artists and all philanthropists would understand, however sorrowfully. Hesse-Wartegg, a German privy councilor and consul general, repeatedly in the United States, noted that many of the young mulatto women he saw on a boat trip through the Louisiana sugar district were of a different variety from the black deckworkers. One of them, *eine schwarze Schonheite* (a black beauty) with a scanty corset, fascinated the German. Her name was Calypso, and she spoke only French. She had big, sparkling eyes; a full, half-opened mouth with "an odd, but delightful appearance," and "a certain radiance."[8]

The oily appearance of blacks, which Arthur Bradley had noticed in Virginia, struck another observer near Titusville, Florida. George Barbour, American journalist and railroad official, confidently asserted that the oiliness, and a tendency to be fat, were caused by the eating or drinking of fresh cane syrup, for while he found the syrup "slightly sickish, the bears, hogs and darkeys" loved it.[9]

The contrast between white linen and the color of skin of Africa American waiters struck the eye of the Italian diplomat, Carlo Gardini, whose southern travels, in the 1880's took him to Alabama, Louisiana, Missouri, Tennessee and Virginia. The skin color ran through all gradations "from ebony black to the lightest shade of coffee."[10]

The physical appearance of the average black did not, one gathers, prove attractive to most nineteenth century observers. Among the exceptions was an Edinburgh civil engineer, Archibald Sutter, who traveled as far South as Atlanta in 1881. On a black church outing at Alton, Missouri, he saw nearly white, captivating women, two men whose heels did not "stick out behind" more than the heels of whites, and better figures than among their "white brethren."[11]

Attractive African American women were, however, scarcely the rule in North Carolina, at least among those that A. L. Bassett saw when he returned to his native state in 1881 after having spent much of his life at the North. The southern repatriate was amazed at the thick skulls of the bare headed black women who walked undisturbed in the hot summer sun with their

> woolly hair plaited in about twenty short plaits, rarely more than two or three inches long, or else . . . divided in the same number of pieces and wrapped tightly with cord until the skin is pulled up in visible hillocks of sombre hue. This is done to make the hair grow.[12]

Comparison between physical features of African Americans and American Indians was attempted by only a few outsiders. One of these was Edward Augustus Freeman, the English historian, yet what he had to say was not very enlightening. Such Indians as he saw impressed him as being "less ugly than the Negroes. But then they lacked the grotesque air which often makes the Negroes ugliness less repulsive."[13]

The "absolutely bestial aspect" of some African Americans, especially those who begged in the streets, led a French royalist and author, Gabriel Paul Le Viconte D'Haussonville to adopt the "Darwinian theories and to understand why all acquaintance" between a white woman and a blackman "should be regarded as the final degree of perversity and degradation." D'Haussonville arrived in America in 1882 "completely a Negrophile" and convinced that there was no difference between Negro and Caucasian except color of skin. It took only a short stay at Richmond, however, to change his thinking to the point that he had to overcome a certain physical repugnance in order to accustom himself to the black hands which made his bed and served his bread.[14]

The bestial appearance of the African also struck Iza Duffus Hardy, an Englishwoman who was in Florida, mainly around Orlando, in 1885–1886. She employed an old African American maid with a "good natured black, monkey face and friz of wool", reminding Miss Hardy of "one of those dark shiny bronze statuettes of the typical Negress, come to life." She was, however, "the proprietress of three cottages," and in addition, she and her husband had "three thousand dollars in the bank."[15]

The view of W. E. B. Du Bois,[16] the most brilliant of African-American intellectuals, differed radically, as might be expected, from that of Iza Hardy, D'Haussonville, and most of the other Caucasians. Born at Great Barrington, Massachusetts, Du Bois was reared in a community and in a region where blacks were about as plentiful as sheep among a pack of wolves. His first intimate contacts with fellow blacks came in the fall of 1885, when he journeyed to Nashville to attend Fisk University. He admits that he was thrilled to see so many of his own color. The various shades of the African Americans struck him as extraordinary. As befitted a seventeen-year-old, he was quite attracted to the black girls at Fisk. He had not remembered seeing such beauty among the white girls of the North. One of these blacks was as beautiful as any "human being could possibly have been." It took Du Bois only a short while to discover that the beauty of the black woman at Fisk was not universal. In rural Tennessee, he met a thin, homely girl of twenty, with a "dark brown face and thick, hard hair." Yet he apparently saw no beast-like creatures.[17]

Blacks exhibiting "cheerful," "open" faces and appearing glad to be alive were seen by Leon Paul Blouet ("Max O'Rell") at Jacksonville and Saint Augustine. He had difficulty in distinguishing between them, for to him they, like French gendarmes, all looked alike at a glance. Generally, they had great dark eyes and rolled the whites thereof "in their own droll fashion." They swayed when they walked, with heads thrown back and toes turned out (one remembers that Virginia blacks, according to Mary Allan-Olney, had turned in toes). White teeth, "framed in thick retroussé lips," were constantly displayed. African American voices were musical, "sweet but monorous," "so pleasing compared to the horrible twang of the lower class people in the North." Obviously a romantic, Blouét found blacks so picturesque that he forgot their color and fell to admiring them, especially the "Negresses," who were "good, merry looking creatures with faxoon faces and forms, supple, light, graceful gait and slender waists," often "quite pretty." With the possible exception of Du Bois, no other outside observer saw African Americans in such a favorable light.[18]

That one could not easily generalize concerning African Americans' appearance became clear to the New England writer and philanthropist, Lillie Wyman, who toured the "Black Belt" in 1889–1890 and perhaps also in 1891. She had seen jet blacks, dark browns, mulattoes, and quadroons. Most had full lips and "prominent jaws of the familiar Negro type." Many were so ugly that upon first impression she viewed the whole race unfavorably. But others had fine eyes, well shaped hands, and chins, cheeks, nostrils, and lips that were curvaceous and not "without beauty." Interestingly enough, she thought the only modifications wrought by white blood in many mulattoes and quadroons were the lengthening of the hair and slight "improvements" in features and complexion. On the other hand, some of the "comely quadroons established traits of features and coloring of skin [comparable] to those of the French Canadians."[19]

Nineteenth century ethnology apparently influenced William Chauncy Langdon, a visitor to the South in late 1890 or early 1891. He concluded that the African American was not an undeveloped "Anglo-Saxon" nor "Celt" nor a "Scandinavian" with a black skin. "No ethnic reasoning can be safely based on any such assumption. Rather, the Negro was a wholly distinct race, wherefore the obstacles to his social and political equality were not factious but anthropological."[20]

Wide mouths make big grins, or so it seemed to the Very Reverend Samuel Reynolds Hole, author and Dean of Rochester, who visited the South in 1894. Approaching Washington from Maryland, he saw "little niggers . . . grinning at the doors of their homes who reminded him of the saying about the "man in 'the Midlands'". "They had some thoughts of widening his mouth, but they found that it would be necessary to move his ears, so they gave it up."[21]

Mulattoes continued to attract a great deal of interest among outsiders. Paul Bouget, a French writer who visited Florida and Georgia, in the spring of 1894, saw the typical, black, thick-lipped African Americans, but took more interest in a yellow-faced man, "nearer neighbor of white blood than the Negro's," whose straight hair and "aquiline" nose led Bouget to recall that he was said to be the son of a prominent white man. Bourget had heard that southern whites greeted the idea of race mixture with utter disdain, but now saw clear evidence of this hypocrisy.[22]

A northern theologian and educator, John C. Campbell who spent nearly a quarter of a century among the southern highlanders, tells the story of a small child in one of "the Negroless areas" of the Highlands who saw an African American for the first time. The terrified child dubbed the black "a no-tail bear." Campbell himself is noncommittal, but the child's view was certainly close to that of many post-emancipation outsiders in the South.[23]

With respect to physical appearances, the position of twentieth century observers was to be very different from those of the nineteenth century. Aside from a small, but significant, sign that twentieth century observers were rejecting the bestial theory of the African's physiology, the other important fact to be noted is the dwindling number of outsiders who even bothered to comment on the physical appearances of African Americans. To suppose that this reflected a growing awareness that physical differences between races were of little importance would be extreme optimism. Such a supposition would, indeed, take us even beyond our own times. The more likely explanation is that increased African American migration to the North, and the appearance of more blacks in European capitals, not to mention earlier travel reports, had made African Americans a less novel sight by the early 1900s than they had been in the aftermath of reconstruction.[24]

NOTES

1. Mary Allan-Olney, *The New Virginians* (2 vols., Edinburgh: William Blackwood and Sons, 1880), I, 3–6. Miss Allan-Olney, an English woman of letters, an extremely harsh critic of blacks, settled on a farm near Lynchburg, Va., where she remained for approximately three years. Fletcher M. Green in Thomas D. Clark, ed., *Travels in the New South, a Bibliography* (2 vols., Norman, Oklahoma: The University of Oklahoma Press, 1962), I, 8.

2. Arthur Granville Bradley, *Other Days: Recollections of Rural England and Old Virginia 1860–1880* (London: Constable and Co., Ltd., 1913), title page: Arthur G. Bradley, *Sketches from Old Virginia* (London: MacMillan and Co., Ltd., 1897), 249–250, 253–254. Bradley was the son of a dean of Westminster. Educated at Trinity College, Cambridge, he wrote for MacMillian's and other magazines. His published works include *Life of Wolfe*, 1895, and *Owen Glyndur*, 1901. Especially fond of Virginia, Bradley was there much of the time period between 1860 and 1890 and spent many hours listening to reminiscences, including those of Negroes. *Who's Who*, 1902 (London: A. and C. Black Co., 1902), 188.

3. William Saunders, *Through the Light Contingent*, (2nd ed.; London: Cassell, Petter, and Galpin, 1879), 78–80. Saunders (1823–1895), son of a businessman of Bath, started the Plymouth *Western Morning News* in 1864 and founded the Central News Agency. He was in the U. S. in 1877–1878, his itinerary included Virginia, North Carolina, Louisiana and Georgia. Well known in the politics of his day, he entered Parliament in 1855, and gradually became extremely socialistic in his views. *Dictionary of National Biography* (ed. By Leslie Stephen and Sidney Lee; reissue, 22 vols., London: Smith, Elder and Co., 1908–1909, 2d—5th Supplements, Oxford: University Press, 1912–1949) L. 331.

4. George Augustus Sala. *America Revisited* (New York: I. K. Funk and Co., 1880), 190. Sala (1828–1895), born of slaveholding parentage in the West Indies, "an ardent sympathizer with the South," when he visited the United States in 1863–1864, declared in 1880 "my heart is still in the South." Sala first wrote of his experiences in letters to the London Daily *Telegraph*. Sala, *America Revisited*, 1; Fletcher M. Green in Clark, ed., *Travels in the New South*, I, 102.

5. Campbell first went to India in 1842 and was in and out of the country for some thirty years as a magistrate, district commissioner, and finally lieutenant-governor. He had a reputation for working in the best interest of Indians. Campbell wrote a multi-volume *Ethnology of India* (1864–1865), *Dictionary of National Biography*, Supplement, I, 383–385.

6. George Campbell, *White and Black: The Outcome of a Visit to the United States* (New York: R. Worthington, 1879), 196, 284.

7. Oscar Handlin, ed., *This Was America* (Cambridge, Mass: Harvard University Press), 333–334. Boissevian (1842–1927) came to the United States in 1880 as correspondent of the Amsterdam *Algemman Handelsblad*, which as editor he subsequently made one of the most distinguished liberal journals on the continent of Europe. His survey of economic and social conditions in the United States included Louisiana and other parts of the South. *This War America*, 333.

8. Ernest Von Hesse-Wartegg, *Mississippi-Fahrten Raisebilder aus den amerikenischen Suden* (1879–1880), (Leipzig: Carl Reissner, 1881), 22–23, 256. Quotations are the present author's translations. Hesse-Wartegg (1854–1918), born in Vienna, was an author and world traveler as well as a diplomat. In 1909 he published another book about the United States, *America als neueste Weltmacht dar Industrie*. He spent much of his latter years in London. *Wer ist's*. (Leipzig: H. A. Ludwig Degener, 1908), 559.

9. George M. Barbour, *Florida for Tourists, Invalids, and Settlers* (New York: D. Appleton and Co., 1882), 36. As a special correspondent for the Chicago *Times* Barbour accompanied U.S. Grant's tour through Florida in January, 1880. He was later a commissary officer for the South Florida Railroad and friend and adviser to Seth French, Florida State Commissioner of Immigration. Thomas D. Clark in Clark, ed., *Travels in the New South*. I, 142: Barbour, *Florida for Tourists*, title page.

10. Handlin, ed., *This War America*, 343–348. Gardini, author of the popular *Gli Stati Uniti* (1891), had many contacts with the United States prior to his visit. For a time he was actually American consular agent in Bologna.

11. Archibald Sutter, *American Notes*, 1881 (Edinburgh: Williams Blackwood and Sons, 1882), I, 52–53, At the time of his visit Sutter was an associate member of the Institution of Civil Engineers, London, and Inspector for H. M. Inclosure of Commission.

12. A. L. Bassett, "Going to Housekeeping in North Carolina." *Lippincott's Magazine*. XXVIII (August, 1881), 205–206.

13. Edward A. Freeman, *Some Impressions of the United States* (London: Longman, Green and Co., 1901), 1, 150. Freeman (1823–1892), who became regius professor of modern history at Oxford, published some forty books. He was described as a liberal humanitarian, but especially critical and impatient, and tending to be hasty,

cocksure and dramatic. *Dictionary of National Biography,* Supplement, II, 247–251; G. M. Dutcher and others, eds., *A Guide to Historical Literature* (New York: The MacMillan Co., 1931), 495.

14. Gabriel Paul D'Haussonville, A *Travers, LesEtats-Unis: Notes et Impressions* (Paris: Ancienne Maison Michel Levy Freres, 1883), 152. D'Haussonville (1843–1924), the son of a conservative French deputy and historian, was himself a leader of the Orleanist Party in 1891–1894. His published works include *Socialisme et Charité* 1895), AND *Ombres Francaises et Visions Anglaises* (1914). *Encyclopedia Americana,* 1963, ed., XIII, 761.

15. Iza Duffus Hardy, *Oranges and Alligators: Sketches of South Florida Life* (London: Ward and Downey, 1886), 101–102. Iza Duffus Hardy, novelist, was the only daughter of Sir Thomas Duffus Hardy, deputy keeper of the Record Office, 1861–1878, and editor of medieval documents. Most of her own time was spent traveling and writing under such titles as *A New Othello, Love in Idleness, and A Butterfly. Who's Who,* 1904, 671).

16. W. E. Burghardt Du Bois, Dusk *of Dawn: An Essay Toward an Autobiography of a Race* Concept (New York: Harcourt, Brace and World Co., 1940), 24. William Edward Burghardt Du Bois (1868–1963) reportedly had French and Dutch ancestry, but proudly identified himself with African Americans. He received a Ph.D. from Harvard in 1895, with a dissertation on *The Suppression of the African Slave-Trade to America* (1896). This volume, his work on the Philadelphia Negro (1899), his *Atlanta University Studies* (1897–1911), and his *Black Reconstruction* (1935) were his most scholarly publications. *Souls of Black Folk* (1903) established his reputation as a stylist and crystallized the revolt of Negro intellectuals against the compromises of Booker T. Washington. Du Bois was, among other things, editor of the NAACP organ. *Crisis,* professor of economics and history at Atlanta University, 1897–1910, and head of the sociology at Atlanta, 1932–1944. He was known as a bitter, eloquent radical with an encyclopedic mind. Francis L. Broderick, W. E. B. Du Bois, *Negro Leader In a Time of Crisis* (Stanford, Calif.: Stanford University Press, 1959); Elliott M. Rudwick, W. E. B. Du Bois: *A Study of Minority Group Leadership* (Philadelphia: University of Pennsylvania Press, 1959); W. E. B. Du Bois: *Autobiography* (New York: International Publishers, 1968).

17. W. E. B. Du Bois, "A Negro Schoolmaster in the New South," *Atlantic Monthly,* LXXXIII (January, 1899), 99, 100.

18. Max O'Rell and Jack Allyn, *Jonathan and His Continent, Rambles Through American Society,* trams. Paul Blouét (1848–1903), born at Brittany, was an officer in the Franco-Prussian War. In 1873, he went to England as a newspaper correspondent. He taught at Saint Paul's School and the University of London (1876–1864), but gave up teaching with the success of his first book, *John Bull and His Island* (1883). Blouét lectured in the United States in 1887 and 1890. He spent much of the winter and spring of 1889 in Florida. *Encyclopedia Americana,* 1963 ed., IV, 118.

19. Lillie B. Chace Wyman, "Colored Churches and Schools in the South," *New England Magazine,* III (February, 1891), 788, IV (June, 1891), 526–527. Mrs. Wyman (1847–1929), born at Valley Falls, Rhode Island, and educated in New England private

schools, was for ten years a trustee of the Rhode Island Institution for the Deaf. Her works include *Poverty Grass* (1886), *American Chivalry* (1913), and A *Grand Army Man of Rhode Island* (1925). *Who Was Who* (3 vols., Chicago: A. N. Marquis Co., 1963), I, 1388.

20. William Chauncy Langdon, "The Case of the Negro, "*Political Science Quarterly*, VI (March, 1891), 31. Langdon (1831–1895), born at Burlington, Vermont, a harah critic of blacks, was educated at Transylvania College, Kentucky. After teaching astronomy at Shelby College, Kentucky, 1850–1851, he was an examiner in the United States Patent Office, 1851–1856; a leader in YMCA activities in the 1850's and an Episcopalian theologian, 1858–1895. *Who Was Who—Historical Volume*, 1606–1896 (Chicago: A. N. Marquis, 1963, 302.

21. Samuel Reynolds Hole, *A Little Tour in America* (London: Edward Arnold Publishers, 1895, 277). Dean Hole (1819–1904), a moderate high-churchman educated at Oxford, became very popular as a preacher and speaker. Besides books he wrote several hymns including 'Father, forgive,' which sold nearly 30,000 copies. *Dictionary of National Biography,* Supplement, I, 282–283.

22. Paul Bourget, Outre-*Mer: Impression of America* (London: T. Fisher Unwin, 1895), 387, 396. Paul Charles Joseph Bourget (1825–1935), son of an eminent mathematician, was himself a Catholic conservative who wrote novels, short stories, plays, poetry, criticism, and travel books. His dogmatism has been regarded as disastrous to his creative writing. *Encyclopedia Britannica*, 1965 ed., IV, 24.

23. John C. Campbell, *The Southern Highlander and His Homeland* (New York: The Russell Sage Foundation, 1921), 95.

24. Edward Atkinson, *North American Review*, CLXXXI, 202; Ray Stannard Baker, *Following The Color Line: American Negro Citizenship in the Progressive Era* (reprint: Albert Bushnell Hart, *The Southern South* (New York: D. Appleton and Co., 1910), 111.

Chapter Two

The Opportunity to Earn a Dollar

The economic fortunes of African Americans have been inextricably bound up with both their social ills and their social progress. They also had and continue to have profound consequences for this nation. In the main blacks in the South remained tillers of the soil. By 1877 numbers of them had become self-sufficient farmers owning their property and sometimes employing fellow blacks to work sizeable acreages. The great majority, however, were either tenants, croppers, or wage or day laborers. Often they worked on cotton or other plantations as they had in the ante bellum period.

The prominence of croppers and tenants was largely a new feature of southern agriculture. The end of slavery and the failure of the post-war wage contract system—a failure that Professor Hammond in *The Cotton Industry* attributed to the ignorance of blacks—had produced a mushrooming of tenancy. The tenant was, to put it simply, a semi-independent farmer, generally owning his implements but renting land for which he paid either money, rent or, more often, a portion of the crop. A lower type of tenancy, that of the cropper, was more common among blacks. The cropper can best be described as half tenant, half laborer, in that he owned no implements and substituted labor for rent. How African American agriculturists fared under those new circumstances we learn from our outside observers.[1]

The Sea Islands of South Carolina were inhabited mainly by African Americans who formed "independent and self-supporting rural communities" of great interest to Sir George Campbell and other observers. Cotton cultivation there was characteristically in the hands of independent black farmers. It is likely, though, that many of the blacks that Laura Towne saw busily picking cotton in 1878 were day laborers.

The Island blacks labored under great disadvantages in that long staple cotton and rice had declined and their land was not suitable for short staple cotton. Many of them supplemented their income, Campbell observed, by occasional labor at the ports and in the phosphate industry. They were fortunate in having the assistance of "Northern and other whites who do for them those things which they cannot do for themselves." Northern dealers ginned and bought their cotton, and white storekeepers maintained a "wholesome system of ready-money payment" that was better for the blacks than the crop-lien system under which landlord or merchant advanced supplies and took control of the crop.

In the South generally African American farm hands or wage laborers, particularly those who were on small farms under the immediate supervision of their employers, "worked exceedingly well," Campbell thought. Inept black workers might be found on the larger farms, where supervision was insufficient, but this fact was not a reflection on the African race; under like conditions "most such races would be guilty of the same inefficiency." Farm hands earned about fifty cents a day, "six or eight times the wages of a coolie in India." This wage coupled with cheap food, inexpensive shelter (croppers, and sometimes day laborers, were often provided with homes by landlords), and a climate requiring little for fuel, meant that the African American farm worker was, in truth, "very well off."[2]

A contrary view was presented by Edward Hogan, a northern writer who was in South Carolina, Georgia, North Carolina, and Virginia from 1879–1890, and concluded that the condition of the African American farmhands had not improved radically since slavery. Unlike Campbell, Hogan regarded the wage of fifty cents per day as far from satisfactory. In South Carolina, especially, farm workers faced serious economic difficulties. Cotton cultivation, which Campbell had found suited to the blacks because it was practicable upon a small scale and gave year round employment, Hogan believed to be an unsteady means of livelihood. He saw little progress for blacks as long as they were bound to the cotton field.[3]

African American earnings as sharecroppers were meager, often below subsistence level, in the "Yazooland" of Mississippi and in the Alabama cotton fields, according to Hesse-Wartegg. Most of the blacks he saw were cultivating very small patches of land, and few owned livestock.

On the Louisiana sugar and rice plantations Hesse-Wartegg found the economic condition and morale of African Americans more encouraging. At Governor H. C. Warmoth's "Magnolia, the greatest sugar plantation in Louisiana," the blacks were grouped and counted each morning, as under slavery, and marched onto the fields by the white overseers. Baskets on heads and tools on shoulders, they were gay and vivacious, singing and dancing as they moved to work. All of this deeply impressed Hesse-Wartegg, who commented that "the Negro generally shows in his daily performance a certain, Tournure,' a burlesque elegance, which contrasts sharply with the sullen rude ways of the white plantation workers."[4]

The usual ratio of labor to land on sugar plantations was one black worker to every seven acres. African American men might expect eighteen dollars per month and free living quarters, considerably more than the twelve to sixteen dollars a month generally paid cotton laborers. Black women did the same work for only fifty cents per day. For work at night, or in excess of eight and one-half hours per day, black men were paid fifty cents per hour.

In Plaquemine Parish, Louisiana, Hesse-Wartegg visited a rice plantation whereon the workers were mainly African American women, "black" 'Guinea wives,' with thick lips, stupid faces and bulky figures." They marched onto the fields with thin aprons draping to their knees. Seeds were carried in these aprons or in little baskets and sowed by hand in the furrow. The crop was harvested by blacks of both sexes who cut the stalks with 'rice hooks' and then bundled them. For Hesse-Wartegg the harvesting was, like most other things connected with African Americans, "a picturesque sight."[5]

Charles Beadle, an Englishman who came to the United States in 1887 and traveled all over the country, his stopping places including Charleston and the Louisiana sugar country, also saw blacks working on plantations. His total impression was that, despite some improvement, African Americans were "pretty much as they were in slave-days," except that they were not slaves and the overseers had no whips.[6]

Another observer who agreed that emancipation had not greatly changed the African American's economic position was Henry M. Field of New York, a liberal Presbyterian minister and writer of travel books. Blacks were still bound to the land and to their old enslavers. Their readiness to work under the new conditions disproved the notion of their enemies that "black labor must always be forced labor." On this point he was substantially in accord with Sir George Campbell, who detected serious laziness only among black women.[7]

The wages of "fifty and sixty" cents a day which African Americans generally made throughout this whole period did not impress Samuel J. Barrows, a northern clergyman, as enough to permit the farm laborer to accumulate anything. The tenant fared little better than the farmhand. The average black who worked twenty-five or thirty acres of land paid at least a bale of cotton, worth about fifty dollars, as rent. Some blacks paid "as much as two or two and one-half bales." The annual rent might equal half the value of the land, which could be bought for five to seven dollars an acre. Prices of supplies were a further problem. A black farmer in North Carolina paid eleven cents per pound for sugar which in Pennsylvania could be bought for six and one-half cents. Such profit making helped to convince Barrows that African Americans on the farm were still largely in financial "bondage."[8]

Although the systems of tenancy and sharecropping came about largely as a response to the loss of slave labor, African Americans were less numerous than whites among farm tenants in the South as a whole. The tenant had to possess at least limited means because he was generally expected to own some equipment, and to shoulder some responsibility because he controlled day-to-day cultivation and labor and handled a large share of the financial operations. Most rural blacks could not meet either criterion. George K. Holmes, an agricultural statistician who studied southern tenancy in 1893, concluded that the black tenant had more to overcome than the white one. While both lived on the next crop, the African American's one-or-two mule holding was on a scale so small that "his net product of wealth gives him no more than a poor subsistence." Overall, the tenant system did not, Holmes decided, compare favorably with the previous slave system. African Americans had been better housed and fed as bondspersons, and were now "almost as helpless as a child." For money to pay their taxes, buy their mules, feed their family, and even bury a wife and children, blacks depended upon the merchant who held the lien on their crop.

The financial woes of African Americans were attributable, in Holmes' opinion, to their own improvidence and laziness, as well as to the defects in the tenant system. The high prices they paid for supplies resulted partly from their untrustworthiness; not infrequently, after a living had been advanced to them, they were missing at cotton-picking time, or carried off cotton in the night without accounting for it to the merchant. African Americans as a whole preferred tenancy to wage labor, so much so that in some areas the white owners found it difficult to hire the superior laborers for wages. Holmes predicted, however, that for either white landlords or black workers to improve their condition the wage system must gain upon the tenant system.[9]

Economist Matthew Brown Hammond, who studied the agricultural situation in Georgia and Texas arrived at conclusions similar to Holmes'. The crop-lien system was "chiefly responsible for the backward condition of southern agriculture, and the inefficiency and unreliability of black labor had been great drags on the prosperity of the southern states." The southern black men were usually docile but lacked energy and ambition. Their standard of living was as low as it was in slavery days, and they seemed "hopelessly content" with their bare subsistence. The best workers were the ex-slaves who had been trained to work diligently "On the big plantations along the Mississippi, the manager's authority was little short of compulsion" and reminiscent of slavery, African Americans were fairly effective workers. Under looser arrangements the situation was much worse.

Poorer farming can be scarcely found than exists in those parts of the cotton belt where the absentee proprietor has rented out his land to the Negro 'croppers' and has left them free to manage the plantations in their own way.

Independent black farmers, "industrious, thrifty, and progressive agriculturists," could be found "throughout the cotton belt," but they were only the "notable exceptions to the general rule of Negro shiftlessness and idleness."[10]

As against the pessimistic impressions of Holmes and Hammond, both professionally trained students of southern agricultural labor, no great weight, perhaps, could be given a journalistic, if not promotional report, by Day Allen Willey, who was in the South at the close of the century. African Americans were, according to Willey, "creatures of climate" especially suited to the southern states, which were similar in many particulars to Africa. "Where employed either as time workers or on share the negroes as farmers seem to be most capable." Some men earned as much as seventy five cents a day, women and boys, fifty or sixty cents. On the principal plantations Willey found the blacks faring well, with little evidence of sickness, suffering, or want among them. Best of all, they appeared happy, contented, and comfortable, in contrast to the misery, immorality, and destitution frequent among their race in the cities; indeed, "in Nature lies the best solution of the 'negro problem'." Willey did see room for improvement in the condition of rural blacks, especially in the Carolinas and Louisiana, where the supply of labor was over abundant. This should be remedied, he felt, for there was enough uncultivated land in the South to give "every colored man in this country employment."[11]

Though most African Americans in the late nineteenth century South were tillers of the soil, a good many were found in other occupations, sometimes in the country, more commonly in the towns. In Virginia Arthur Bradley remarked, with some nostalgia and inaccuracy, that by 1880 most of the African American labor had disappeared from the rural districts and flocked into the big cities for factory or domestic work. "Agriculture of a large and careless sort is almost dead, killed by its own futility."[12]

South Carolina blacks might find jobs in mining phosphates, which were processed into fertilizers. Pay was $1.75 a day, or ton. The phosphate mines off Eddings Point, near Charleston, were "setting all the boys wild," Laura Towne observed from "Frogmore" in August, 1877. Though at least one of these blacks returned "sick, crestfallen, and disappointed." Sir George Campbell reported that many of the Sea Islands farmers made "ends meet" by occasional labor on the "great phosphate beds, which have become a large source of industry and wealth to that part of the country." As Professor Joel Williamson put it, "Negroes struggling to retain their small farms on the Sea

Islands during the hard years following emancipation must have viewed the rise of the phosphate industry as providential."[13]

At Greensboro, North Carolina, and at Richmond, Virginia, William Saunders saw large numbers of African Americans working successfully. The Greensboro blacks were making wooden handles, presumably for tools, and earned from "two shillings to three shillings" (about fifty to seventy-five cents) per day, approximately the going rate for farm labor. Saunders saw nothing to criticize in this, but felt rather that the abundance of this cheap labor should be an encouragement to industry in the South. A large flour mill at Richmond employed many blacks. The proprietor said that they were more regular in attendance than white men and be therefore gave them preference.[14]

In Virginia, evidently in Richmond, George Campbell visited a factory that produced chewing tobacco wherein African Americans did by far the greater part of the work. "Tobacco seems to be specially their vocation." (This had been true in the ante bellum period also.) "Most of the foremen are white and some of the work is done by white and black men mixed." Campbell saw no mixture of white and black women, and assumed that it was not allowed. Cigars were not made by African Americans, that being "one of the skilled things they do not do." (Sir George was perhaps unaware that the manufacture of cigars received little attention in the Virginia-Carolina area.) Wages at the factory were "about a dollar a day for moderately skilled work, and sometimes more, but employment was not very regular, averaging perhaps four days a week. All informants agreed that the black workers were fond of amusements, "including fishing or other excursions." Though Nannie Tilley questions the extent of "melodious singing" among African American tobacco workers, at Richmond, especially the women, were set to sing for Sir George's benefit, "and they certainly do that very well."[15]

In the great flour mills of Richmond Campbell found that most of the labor was black, but the "really skilled work must be done by whites. I saw a good deal of work in which black and white men are employed indiscriminately, and are paid the same. There are said to be no signs of jealousy between the two races."[16]

In iron foundries Boissevain saw black and white laborers working together, but in textile mills he saw no African Americans. Like Campbell, he observed that the preparation of tobacco was entrusted almost exclusively to the blacks; unlike Campbell, he asserted that they also made cigars.[17]

African American children, as well as men and women, were observed performing such operations as sorting and rolling up leaves in a Virginia tobacco factory visited by W. H. Russell as one of a party headed by the Duke of Sutherland and the Marquis of Stafford in 1881. "A happier looking people could not be seen, and at times their feelings of contentment burst out into song." Their 'half comic, half religious . . . extraordinary melodies" were sung with "a great sweetness."[18]

Though hardly outstanding as a student of African American affairs, the most famous foreign analyst of the American scene in the late nineteenth century, James Bryce, did notice the African American's role in tobacco manufacture, presumably in Virginia. Blacks handled tobacco better than the whites and appeared to monopolize the less skilled departments of the tobacco industry. They were not good in textile mills, where the whirr of the machinery was said to daze them or put them to sleep. Many African Americans were working in the mines and iron foundries of southeastern Tennessee and northern Alabama. Although generally poor, they seemed to be getting along well and some belonged to the trade unions. Everywhere Bryce traveled, in the Border States as well as in the Deep South, he observed that the division between blacks and native whites was sharper and more permanent than that between European immigrants from abroad.[19]

The African Americans of Farmville, county seat of Prince Edward County, Virginia, were studied by W. E. B. Du Bois during the late summer of 1897. The town contained 1,443 blacks and 961 whites according to the Census of 1880. Most of the African Americans in Farmville depended upon the industrial "chances" of the town, but many did hire out as farm laborers during spring and summer, the standard wage being fifty cents a day.

The chief industry in Farmville was tobacco. Storage was provided in warehouses, and the product was sold by companies composed of black as well as white stockholders. Men, women, and children worked in the tobacco houses untying the bundles and placing them in position. They then drew out the stems. Next the children tied the stemless strips into uniform bundles which were weighed, stretched on sticks, and hung up in the drying room for from eight to twelve hours. When thoroughly dried and cooled, the tobacco was again steamed as it hung, and then cooled for two more days. Finally it was steamed a third time, straightened, and quickly packed in hogsheads.

The women and men who steamed tobacco get fifty cents for every hundred pounds. They could, with the aid of children, stem from 100 to 300 pounds a day each, thus earning $2.50 to $9.00 a week or more, for five to seven months in the year. The men who prized, steamed, and packed tobacco received seventy-five cents to one dollar a day for eight or nine months. The "better" classes of women, Du Bois learned, did not like to work in the factories, as the surroundings were said to be unsuitable. Unfortunately, the factories kept many children from school all or part of the time.[20]

Railroad construction employed many African Americans as the southern rail network developed during the last third of the century. About 600 African

Americans primarily from Georgia worked in the constructions of the South Florida Railroad in 1880–1881, mainly in unskilled capacities. Most of them made one dollar per day, but the "spikers," who drove the track spikes, and the sub-foremen received $1.25 to $1.40 per day. The "older darkies of about forty or fifty years, especially the genuine blacks," impressed George Barbour, the commissary officer who observed them, as the best laborers. The "young darkies," especially "the 'yellow fellers,'" seemed to enjoy singing and dancing more than work and never averaged over fifteen days' labor in the month. Pay day, the tenth of each month, was "the great day." In place of working the blacks gathered at an early hour at the pay offices "scuffling, dancing, shouting, singing—a happy crowd indeed." The payrolls exhibited their "lamentable condition of ignorance," less than ten per cent being able to sign their names. Yet the condition among thirty or forty "poor white" laborers was even worse, less than four percent (i.e., only one) being able to sign. Old African Americans would admit their inability to write, while the whites would lie, offering some excuse such as hurt or dirty hands for failure to sign. African American railroad men in Kentucky (and elsewhere) by 1880 were also performing satisfactorily as firemen and brakemen.[21]

About one third of southern blacks were fit "to be trained for mechanical employment of a fairly high grade" though the others, "particularly those of the Guinea type," were not. Such was the opinion of the Dean of the Lawrence Scientific School at Harvard, Nathaniel Southgate Shaler, who was in his native South at the close of the century. Many African Americans should forsake the land and seek employment in industry, Shaler believed. "The simple, yet valuable lessons of the soil-tiller they have had." Whereas agriculture could never afford African Americans the opportunities they needed to raise their social and economic level, in industry they could use both "head and hands to help one another to profit of mind and pocket." Shaler counseled against any effort to enter the professions, for there the African Americans' race was bound to weigh against them. They would be hindered and shunned by their fellow southerners. Shaler's advocacy of industrial employment for African Americans ran directly contrary to the views of D. Allen Willey who argued that their congregation in urban areas could lead only to moral degradation and economic misery.[22]

Since learning a skilled trade called for a certain talent and a degree of advanced training, it must have been a considerable achievement, ample to give a feeling of independence and worthiness, for a nineteenth century African American to master a trade. Few observers saw racial discrimination as playing any part in the advancement or lack of advancement of African Americans in the trades. Campbell found whites tolerant of black craftsmen. The Reverend Mr. Field boldly asserted that in most places, especially in

Georgia, African Americans could enter any trade, and if they became skilled mechanics could find plenty to do. There is little doubt that Field exaggerates the matter. As several scholars have pointed out, a good many whites insisted that the African American was temperamentally unfit for skilled mechanical work, and there was opposition among white workers to the employment of blacks.[23]

Nevertheless, African American craftsmen observed by Samuel Barrows were obviously not the victims of severe discrimination. The good reputation of the blacks in the trades was in great measure due, Barrows thought, to the influence of such schools as Hampton, Tuskegee, and Atlanta. Tuskegee had, for example, turned out a number of printers patronized by both black and white. One of them had "a printing office" at Montgomery, and another "an office in Texas." African American brick makers in Washington were earning from four to five dollars a day. Hod carriers received $1.50 per day. A black trained in the industrial department of Atlanta University had constructed a school in Alabama. His earnings were about $2.50 a day.[24]

Du Bois also found little bias against African Americans in the trades. The entire brick making business of Farmville, Virginia and vicinity was in the hands of an ex-slave who was said to have bought his own and his family's freedom, to have purchased his enslaver's estate, and eventually to have hired his former enslaver to work for him. In his brickyard he employed some fifteen hands, mostly boys under twenty, paying them about twelve dollars a month, with extra pay for overtime. The brickyard operated about half of the year, producing from 200,000 to 300,000 bricks. More than half of the brick homes in and near Farmsville, it was estimated, had been constructed by this black's firm, which had "repeatedly driven white competitors out of business." Two African American blacksmiths and a black wheelright also did well in Farmville, sometimes taking in five to eight dollars a day. All of this pleased Du Bois.[25]

The services of a black carpenter were used in North Carolina by A. L. Bassett. Called upon to repair some furniture, he "came promptly for a day or two did his work well, and was paid at once." He then disappeared, leaving the job only half done, and avoided Bassett for several days. When finally captured he laughed and said it was "too warm to work." Bassett saw no more of this *nouveau rich* carpenter.[26]

The assistance of an African American blacksmith was sought by the well-known novelist, essayist, and editor, Charles Dudley Warner in the course of a horseback tour of Virginia, North Carolina, and Tennessee in 1888. Even though the black had on hand no shoes and no nails, he undertook to make a shoe and to "crib" four nails so that Warner might be on his way. This he did despite the opposition of a local white who was also demanding his services.

Warner, understandably enough, admired the skill and the courtesy of the blacksmith.[27]

Sir George Campbell, complimentary to African Americans in most endeavors, found them seriously lacking as artisans and craftsmen. There were, to be sure, African American carpenters, blacksmiths, and bricklayers who did a fair job, with the tolerance of whites, but most of the skilled trades wee in Caucasian hands. Whether black failure was attributable to natural defects or to "want of cultivation," he could not say. He would, however, grant that they had just come from a low and oppressed condition and thus time would be required for them to prove their ability to work in areas requiring accuracy and care.[28]

In terms of numbers employed the various forms of personal service remained much more important as African American occupations than were industry and the skilled trades. By far the largest economic group outside agriculture was in such service. Theodor Kirchoff, a German writer in the United States about 1875–1877, noted with obvious inaccuracy that in restaurants North and South the waiters were invariably black. Their efficiency left much to be desired, a loud voice being required in most instances to summon them. Leon Blouet, at Jacksonville, complained about his black waiters. One who was extremely obliging once allegedly brought him a glass of water containing a snake. When Blouet protested, he was assured that the reptile was dead. When he further protested that the snake might have left eggs, the black reexamined the glass and announced that the snake was a male. Blouet also observed that the black waiters working in almost all of the hotels south of Washington were extremely slow—it was the guest who did the waiting. On the other hand, Carlo Gardini received acceptable service, as did James Fullarton Muirhead, who was in the South first in 1888 and again in 1890–1893. The black waiters seen by Muirhead displayed an "expansive geniality" in contrast to the "supercilious indifference," if not positive rudences of his pale colleague, and were "indefatigable" in ministering to one's wants, and dressed more neatly than the "greasy" European waiter.[29]

At "Frogmore" and at Penn School, Laura Towne used several African American servants. One slept in the next room to hers at night, and two others were close at hand in the event of trouble. Except for one black boy who had a "don't care" attitude, all the servants were "comforts" to her, especially the African American woman who slept near her.[30]

Similarly, the old black servants who surrounded Arthur Granville Bradley in Virginia "were for general purposes as reliable and trustworthy as good English farm servants. Their families had generally got out of hand, but the older darkies were often the very models of honesty."[31]

African American servants were employed in various capacities by Mary Allan-Olney and in the Virginia homes she visited. She was, to reiterate, a harsh critic of African Americans and could not find much to say in favor of even this group. The sight of black waiters putting down white plates on a dining table struck her disagreeably, for she found herself looking instinctively to see whether their thumbs had not left a black mark. Her Virginia host ridiculed this notion, but Mary Allan-Olney retorted that they were biased observers having been surrounded by black servants since infancy. She conceded, however, the friendliness of a "barelegged Negro girl" who stared and grinned as she served ice water. Once she had occasion to hire an "old nigger" who knew how to use the spade—"some can only hoe"—to dig holes for trees. An amusing character who claimed to be an ardent seeker after truth, he worked fairly well for a day or two, then abandoned his job without notice. Eventually he explained that he didn't feel like digging "'no mo' o' dam holes . . . It jes' like digging graves.'" The same type of irresponsibility was displayed by her black washerwoman, cook, and stable boys. For the most part their work was sloppy, and on many occasions they did not report for duty.[32]

That the black servant class was poor, "uncertain, indolent, and negligent, unless closely and incessantly watched" was also the opinion of the Chicago journalist, George Barbour. They were given to falsehood and petty theft (a point made also by Mary Allan-Olney), they would leave without warning even if badly needed, and they were wasteful of supplies. Their only praiseworthy quality was an "easy good-nature" Barbour deemed "the silent, neat, careful, polite Chinese" far preferable, and alleged a general desire in Florida to replace African Americans with Chinese immigrants.[33]

The worthlessness of black servants was the primary reason their wages were low, A. L. Bassett concluded. The better trained ones went to the larger cities, mainly in the North, leaving behind the rough, ignorant sort. These, though paid little, managed to get a good deal in other ways. The Bassetts' cook, for example, fed her three children in their kitchen, despite remonstrance, and clothed them from their wardrobe. In addition, everything had to be kept under lock and key—something the Bassetts had not experienced in the North.[34]

The fact that most African Americans outside agriculture not only worked in servile occupations but also seemed to enjoy doing so disgusted and angered the French traveler, D'Haussonville, who came to the South a Negrophile, and left almost a Negrophobe. Reflection led him to suppose that the African Americans' servility stemmed from their oppression in slavery, and that the newer generation might change. Yet "the Negro population will remain inferior to the whites; it will become for the South the same as the immigrants, Irish, and others, were for the North, agents of work and thus of progress."[35]

African American servants were, in the experience of Iza Duffus Hardy, often very satisfactory, the better one being preferable to whites. Unfortunately, there was a shortage of the industrious and an abundance of the "slow, indolent, shiftless, untidy, and extravagant" ones. Black workers in Florida generally "get good wages and find plenty of employment; indeed the demand for labor is chronically greater than the supply, especially in the line of domestic help.[36]

The economic status of the better situated African American servants was adjudged favorably also by Blouet. Black train porters, pretty much a class unto themselves, often made ten to twelve dollars a day in tips, some amassing $2,500 to $3,000 a year independently of their regular salary. Their politeness was universally acknowledged by outside observers though Blouet sensed, no doubt correctly, that much of it was feigned for the sake of the financial reward. Black maids, though they were often too noisy (an opinion shared by Muirhead), did rather well from tips, and so did bellhops.[37]

The blacks of Farmville looked upon servant work as a relic of slavery, degrading and inadequately paid, and undertook it only from sheer necessity and as a temporary makeshift. Such was the conclusion of Du Bois, a conclusion contradicting that of most Caucasian observers elsewhere. Interestingly enough, however, the more affluent black families of Farmville were themselves beginning to hire servants. Ten regularly hired one servant each, and several others had a woman to help occasionally. Du Bois heard no objections to this type of service, and offered none himself.[38]

Very few outside observers commented on African American professional people. One obvious reason was the scarcity of such persons in the rural South, particularly. It is possible also that most observers thought that African Americans should deemphasize or shun the professions, and tended to ignore those who did not. Even the African American observers, who furnish some of the most instructive impressions of professional people, were not all sympathetic to them.

A doctor "of their own" on St Helena Island, presumably an African American, was first mentioned by Laura Towne in 1884. Five years earlier the blacks had spoken to her about "sending away a young man to learn to doctor them, and they propose to raise money for his support, in the church." (Whether or not the new doctor was the first of this project is unclear.) He had not yet obtained an office, but had begun practicing, and would soon be available to all who needed him. He charged very little—"fifteen cents for ten powders" was one example. Mrs. Towne was apprehensive lest he find the venture disastrous and leave.[39]

In Washington, D. C., African Americans enjoyed a "commendable" professional status according to the African American observer, Mifflin Gibbs. Gibbs himself was an admirer of Booker Washington and a critic of emphasis on the professions. One of the African American lawyers in Washington was, in the words of T. Thomas Fortune, a "ripe scholar and a gentlemen," was not wholly sympathetic to educating blacks for the professions, but happy to applaud the successful. Apparently, the black lawyer taught in addition to practicing at the bar. He had both black and white clients and had started his own insurance company.[40]

In Montgomery, Alabama, Samuel Barrows met an African American physician with a thriving practice. At Selma, there was also a doctor who had graduated from the local black college. Two black physicians were found in Birmingham, and seven in Baltimore. Birmingham also had a black dentist. At least one black lawyer practiced in the city and six in Baltimore. Selma had a pharmacist who had been trained at Howard University. All of these professional men, in Barrows' view, enjoyed the confidence and support of their African American clientele.[41]

At Farmville, Du Bois found no African American physicians nor lawyers. Preachers and teachers were the only representatives of the "learned professions." The preachers enjoyed the greater respect and prestige, along with the higher salaries. The two leading preachers in the town, both "young and progressive" graduates of theological seminaries, were paid $480 to $600 a year plus a home in one case. The "ignorant but picturesque" black ministers were confined to the smaller churches, or to rural areas where they cared for two or three congregations; such ministers received salaries ranging from $75 to $300 a year. African American teachers in Farmville, of whom an increasing number were young women, earned $100 to $250 a year, often supplemented by other work during vacation. Farmville seemed typical of the small, black-belt towns.[42]

African Americans were employed to a very limited extent in public service as policemen and clerks. George Sala saw a good many policemen on duty near the White House and the Capitol in Washington. Hesse-Wartegg first observed black public employees at Memphis, mainly policemen. In Petersburg, Virginia, Sir George Campbell remarked: "I notice that generally most of the United States employees [sic] are blacks, while the State and municipal employe's [sic] are whites." Even the street sweepers were Caucasian in Petersburg. At Columbia, South Carolina, Campbell encountered a black "Trial Justice" and "a coloured man, apparently connected with the city waterworks," who seemed very sensible and intelligent, at least on political matters. The town jailer at Farmville, Virginia, was black. This job, together with business and farm activity, had made him quite prosperous. But by the end of the century it appears that, except in jobs involving manual labor, the relatively few African Americans in public service had greatly diminished.[43]

Among the most observed of African Americans were the Mississippi River deckhands and levee workers. Those that Hesse-Wartegg saw were invariably sweaty and ragged, but seemed to work hard, with little rest. Aboard the Steamer Vicksburg the chief mate cursed and drove them as they worked frantically loading and stacking goods. It was a "sorrowful sight." Their pay of one dollar per day was likely to go almost immediately to the barkeeper. What was left, if any, was supposed to be used for shelter, food, and clothing for a wife and children.

On his boat trip through the Louisiana sugar country Hesse-Wartegg encountered more African American workers. They too, were black and ragged and apparently hard working when they worked. They might have worked eight or ten hours but were so lazy that two hours every day or two at twenty cents an hour was enough for them. Their diet was meager, and they slept "in any unoccupied house."[44]

The Robert E. Lee employed sixty or seventy black deckhands when Chaplain Cowan rode it from Vicksburg to New Orleans. Stationed on the lower deck, where no one else except the host's officers ever ventured, the hands scurried "here and there," working, quarrelling, or fighting. By contrast the hands seen by a New York journalist, Julian Ralph, were "a dull and almost barbaric looking crew" who received the standard wage of a dollar a day for "their almost superhuman work—the very hardest I ever saw performed anywhere or by anybody." This was a remarkable impression, considering that Ralph had traveled widely in the United States and in Europe. But, these blacks drank up all their earnings at Natchez and New Orleans.[45]

Some African Americans sought to eke out an existence, or to supplement their incomes, by singing, dancing, or just plain clowning for white observers, especially outsiders. Chaplain Cowan and the northern officers of his party paid "a handful of nickels" to a young black "who shook it down [danced] right merrily" at Milan, Tennessee. At Asheville, North Carolina, Charles Dudley Warner paid to see "Happy John," supposedly an ex-slave of Wade Hampton, and his companion Mary, a "bold, yellow girl," put on a show singing, dancing, and banjo and guitar playing. What most impressed Warner was that John, an already dark African American, painted his body even blacker to give a hilarious portrayal of the "nigger side" of African American life.[46]

Blacks peddling cotton, produce, and molasses were seen all over the South from Washington to New Orleans. At Huntsville, Alabama on Saturdays, the usual market day, William Wells Brown, a pioneer African American historian, saw them with their wares on their heads or in wagons, and recorded one of their chants:

> Here's yer chitlin's [hog intestines],
> Fresh an' sweet,
> Who'll jine de Union?
> Young hog's chitlin's hard to beat . . .
> Methodist chitlin's, jest been biled . . .
> Baptist chitlin's by de pound . . .
> As nice chitlin's as ever was found . . .

African American newsboys, juvenile representatives of the street vendor class, monopolized the trade in Washington.[47]

George Sala stayed in an African American hotel, Wormley's in Washington, which he described as "one of the quietest, most elegant, and most comfortable hotels in the Federal capitol." Sala met Wormley, a man of gentle manners and great administration abilities." He was typical of the "better" Washington blacks, who were not only "invariably civil and obliging, but in many cases [also] very bright and intelligent."[48]

Booming African American businesses in the nation's capital were noticed also by two blacks, Mifflin Gibbs and T. Thomas Fortune, and by Henry Loomis Nelson of *Harper's Weekly*. Black insurance men and bankers were doing well. Fortune had occasion to sit in the banking offices of William Mathews and Joseph Rainey, ex-congressman from South Carolina. As he sat, a number of patrons came and went, the majority being Caucasian. Many were seeking loans. "They all spoke with the utmost deference to the colored gentlemen" who ran the financial institution.[49]

In both the upper and the lower South African Americans practically monopolized barbering. Many were getting rich cutting heads, mainly of whites. A black barber at Montgomery, an ex-slave, had done so well that he bought one of Jefferson Davis's former plantations in Mississippi. At Farmville, Virginia, the leading barber was the wealthiest African American in the town, reputedly worth something like $10,000. The other barber shops in the town—there were four more, which Du Bois thought rather too many for the trade—were all run by African Americans. The average income of a full-fledged barber was $5 to $15 a week, of an assistant, $3 to $5 dollars. The work of black barbers seemed satisfactory to all, though Johannes Baumgarten thought they ran their fingers through the hair more than German barbers did.

Blacks at Farmville also operated grocery stores, restaurants, repair shops of all kinds, laundries and hotels, a total of thirty-two separate enterprises employing about forty persons besides the proprietors. African American grocery stores were also seen at Birmingham and Tuskegee, Alabama and at Selma a black pharmacist had built a drug store.[50]

African American financial institutions included a "building association" at Atlanta with branches elsewhere. Similar associations existed in Montgomery, Selma, Baltimore, and Washington. A bank chartered at Chattanooga gained in its first year 1,000 deposits ranging in amount from two cents to $1,000. In general, however, as William Wells Brown noted, the failure of the much heralded Freedmen's Bank at Washington had made blacks skeptical of such institutions. This he regretted inasmuch as a tendency to be spendthrift was manifesting itself among the race.

Viewing the situation of African American business from Farmville in 1897, W. E. B. Du Bois was led to remark: "The individual undertaker of business enterprise is a new figure among Negroes, and his rise deserves to be carefully watched, as it means much for the future of the race." Du Bois's assertion that the African American businessman was a new figure in 1897 is matched for its unenlightenment only by Sir George Campbell's earlier claim that he had "not been able to hear of a successful Negro merchant—the shop-keeping business in the most Negro districts is almost entirely in the hands of whites." He had "scarcely found a Negro who had risen in the mercantile world higher than an apple-stall in a market."

On the subject of African American property holding the outside observers provided a good deal of scattering and unsystematic information. Such property holding was not a new thing. In Maryland, for example, blacks had paid taxes on at least a million dollars of real property in 1860, and free blacks in New Orleans had owned more than $15,000,000 worth. The accumulation continued and became much more widespread in the post-war era. The English journalist, William Saunders, observed that a large number of Richmond blacks owned the property they occupied. In Alabama the assessed value of black property, about 1878, was seven million dollars. When Saunders asked some of the more prosperous, intelligent blacks how they were getting along as compared with former times, a typical reply would be:

> Well, sir, most of us are doing better
> But some are doing worse. Those who
> Can't take care of themselves are going
> To the bad faster than before; but if a
> Man can take care of himself, he now has
> the chance.[51]

Barrows felt that African Americans were much better off as property owners in the upper than in the lower South. A black bishop in North Carolina told him that "our people are buying land wherever they can get it" at prices usually of ten to fifteen dollars an acre. "The bishop, himself, has a little farm of thirty-three acres near Salisbury that cost thirty-four dollars an acre." "I'm so anxious to see my race improve," the bishop said, "that I should like to have a great deal more done, but in view of the small wages we get for labor we are doing pretty well."

Whatever the comparison with the upper South, Barrows' own data showed much property holding by African Americans in the Deep South. He understood that fifty per cent of the black people in Marion County, Georgia, owned their homes, and some had large plantations; that in Sumter and Terrell counties blacks lived mostly on their own farms; and that in Bullock County, Alabama, one black owned 300 acres. Property holding in urban areas included, according to Barrow's information, home ownership by "all the colored people" in a "small city of 10,000." In Terrell County; "nearly all" the blacks owned their own homes in a township of Lee County, Alabama, and large numbers did so at Montgomery and Chattanooga.[52]

The significance of land ownership for blacks was understood by the African American politician, Mifflin Gibbs, whose position as Register of the U. S. Land Office for the Little Rock District afforded him a good deal of experience in the settlement of blacks on the public lands. He believed that the ownership of land and homes was for African Americans an important factor, making them taxpayers, encouraging reverence for the law "and protection of the public peace," giving them a mutuality of interest with other members of the "body politic," and impelling business and trade to seek them out. Du Bois found likewise that in Farmville the holding of property, together with the operation of a comparatively large number of businesses, had given the town's blacks a degree of economic importance which had even brought many white men to say "mister" to the preacher and teacher, and to raise their hats to black ladies.[53]

In the immediate transition from slavery to freedom, the necessity of earning a living was, perhaps, the African American's most pressing challenge. Indeed it was vital for survival. On the farm, where most of them remained, and in the towns, where they worked mostly as servants, they managed to successfully meet the challenge and to obtain an economic base for their social and cultural activities.

The emancipated African American, Booker T. Washington asserted, needed the opportunity to earn a dollar more than the opportunity to spend one in an opera house. Wisely used, this dollar, whether the product of farm or factory, would win respect and a degree of power for the race. Social equality Washington would gladly abandon for economic security.

Washington stressed the training of mechanics as well as farmers, but most southern blacks in the early 20th century remained in the country and would still have to look to the soil for their livelihood. Those who did make it to the cities were more likely to become servants than industrial workers, and even mechanics trained at Tuskegee and Hampton found most of the doors to the South's growing industries were closed to them.

While American agriculture, as a whole, enjoyed a good deal of prosperity in the Progressive Era, African American agriculture remained largely involved in the unprofitable tenant system or continued as a subsistence laborer. The standard wages in 1902 was seventy-five cents a day, according to Thomas M. Young, a representative of the British textile industry, North and South, and observed plantations in the vicinity of New Orleans. The blacks seemed fairly good workers, thriftless but honest. Considering that the farm laborer paid no rent, and lived on a meager diet, Young thought the standard wage more than adequate. An exemplary a food budget for a black family of five for a week would be:

10 pounds of bacon at 12½ cent	$1.25
12 pounds flour	$ .40
12 pounds Indian meal	$ .30
1 quart of molasses	$ .12
1 pound of coffee	$ .12
2 pounds of sugar	$ .14
salt, etc	$ .10

In a family with a baby the budget would be slightly higher.[54]

Professor Kelsey, who went to the South specifically to study the African American fanner, reported that most of them were diligent workers, rising at four or five in the morning and going directly to the fields without food. Some returned home around eight or nine for grits; others worked until noon, when they ate grits and fish, or occasionally corn bread and molasses. Milk was very seldom drunk, even when a cow or two was owned. The farm day ended at sundown with a meal of pork fat, collards, turnip greens, and cornbread.

Kelsey found that blacks in the main were poor agriculturists. The cause was ignorance, not laziness. Their farming, characterized by poor tillage of the soil, lack of crop rotation, and absence or improper use of manures, was "very unscientific." Employment of expensive mules—which many blacks mistreated-instead of horses was both a practical and financial liability. Hampton and Tuskegee graduates had worked improvements, but they were insufficient to the need, and the general condition was not good.

Kelsey advocated "local interest groups" among blacks to enhance agricultural knowledge and thus to increase income for African American farmers. Such groups had been organized in Alabama and in Texas, and the Texas group, known as the "Farmers Improvement Society," had won a great deal of success with a program of abolishing the credit system and stimulating improvements in farming, cooperative buying, sickness and life insurance, and purchases of land and homes.[55]

Sir Harry Johnston saw a great deal of energetic and praiseworthy activity among African American farmers of Alabama. The poultry of the tenants and independent farmers was excellent, including "Leghorns, Buff Orpingtons, Plymouth Rocks," and other good breeds of chickens, as well as a large number of turkeys, geese, and "guinea fowl." Comparing conditions of the black agriculturists and the English poor, Johnston found the southern blacks to be "greatly superior in comfort, happiness, and even in intellectuality."[56]

On a sprawling plantation at Hawkinsville, Georgia, Ray Stannard Baker noticed that few of the tenants took advantage of the opportunity to supplement their twelve to fifteen dollars a month incomes by raising crops on their own small garden plots. He judged that indolence and lack of ambition were largely to blame, but also that the steady work demanded by the planter left little time or energy for other endeavors. Some of the more industrious tenants had, however, graduated to ownership of their own farms near the greater plantation. Indeed, one black man owned more than a thousand acres of land; another owned both a plantation and a store and rented out land to tenants on the same system employed by whites; and a third owned a spread of land worth $2,000, a large house, a one-horse syrup mill, and mules, horses, and equipment worth hundreds of dollars. African American holdings such as these were, Baker acknowledged, notable exceptions to the general rule, but their number had increased significantly.[57]

Though masses of southern blacks were still laboring on the plantations, historian Albert Hart observed that the demand for plantation labor exceeded the supply. One partial reason, at least in certain localities, was a meager but continuing exodus to the cities. Another was suggested by a planter, himself an African American, who told Hart that "If a Negro can get what he wants without working he will do it." Apparently the living standards of a great many blacks were so low that they could exist without substantial labor. Yet Hart and several other observers denied that the weight of the evidence was on the side of African Americans. Even in winter he saw blacks tending gardens, taking care of stock, and repairing houses and barns. It was true that an African American's farm was "generally more slovenly than a white man's, but the crops are raised;" and the black farm laborer was superior to the "fellahin of

Egypt, the Ryots of India, and the lowest end of the Mountain whites and the remnants of the lowland Poor Whites."[58]

In the late nineteenth century, the relatively small number of African Americans employed in industry was mainly in tobacco factories and mines. There were few, if any, in textile mills. By 1902 when Thomas Young, the British student of the textile industry visited South Carolina, blacks were working in the "picking (opening and blowing)" room of the mill at Columbia. Theirs was the only in-door mill work which Young saw performed by African Americans. Like farmhands, they were paid seventy-five cents per day.

Young was curious to know why there were not more African Americans in the cotton mills. Having seen whites and blacks working together "on good terms" on a "lever trolley" at Cooleemee Station, between Charlotte and Winston-Salem, North Carolina, he could not believe that "race feeling" was the answer. The African American, Young was satisfied, simply did not choose to work in the cotton mills. The "general attitude of his race" was expressed, Young thought, by a Columbia black who denied that "cotton mills were ever meant for colored people." The African American had "a child's impatience of any monotonous occupation" demanding constant application and continued vigilance; he disliked the mill air, "laden with moisture and fine particles of lint cotton;" he loved sunshine and "the open sky;" and, finally, he saw more dignity in wearing the dress of a waiter, or a porter, than in "standing for eleven hours a day in front of a . . . group of looms." "Even if he were driven to the mills, the African American's natural antipathy to such work" would make him a poor workman. And he was unlikely to be so driven, his needs were met by four days' work a week in the fields.[59]

When Albert Bushnell Hart inspected the cotton mills at Charleston and Columbia, about five years after Young had been there, the first thing he noticed was that the laborers were exclusively white. Aware that the mills at both places had attempted to use blacks, that blacks had tried to operate their own mills, and that every one of these experiments had seemed to fail, Hart sought explanations. Ignorance was said to be a major factor, "together with the African American's irregularity." The ill success of blacks in the mills was not, Hart cautioned, to be attributed to racial traits; southern poor whites did not make "by any means the best mill help, and their output of yards per hand" was "considerably less than that in the Northern states."[60]

In the mining camps near Birmingham, Alabama, African American workmen did roughly fifty per cent of the unskilled labor in 1907, when a northern-born camp physician reported upon the situation there. All had come from the farms in a rather steady stream since about 1877. A few of the younger black workers were second generation miners born in the camps. Much of the work force consisted of ex-convicts, the reason being that almost all the state's black convicts were sent to the coal mines for work, and large numbers upon being paroled or completing their sentences returned to the mines. If he were willing to endure hard, filthy work and a poor environment, physical, moral, and educational, an African American could do very well economically as a miner. The pay in 1907 was three to six dollars per day. Few, if any, black public school teachers, or preachers, or mechanics, let alone farm laborers, could equal such wages.[61]

About a year after the camp physician's report on conditions in the Birmingham area, Sir Harry Johnston arrived there, visited coal mines, iron mines, iron foundries, and steel works. Approximately fifty percent of the laborers in the foundries and in steel, about fifty five percent of the coal miners, and some ninety percent of the iron miners were African Americans. They appeared to work well, hard, and long, and to earn very good wages. Many blacks in that area and elsewhere were also making good wages constructing and repairing railroads.[62]

At Galveston, Texas, in 1916 Mildred Cram observed a number of blacks working amid the cotton compresses, threading and securing the containers. Characteristically, the blacks sang. Their attitude seemed to Mrs. Cram alarmingly careless, for "one misstep, on miscalculation" and the giant presses would have rolled them out "as flat and as featureless as pancakes."[63]

African Americans were excited about the growing development of the oyster industry when Professor Kelsey visited the Virginia Tidewater in 1902–1903. The industry had a twofold effect on the blacks; it brought them a considerable amount of money which had been wisely invested in homes and small farms, but at the same time drew many young boys out of school to work at "shucking" oysters. In addition, the work, although irregular, had attracted many farm hands to the detriment of the more permanent agricultural activity. Though Kelsey would not say that the bad results outweighed the good, he believed the blacks in their quest for the dollar were not giving enough thought to the relative long-range possibilities in the oyster industry as compared to agriculture.[64]

A prosperous business of basket making had been developed by the blacks on St. Helena Island employing methods "used by their African ancestors" and concealed from all but the most trusted whites. Rossa Cooley saw the instruments, a sharpened bone and a knife, with which they worked native reeds and palmetto into baskets that were widely used in the North as well as the South. Miss Cooley called the activity a tribute to the African American's "self-respect."[65]

The activities and the economic status of African American engaged in various forms of personal service probably changed little in the early years of the twentieth century. There were, however, small modifications quite disturbing to whites, whether outsider or native, in the demeanor of many servants, especially those who worked in places of public accommodation. Henry James noticed and disapproved a new attitude among black porters and coachmen at New Orleans but remarked that they displayed the customary servility when their white supervisors were around. To Mildred Cram the lack of servility among black bellboys, waiters, and porters at Baltimore and Savannah was shocking. She had expected the old "Uncle Remus" type of subservience and instead encountered "playboys of the Southern world."[66]

More tolerant and analytical than the other observers of servant behavior were Ray Stannard Baker and Albert Bushnell Hart. Baker, who had no particular objection to the new mood, met at Atlanta intelligent African American waiters and elevator boys who said that conditions in the South had become unbearable and that they wanted to go North. Like Du Bois somewhat earlier, Hart attributed the poor quality of domestic service mainly to the fact that the "better" blacks shunned degrading work.[67]

Mrs. Tweedie noted a growing interest in the professions among African Americans, though she seemed to have had difficulty in reconciling herself to the existence of these "modern darkeys." Whereas in 1900 one hardly saw a black person who was not a servant, by 1912 they had entered almost all the professions, at least in the cities. The young black porter at a private club in New Orleans turned out to be a law student. At Birmingham, Sir Harry Johnston passed the office of several black physicians, dentists, and pharmacists. At Washington there were lawyers, surveyors, engineers, and architects. Furthermore, black members of several of these professions could, he gathered, be found in small numbers in most of the larger southern towns. Albert Bushnell Hart, who saw black physicians and teachers almost everywhere he went, confirmed this encouraging development.[68]

Many of the supporters of Booker T. Washington probably feared that if the African Americans went into the professions they would, by virtue of their training and the economic status they attained, tend to agitate questions of social equality. Even in Washington's lifetime this began to happen. In 1902 Du Bois, whose more militant days were fast approaching, lead a group of blacks, presumably educators, to the newly opened Carnegie Public Library in Atlanta and demanded to know why African Americans would not be permitted to use it. Sensing that the northern-born educator might push his point too vigorously, one of his more adroit fellows took the floor. In an address flattering to the trustees this Negro asked only for separate but equal facilities, which were subsequently promised. This promise pleased many of the blacks, but fell short of Du Bois' expectations.[69]

At Memphis several years later a black professional man encountered difficulty in trying to secure use of the public library for his son. As a result of his efforts and threats the city proposed to build a branch library for African Americans. The compromise satisfied him or so he told William Archer, the English author, during a buggy ride they took together. He also expressed disappointment that business would prevent his hearing Ambassador James Bryce speak in Memphis. He would have sat in a segregated gallery in order to do so.[70]

Another African American professional man in Memphis, a physician, boldly announced to Archer that he belonged to a well-known southern white family that had filled "sundry political offices." His white father had attached himself "openly and honorably" to his black mother and been driven out of both North Carolina and Mississippi. They fled to Ohio, where they were married. Their son, the physician, had witnessed the ceremony. He himself was not incensed over this family history, but Archer was incensed for him. Because illicit relations between a white man and a black woman were a "humiliation" to the African American, they should be forbidden under severe penalties.

The same physician felt strongly concerning the Washington-Du Bois controversy over African American education. He sided with Booker Washington and agricultural industrial training or "manual training," calling it the first essential for the race, and saying of Washington; "Ah, he is our Moses."[71]

Since emancipation, African American businesses on a small scale had appeared in many parts of the South, and after the turn of the century they grew in number. Booker Washington both urged his fellow blacks to go into business and helped found a Negro business association to foster race enterprises and sound entrepreneurial practices. There was little if any questioning of the desirability of this, at least among blacks. A prosperous African American business community, including a savings institution and insurance companies, developed at Tuskegee. Black merchants even appeared in the Mississippi Delta. Professor Kelsey talked to one whose store was located on the main street of a moderate sized town. This merchant was aware that a black person would not have been allowed such a good location in many other parts of the country. The fact that he was operating prosperously, and had white trade, convinced Kelsey that race relations in the Delta and in other parts of the South were better than one would expect.[72]

On one of Atlanta's main streets Ray Stannard Baker came upon an African American shoe store. Previously he had not known "that there was such a thing in the country." The business, apparently prosperous and well kept, was owned by a stock company organized and controlled wholly by blacks.

The mulatto manager was a graduate of Atlanta University. Busy dictating a letter to his secretary when Baker entered, he took time to explain that the business had been established because the promoters thought it a good opportunity to make money and because many blacks of the "better class" felt that they did not get fair treatment at white stores. African American leaders had urged blacks to patronize the store; hence it was exceedingly prosperous. Like many businessmen, the manager was reluctant to discuss social issues, professing only a desire for protection and to be "let alone, so that I can build up this business."

The "wealthiest Negro in Atlanta," Alonzo F. Herndon, operated the largest barber shop in the city "for whites only"; was president of a black insurance company, one of four in town; and owned or rented some fifty dwellings. He was said to be worth $80,000, "all made, of course, since slavery." Baker talked also with a mulatto druggist who enjoyed "a high degree of prosperity." His establishment served as a post office and had become a favorite gathering spot for African Americans. The credit system was the African American businessman's greatest difficulty, he believed, for many blacks had not learned financial responsibility. This type of irresponsibility had at one time caused him to consider closing his business. He held that the best opportunity for an African American in any area of life was in the South, where the whole race was behind him.[73]

The large number of African American businesses in Atlanta, including hotels, grocery stores, and newspapers, convinced Baker that the African American was "rapidly building up his own business enterprises, tending to make himself independent as a race." It was also clear that Atlanta was by 1906 well on its way toward becoming the financial capital of African Americans—a position it would retain a half-century later. There were, to be sure, "no large Negro capitalists" anywhere at this time. But Albert Bushnell Hart observed that small black capitalists were "very numerous" in the South, a "promising" development.[74]

The city of Birmingham, if the impression of it conveyed by Sir Harry Johnston was reliable, compared favorably with Atlanta and Washington in the number and variety of African American businesses. One of the several black banks was "lined with marble and upholstered with handsome woods." Birmingham also had a black-owned theater for performing artists whose acts, the British consul thought, were "excellent" musical comedies. One wonders if Sir Harry's theater for performing artists was not actually a vaudeville house.[75]

The familiar street vendors, particularly picturesque in New Orleans and Charleston, continued peddling their wares in the twentieth century. Edward Hungerford was made rudely aware of this at 7:00 a.m. in Charleston, when black vendors loudly hawked "swimpy waw, waw" [raw shrimps] or "waw cwab" [raw crabs] or "monkey meat" [a candy made of coconut and molasses]. One might regret the disturbance of sleep, and not care for the itinerant's wares, but he could hardly help enjoy the melancholy music. The streets were clear long before noon.[76]

On the Mississippi River, particularly near Vicksburg, some African American families had turned their houseboats into fish markets. For them catching catfish was a means of income as well as a recreation.

By the First World War many African Americans with musical talent had turned away from impromptu performances in the factory and on the farm, or singing, dancing and clowning for dimes and quarters at street corners, to channel their energies to more financially rewarding ventures, notably in New Orleans and Memphis. Memphis blacks enjoyed the lyrics of W.C. Handy, composer of the "St. Louis Blues," and danced to the tunes of pianist Joe Turner. Julian Street analyzed Handy's music as "Negro 'rags' in fox-trot time" and found that it was generally preferred to the enduring "one-step."[77]

The status of thrift among African Americans was a matter difficult for outsiders to estimate reliably. Clearly large numbers of blacks, especially professional and business people and independent farmers, practiced thrift. But harsh critics like Professor Munsterberg and Clifton Johnson believed that "a reckless expenditure of cash" is a marked tendency of the race, "and it was true that the relatively large sums supposedly spent on female dress, whiskey, and gambling suggest a good deal of thriftlessness among the poorer elements." Charles Bartlett Dyke, a northern educator, undertook to examine the source of African American attitudes toward thrift. To 1,200 black children, one half from cities, mainly of the Chesapeake area, the other half from "the most enlightened rural districts" of Virginia, North Carolina, Georgia, and Alabama, he posed the following questions: "Would you like to be rich? Why? How much money of your own did you have last week? What did you do with it?" The greater number of the rural children exhibited a limited idea of what constituted wealth, and a marked lack of thrift. Their wants were few—a little food, some shelter, a few clothes. Most did not shun poverty, for the preacher taught that the rich could not get to Heaven, and that there was glory in being poor. The fact that urban blacks, where the African American ministry was becomingly increasingly educated, showed almost two to one a greater desire for wealth and disposition toward thrift led Dyke to conclude that the greatest blame for thriftlessness lay with illiterate preachers, and that the remedy was an educated clergy. The problem was, he thought, of the utmost urgency, and "a real menace to the South," because as matters stood the African American's "few demands upon the world" could be met without much exertion on his part, and "the outgrowth of his indo-lence" was vice and crime.[78]

During the 1920s approximately two-fifths of all American blacks still lived in the South, and a substantial majority of them continued to be tillers of the soil. Though they were far from prosperous, the noted French political economist, Andre Siegfried, thought that the African Americans were better off than many whites. The competition of the black farm laborer, Siegfried felt, was partly responsible for the worsening condition of the "poor whites." They had sunk to "a mediocre lot, often living in squalor." Economically and physically, they were the African Americans' inferior. Though no one got rich under the tenant system, Frank Tannenbaum, a student of Latin America and subsequently a professor of History at Columbia University, who examined the American South in 1923–1924, concluded that African American tenant farmers were purchasing land and becoming owners at a more rapid rate than were the more numerous whites. Tannenbaum applauded this development but did not venture to say among whom or why it occurred.[79]

On the Sea Islands immediately after the Civil War a severe drought had added to agricultural woes. Rossa Cooley overheard a conversation between two blacks at Fort Royal Island that summed up the situation. "Dis year too hard!" exclaimed one of them, "But den I hab t'ree or fo' buttons on my coat, an' some men I see has but one!" On St. Helena, the most prosperous of the Sea Islands, the corn crop, cultivated largely by Penn School students, did net $3,000 despite the drought, but most Islanders were canning fruits and vegetables in the event things did not improve. The Island's basket-making industry was also a source of refuge for the stricken economy.[80]

Just prior to the financial Crash of 1929, Arnaldo Cipolla, an Italian writer, saw in the area north of Little Rock, around the Arkansas river, acres upon acres of freshly cultivated cotton fields under black management. The managers were by no means land barons, but they did not appear to be in distress.[81]

Southern blacks continued to hold a virtual monopoly in the occupations involving personal service. A few merited and received recognition in such roles. Thus an old black barber who had been "shaving prominent Birming-ham citizens and cutting their hair since the day that Birmingham was a flag station" was allowed to ride in a parade honoring President Harding in 1921. But many, perhaps most, some observers believed, were more like barbers and waiters observed at Kansas City by the British novelist Walter George. They did not serve, but mostly stood and waited. A group of seven shoeshine boys were at least more entertaining, for they ran their shop to the sounds of a gramophone and "at the proper moment of syncopation, the shiners all together brought down their brushes upon a board!"[82]

A black man who was hired as a stoker or fireman by the Prossinaggs for their home in Washington worked in a similar capacity for many of their neighbors. Allegedly he spent most of his summers loafing, but he earned enough money to buy a good automobile. Three times a day, he drove up, went into the cellar, donned gloves, shoveled the coal, then left again. A young black woman was employed by the Prossinaggs to clean house and wash dishes. They saw very little of her because she generally came after they had left for the day and departed before they returned, or did not come at all. Her absences went unexplained, though she might leave "laconic little notes" on such subjects as how she broke something. From Prossinagg's point of view the black man was efficient, the housekeeper quite unreliable.[83]

Pullman porters and dining car waiters were described by William, Crown Prince of Sweden, on the basis of a train ride south from St. Louis. The waiters he found satisfactory. The porters gave friendly grins and courteous greetings but their service left much to be desired. Prince William was particularly annoyed at one whose job was to regulate bedtime temperatures. Unable to sleep himself, the black was "sublimely indifferent" to the comfort of his passengers.[84]

African Americans were increasingly taking over the manual jobs in public service, particularly at the local level, or so it seemed to Andre Siegfried and John T. Faris. Faris, a Pennsylvania clergyman, learned that "a gang of Negroes, bossed by a white man," had paved one of the main streets of Miami. This degree of skill amazed him. Such work, Siegfried thought, belied the contention by southern whites that skilled labor of any kind had to be done by "the superior race." White employers in and out of government preferred black laborers because they could be paid less and were "more obedient." This preference was increasing the chasm between blacks and "poor whites," who saw the African American as a "brutal competitor" robbing them of their jobs not only on the farm but also in the city.[85]

The really prosperous African Americans in the 1920s were still the professional people, especially urban physicians and dentists, and businessmen such as barber shop proprietors, insurance men and bankers. The presence of successful black banks at Washington convinced the German, Felix Graf von Luckner, that blacks were "making undeniable economic progress," which he applauded. Similarly, Ernst Prossinagg thought it commendable that African Americans had their own professional workers and businesses. The businesses had, he noted, already produced a few black millionaires. All of this was evidence of industriousness among the blacks.[86]

The success of the businessman was part of the economic progress which Booker T. Washington had envisioned in 1895. Washington would have also been pleased to note continuing moves toward thrift among blacks. One evidence was the establishment, reported by Rossa Cooley, principal of Penn School, of the St. Helena Credit Union in 1924. Shares were sold at five dollars each, and the blacks were encouraged to save. Unfortunately the success of the Credit Union was short lived. Miss Cooley explained that on the eve of the Great Depression a white bank at Beaufort failed, shaking the confidence of African Americans in their own saving institutions. If the white men with all their financial experience suffered thus, it behooved the blacks to watch their step. Still, Miss Cooley believed that the Credit Union would eventually function "as it should in a rounded way."[87]

NOTES

1. Works of value on cotton, tenancy, and the plantation after the war included M. B. Hammond, *The Cotton Industry* (1897), Roger W. Shugg, "Survival of the Plantation System in Louisiana," *Journal of Southern History*, III (1937), 311–325, E. M. Banks, *Economics of Land Tenure in Georgia* (1905), Robert Preston Brooks, *The Agrarian Revolution in Georgia, 1865–1912* (1914), and Fred A. Shannon, *The Farmer's Last Frontier* (1945).

2. Campbell, *White and Black*, 155.

3. Edward Hogan, "South Carolina Today," *International Review*, VIII (February, 1880), 116; Campbell, *White and Black*, 149–150.

4. Hesse-Wartegg, *Mississippi-Fahrten*, 77–78, 148, 173, 264, 268–269, 269–270, 284, 296.

5. *Ibid.*

6. Charles Beadle, *A Trip to the United States in 1887* (London: J. S. Virture and Co., Ltd., 1887), 66–68, 197.

7. Henry M. Field, *Bright Skies and Dark Shadows* (New York: Charles Scribner's Sons, 1890), 114–115. Sent South in 1889 for his health, Field (1882–1907) traveled in Florida, Georgia, Mississippi, and Tennessee. Clark, ed., *Travels in the New South*, I, 170. Campbell, *White and Black*, 143, 145, 159, 297.

8. Samuel J. Barrows, "What the Southern Negro Is Doing for Himself," *Atlantic Monthly*, LXVII (June, 1891) 805–806. Barrows (1845–1909), born in New York, studied at the Harvard Divinity School, and was pastor of Unitarian churches in Dorchester and Boston, Mass. He edited the *Christian Register* (1881–1897), and in 1897 was awarded a Doctor of Divinity degree by Howard University, "the Capstone of Negro Education." He also served a term in Congress, 1897–1899, as a Republican, and was internationally prominent in the movement for prison reform. *Who Was Who in America*, I, 62.

9. George K. Holmes, "The Peons of the South," *Annals of the American Academy of Social and Political Science*, IV (1893), 270–271. Born like W. E. B. Du Bois at Great Barrington, Mass., Homes was admitted to the Massachusetts Bar in 1877. He was special agent in charge, Division of Farms, Homes and Mortgages, U. S. Census

of 1890, and subsequently agricultural statistician and member of the Corp Reporting Board of the U. S. Department of Agriculture, 1905–1924. *Who Was Who in America*, I, 581.

10. M. B. Hammond, "The Southern Farmer and the Cotton Question," *Political Science Quarterly*, XII (September, 1897), 465–467. Hammond (1868–1933), born at South Bend, Indiana, was educated at the Universities of Michigan, Wisconsin, Tubingen, and Berlin, and received the Ph.D. in economics from Columbia in 1898. He taught at the Universities of Missouri, Illinois, and Ohio State, was a member of various commissions, and was labor adviser to the U. S. Food Administration in 1913. His books included *The Cotton Industry* (1897) and *Railway Theories of the Interstate Commerce Commission* (1911). *Who Was Who in America*, I, 513–514.

11. D. Allen Willey, "The Negro and the Soil," *Arena*, XXIXX (May, 1900), 558–560. Born in Rochester, New York, and educated at the University of Rochester, Willey began as a reporter and became city editor of the Rochester *Democrat and Chronicle*. In 1890 he moved to Baltimore, where he edited the Baltimore World, and was assistant editor of the *Manufacturer's Record*. *Who Was Who in America*, I, 1350.

12. Bradley, *Other Days*, 396.

13. Joel Williamson, After Slavery: *The Negro in South Carolina During Reconstruction 1861–1877* (Chapel Hill, The University of North Carolina Press, 1965), 161. Towne, *Letters and Diary*, 273, 275, 276. Campbell, *White and Black*, 155–157. Williamson, *After Slavery*, 161.

14. Saunders, *Through the Light Continent*, 75–76.

15. Joseph Clarke Robert, *The Tobacco Kingdom: Plantation, Market, and Factory in Virginia and North Carolina, 1800–1860* (1937); reprint, Gloucester, Mass.: Peter Smith, (1965), 197–208. Campbell, *White and Black*, 285. Cf. Nannie May Tilley, *The Bright-Tobacco Industry, 1860–1929* (Chapel Hill: The University of North Carolina Press, 1948), 318–319, 490. Taking up where Robert left off, Tilley gives a good survey of the industry down to the Great Depression.

16. Campbell, *White and Black*, 288.

17. Handlin, ed., *This Was America*, 336.

18. W. E. Russell, *Hesperothen; Notes from the West,* (2 vols; London: Sampson Low, Marston, Searle, and Rivington, 1882), 1, 97. Educated at Trinity College, Dublin, Russell became famous as a war correspondent of the London *Times*. His *My Diary North and South* (1863) has been widely used by American historians. John Black Atkins, *The Life of Sir William Howard Russell* (London: J. Murray, 1911); Robert Furneaux, *The First War Correspondent, William Howard Russell of the Times* (2nd ed.; London: Cassell and Co., Ltd., 1945).

19. James Bryce, *The American Commonwealth* (2nd rev. ed., 2 vols.; New York: The Macmillan Co., 1918), XI, 514–515. Bryce (1838–1922) won the Arnold prize at Oxford in 1864 for his essay on the Holy Roman Empire. He taught civil law there from 1870 until 1893. First elected to the House of Commons in 1880, he was a member of Gladstone's cabinet in 1892; president of the Board of Trade under Lord Rosebury in 1894; administrator in Ireland until 1907; ambassador to the United

States, 1907–1913. He was the author of numerous works, including *The Relations of the Advanced and Backward Races of Mankind* (1902). *Dictionary of National Biography*, 1922–1930 Supplement, 127–135.

20. W. E. Burghardt Du Bois, "The Negroes of Farmville, Virginia: A Social Study," United States Department of Labor, *Bulletin*, III, No. 14 (January, 1898), 3, 19.

21. Barbour, *Florida for Tourists*, 232–233, 235–237, Cowan, *A New Invasion of the South*, 34.

22. N. S. Shaler, "The Future of the Negro in the Southern States," *Popular Science Monthly*, LVII (June, 1900), 148–149, 154–155; Wiley, *Arena*, XXIII, 558–560. Shaler (1841–1906), a native of Kentucky and a Harvard graduate, served two years as an artillery officer in the Union army. As professor of paleontology and geology and a dean he became a major figure of Harvard. Dumas Malone, ed., *Dictionary of American Biography*, (20 vols.; New York: Charles Scribner, 1936), XVII, 17–19.

23. Field, *Bright Skies and Dark Shadows*, 167.

24. Barrow, *Atlantic Monthly*, LXVII, 807.

25. Du Bois, United States Department of Labor, *Bulletin*, III, No. 14, pp. 17, 18.

26. Bassett, *Lippencott's Magazine*, XXVIII, 207.

27. Charles Dudley Warner, *On Horseback: A Tour in Virginia, North Carolina and Tennessee* (Boston: Houghton, Mifflin, and Co., 1880), 106. Warner (1829–1900), well-known man of letters, was born at Plainfield, Massachusetts, and educated at Hamilton College and the University of Pennsylvania. For a sketch of him see *Dictionary of American Biography*, XIX, 462–463.

28. Campbell, *White and Black*, 138–139, 298.

29. Baumgarten, compl., *America*, 316–321; O'Rell, *Jonathan and His Continent*, 287–288; Handlin, ed., *This Was America*, 348; James Fullarton Muirhead, *America The Land Contrasts* (London: John Lane 1898), 39–40, 253–254. Muirhead (1853–1934), educated at Edinburgh University, was most noted for editing the English editions of *Bedeker's Handbooks*, a job he held for over thirty-five years. He married the great-granddaughter of Josiah Quincy. *Who Was Who, 1929–1940*, p. 980.

30. Towne, *Letters and Diary*, 267–269.

31. Bradley, *Other Days*, 362.

32. Allan-Olney, *The New Virginians*, I, 26, 36, 137–143, 189–190.

33. Barbour, *Florida for Tourists*, 227.

34. Bassett, *Lippincott's Magazine*, XXVIII, 206–207.

35. D'Haussonville, *A Travers, Les Etate-Unis*, 153.

36. Hardy, *Oranges and Alligators*, 100–101, 109–110.

37. O'Rell, *Jonathan and His Continent*, 276–282.

38. Du Bois, United States Department of *Labor, Bulletin*, III, No. 14, p.21.

39. Towne, *Letters and Diary*, 297, 307.

40. Mifflin Wistar Gibbs, *Shadow and Light: An Autobiography* (Washington, D.C.: The author, 1902), 366. Born in 1823 in Philadelphia, Gibbs worked in Baltimore as a free youth, observing there some of the most dramatic operations of the "Underground Railroad." He later became an anti-slavery lecturer. He was a carpenter, contractor, merchant, railroad builder, and was in California in the years immediately following the discovery of a gold as a superintendent of mines. He

witnessed Reconstruction in Florida, and actively participated in it in Arkansas. He held various local and federal appointments including that of United States Consul to Madagascar. Gibbs himself was an admirer of Booker Washington and a critic of emphasis on the professions. *Gibbs, Shadow and Light*, v-vii. T. Thomas Fortune, *Black and White: Land, Labor and Politics in the South* (New York: Fords, Howard, and Hulbert, 1884), 183. Fortune was born in Florida, the son of a Reconstruction legislator, and graduated from Howard University. Shortly thereafter he moved permanently to the North, where he entered the newspaper business. He wrote for the New York *Sun*, then edited the black owned New York *Globe* and New York *Age*. Fortune was strongly Caucasian in appearance. At his peak he was the intimate of the best known black business and cultural leaders in the country. He early identified with the principles of Booker Washington, and in later years with some of the ideas of Marcus Garvey. Fortune, was not wholly sympathetic with educating blacks for the profession, but happy to applaud the successful. He was in the South for a considerable period between 1880 and 1884. Richard Bardolph, *The Negro Vanguard* (1st Vintage ed.; New York: Vintage Books, (1961), 129–130.

41. Barrows, *Atlantic Monthly*, LXVII, 813.

42. Du Bois, United States Department of Labor, *Bulletin*, III, 14, pp. 16–17.

43. Campbell, *White and Black*, 281, 317–318, 327. Du Bois, United States Department of Labor, *Bulletin*, III, No. 14, p.18.

44. Hesse-Wartegg, *Mississippi-Fahrteh*, 18, 252.

45. Julian Ralph, *Harper's Weekly*, XXXVII (January, 1893), 39. Ralph (1853–1903) was "a professional traveler, but his powers of observations were unusually good." Clark, ed., *Travels in the New South*, I, 221–222. Educated in New York, he was on the staff of various New York newspapers beginning in 1875, and in 1896 became London correspondent for the *Journal*. *Who's Who in America*, 1899–1900, p. 588.

46. Cowan, A New *Invasion of the South*, 36, 51–53; Warner, *On Horseback*, 115–117.

47. William Wells Brown, My Southern Home: or the South and its People (Boston: A. G. Brown and Co., Publishers, 1880), 167, 172–173. Brown (1816–1884), was born at Lexington, Kentucky. His mother was a slave, his father probably a white slaveholder. Having escaped into Ohio in 1834, Brown became active in the anti-slavery and other reform movements. Long afterward, in 1880, he visited Alabama, Tennessee, and Virginia. Brown's reputation rests largely on such works as *The Black Man, His Antecedents, His Genius, and His Achievements* (1863) and *The Negro in the American Rebellion* (1867). *Dictionary of American Biography*, III, 161.

48. Sala, *America Revisited*, 165. Fortune, *Black and White*, 181–182; Nelson, *Harper's Weekly*, XXXVI, 654.

49. Henry Loomis Nelson, "The Washington Negro," *Harper's Weekly*, XXXVI (July, 1892), 654. Nelson, a native of New York, City, became editor-in-chief of *Harper's Weekly*, and was subsequently professor of political science at Williams College. *Who Was Who in America*, I, 890.

50. Du Bois, United States Department of Labor, *Bulletin*, p. 18; Baumgarten, *America*, 400–401.

51. Saunders, *Through the Light Continent*, 76–77.

52. Barrows, *Atlantic Monthly*, LXVII, 813–814; Brown, *My Southern Home*, 200–201.

53. ˜Du Bois, United States Department of Labor, *Bulletin*, III, No. 14, p. 17.

54. Thomas M. Young, *The American Cotton Industry*, 103–104.

55. TBA

56. Johnston, *The Negro in the New World*, 428–429.

57. Baker, *Following the Color Line*, 73, 75, 89–91.

58. Hart, *The Southern South*, 120–123.

59. Young, *American Cotton Industry*, 68–69.

60. Hart, *The Southern South*, 275; Holland Thompson, *From the Cotton Field to the Cotton Mill* (New York, 1906) is one of the better early studies of mill laborers, but Thompson does not qualify as an outsider.

61. A Camp Physician, *Independent*, LXXX, 790.

62. Johnston, *The Negro in the New World*, 436.

63. Cram, *Old Seaport Towns,* 339.

64. Kelsey, *The Negro Farmer*, 33.

65. Rossa B. Cooley, "Aunt Jane and Her People," *Outlook*, XC (October, 1908), 426–427.

66. James, *The American Scene*, 360–363, Cram, *Old Seaport Towns*, 13, 18, 35, 81, 138–139.

67. Baker, Following the Color Line, 27–29; Hart, *The Southern South*, 122–126.

68. Tweedie, *America As I Saw It*, 368–370; Johnston, *The Negro in the New World*, 436, 473; Hart, *The Southern South*, 129–130; Gibbs, *Shadow and Light*, 366; Street, *American Adventures*, 538.

69. W. E. Buoghardt Du Bois, "The Opening of the Library," *Independent*, LIV (April, 1902), 809–810.

70. Archer, *Through Afro-America*, 40–42

71. *Ibid*, 62–65.

72. Kelsey, *The Negro Farmer*, 18.

73. Alonzo F. Herndon and his amazing rise from slavery to riches is a fascinating topic in American business history. His Atlanta Life Insurance Company was once the richest black business in the country. Norris B. Herndon, the founder's son was also once the wealthiest African American in America. Baker, *Following the Color Line*, 39–41, 43.

74. Hart, *The Southern South*, 129–130.

75. Johnston, *The Negro in the New World*, 436.

76. Hungerford, *The Personality of American Cities*, 141–142.

77. Street, *American Adventures*, 483, 495–498, 538.

78. Charles Bartlett Dyke, "Theology versus Thrift in the Black Belt," *Popular Science Monthly*, LX (February, 1902), 360–364. Dyke was born in 1870 at Berea, Ohio, and educated at Baldwin University (Ohio), Stanford, and Columbia, whence he received the M.A. in 1899. Beginning in 1915 he was superintendent of schools at Milburn, New Jersey. His career as teacher and educational administrator took him to

Minnesota and Honolulu and briefly (1899–1900) to Hampton Institute. *Who's Who in America*, 1920–1921, p. 837.

79. Siegfried, *America Comes of Age*, 96–97; Tannenbaum, *Darker Phases*, 118–119.

80. Cooley, "America's Sea Island," *Outlook*, CXXXl, (April, 1919), 739–740.

81. Arnaldo Cipolla, *Nortre America y los Nortre Americans* (trans. into Spanish by Ramon Mondira; Santiago, Chile: Editorial Nascimento, 1929), 236–237. Cipolla (b. 1879) was in the South from 1924 to 1927. Lawrence S. Thompson in Clark, ed., *Travels in the New South*, II, 152.

82. *New York Times*, October 27, 1921, p.1; W.L. George, Hail Columbia: *Random Impressions of a Conservative English Radical* (New York: Harper and Brothers Publishers, 1921), 177. Walter Lionel George (1882–1926), born of British parents in Parish and educated there, became a journalist, serving as a special correspondent of various newspapers in France, Belgium, and Spain, He traveled to Missouri and Alabama in 1920. *Who Was Who*, 1916–1928, 404.

83. Prossinagg, *Das Antlitz Amerikas*, 240–241.

84. Prince William of Sweden, "America froma Pullman Car," *Living Age* (trans. From *Svenska Dagbladet,* Stockholm*)*, CCCXXXV (November, 1928), 200–201.

85. John T. Faris, *Seeing the Sunny South* (Philadelphia: J. B. Lippimcolt and Co., 1921), 144. John Thomas Faris was born in 1871 at Cape Girardeau, Missouri, but was soon taken North, attending Princeton University and the McCormick Theological Seminary of Chicago. As a Presbyterian Minister his first pastoral was at Mount Carmel, Illinois (1898–1903), and he was subsequently active in editing Presbyterian Sunday School publications. He toured all of the south in 1920–1921. *Who's Who in America*, 1920–21, p. 915.

86. Handlin, ed., *This Was America*, 490–491, 497–498. Von Luckner as a youth worked his way around the world as a ordinary seamen. During World War I he commanded the famous commerce raider, *Seeadler*. Afterward he lectured in the United States almost a year and wrote *Seeteufel erobert Amerika* (1928).

87. Cooley, *School Acres*, 123–124.

Chapter Three

Pray, Shout and Sing

African Americans in the United States, long a victim of racial discrimination and oppression, have had to make many adjustments. With little control over their own lives they were (and in a few places still are) considered less than human. In a real sense, it became necessary for them to develop techniques of both physical and emotional survival. Among these was what was originally called American Negro Religion. Very early the church gave African Americans the one and only organized field in which they could release their "suppressed emotions" and develop independent leadership.[1]

At "Frogmore" shortly after the Civil War, Laura Towne heard an old black woman, newly freed, praying a simple but stirring invocation. She implored "Massa Jesus" to come down among her race and lift their heavy burdens. (He would not have to knock at the door, just come right in.) This is an example of the simplicity and emotionalism which have remained vital parts of African American religion.[2]

The evangelical denominations, Baptists and Methodists, with their emphasis on freedom of emotional expression and simple rites, attracted the great masses of the race, as they did of the southern whites also. Thus, in a sense, African American worship has not been unique. There were definite similarities between it and other forms of evangelical religion both in this country and in Europe. It has paralleled, in many particulars, ancient worship practices in Asia, Africa, South America, and among North American Indians. Even the voodoo worship once seen among Louisiana blacks, an import from Africa and Haiti, did not differ radically from the practices of snake cults and "holy rollers" subsequently to be found among some "backward" Euro-American whites.

One of the more unique elements—and one of the most attractive to outsiders—has been the revered Negro spirituals with their dialect peculiar to this country. The development of Negro spirituals was a part of the adjustment blacks made to the new conditions in America. The songs were partly reactions to the oppression which their creators experienced as southern chattels and which their descendants faced under the succeeding caste system. Basically, they represent what Mays and Nicholson, and others call the soul of a people—their "joy and sorrow," "hope and despair," "pathos and aspiration." The race seemed through them to be grasping for a way to relieve its oppression and to survive.[3]

Southern whites were prone to look upon black religion as very different from theirs, so much so that they often made special visits to African American churches to observe the rites. This being so, it is no surprise that the outsiders also exhibited a great curiosity about black religion.

Southern black churches were typically small, unpainted, often windowless buildings, steamy hot in summer, smoky in winter. There were, however, buildings which compared favorably with the more attractive ones in which whites worshipped. Henry Nelson called the black churches of Washington "modest and substantial." William Wells Brown, after observations at Nashville and Petersburg, Virginia, deplored a growing tendency of African Americans to build costly churches "often from the scanty earnings of men in the fields or at service and black women over the washtub." Rossa B. Cooley, a long-time friend of blacks on the Sea Islands, noted that on St. Helena alone there were seven well-constructed black churches, one of brick inherited from whites and six of wood that represented "much effort and sacrifice on the part of their builders."[4]

African American church services, especially in North Carolina, were attended by Sir George Campbell, who also witnessed a convention of black Baptist ministers. The oratory of black preachers tended to "exaggerate the American style," which itself exaggerated the British; but Campbell felt on the whole "considerably edified" by the performances. "They come to the point in a way that is refreshing after some sermons that one has heard." The churches were thoroughly democratic, and were independent of all white guidance and control, affording the blacks a significant experience of self-government. While Campbell did not witness the excessive emotion attributed to worshippers—the few hearty responses to sermons that he heard were not disturbing nor irreverent—he understood it to be an expression of direct communion with God, which was not without merit. Because of this desire for direct communion Campbell predicted that Roman Catholicism would never enjoy much success among African Americans.[5]

The convention of Baptist ministers that Sir George attended was held in a rural church, and proved "a pleasant sight." Campbell understood that black preachers were chosen because they were leaders, rather than the other way around. This group did not, however, deliberate in seclusion. The "whole countryside seemed to have come in to assist, both men and women, and they seemed to be making a time of it, camped about for the day." An African American church at Jacksonville was visited by Abbie N. Brooks, who felt that blacks were more "naturally inclined to religion" than whites were. Sometimes called Silvia Sunshine, Abbie was a northern "lass" whose sickness took her South each winter, mainly to Florida. Most of what she saw of African Americans in various parts of the state in 1878 was not encouraging, but she was impressed with the sermon at Jacksonville. The preacher berated his flock for saving their money, rather than bringing it to him, or rather to the church.

> Last night was Saturday, and you have spent most of yer week's wages, and earnin's, dun put de rest in de Freedmen's Savin Bank, and you don't know as you'll ever see it any moe in dis world: . . . How much did you bring here for de Lord?[6]

Black preaching, and congregational reaction to it, were never heard by William Saunders, to his regret, for each time he visited an African American service a white man preached. The sermons were among the best he heard in America, for white preachers seemed to speak "plainly" to the black congregations. On one occasion blacks even mistook Saunders for a preacher when he protested his lack of calling, they suspected him of being a detective.[7]

African American ministers were grossly inadequate, not at all concerned about "personal holiness"—such was the conviction of Mary Allan-Olney, who perhaps never set foot in a black church. She appears to have gotten most of her information from black servants. African American religious services were, she felt, of "mixed quality, often punctuated by "Oh, I'm so happy!" and invariably ending with 'Hallelujah!' Although seemingly depreciating the songs, she thought them original enough to want to make a compilation of them. She learned that African Americans tended to "line out" their hymns, i.e., to read a stanza of a song, then sing it. This, as William Aubrey noted, was because few of the congregation could read. The "lining out" was done by any literate preacher, deacon, or sister the congregation happened to possess. Aubrey was especially critical of the discourses of the preachers. "Even charity cannot condone the absurdity, the ignorance, and the irreverent parodies of sermons by unlearned but fluent and conceited preachers, of whom there are far too many."

One of Mary Allan-Olney's servants, while busily shouting in church, had a chicken stolen from her there. Allan-Olney was not surprised, for she believed that "negroes cannot see any connection between morality and religion." Many persons had "talked glibly about going out to convert the heathen," but in point of fact the blacks were heathens already "at our doors, and we know not what to do."[8]

Also unsympathetic to southern black religion, though for quite different reasons, was the African American physician-historian, William Wells Brown. He attributed "the moral and social degradation of the colored population" of the South largely to their religion. Next to food, he thought religion the dearest thing to a southern black. It would be difficult to erase "the prevailing idea that outward demonstrations, such as shouting, the loud 'amen,' and the most boisterous noise in prayer are not necessary adjuncts to piety." The frivolity displayed in many revival meetings, and the lateness of the hours at which they closed, were injurious to both health and morals. The only remedy he saw was in an educated ministry, signs of which had already begun to appear. Brown's view was shared by Bryce, who noted the "salutary effect on Negro religion" of educated ministers in the Border states. It would be hard, however, to induce "the uneducated, superstitious masses to receive and support an intelligent Christian Clergyman."[9]

The call for an educated clergy found favor with other observers such as T. Thomas Fortune, the black editor, Edward Freeman, the English historian, and Lillian Chase Wyman, the New England writer. Fortune believed, however, that the ministry should not be over emphasized among the professions, and urged African Americans to aim for positions other than those with churches paying "fair salaries." Even at Baltimore the services struck him as "strange." The black minister made a number of errors, including the assertion that the will of Herod the Great had been "taken to Rome to be probated by Augustus." On the other hand, the services at the city's black Episcopal Church, "with tendencies to what is called an 'advanced ritual'," were probably more akin to those of the "better" white churches.[10]

At a "Black Belt" church visited by Lillian Wyman in 1891 the minister's sermon declared his disbelief, traditional in the "evangelistic" sects, in the propriety of educated men for the ministry. Ministers were called of God, not made by education. His own summons had been received in the days of bondage, when it was dangerous for African Americans to transmit the "word of God." The preacher then touched political topics and the current depressing condition of the race. "If there's any world where they don't talk about 'niggers'" he wanted to go there. "That's one thing I love Jesus for. He's going to put an end to all this trouble by and by." This preacher, Mrs. Wyman learned, interpreted the Bible literally, believing that the earth was flat and that the stars sang. The doctrine of evolution he compared to "a flop-eared mule, sure to fling its rider into hell." Even among the educated ministers Mrs. Wyman noted shortcomings. As they became excited in the heat of their sermons, they tended to relapse into ungrammatical dialect.[11]

A more favorable sampling of African American ministers and their sermons was made by the Reverend John Kerr Campbell, a Presbyterian minister from Scotland, who attended black worship at Paris, Kentucky, just northeast of Lexington. He was asked to preach, but declined on account of a later engagement. The black pastor in discussing the creation, fall, and redemption of man began by exploring various prevailing theories of man's creation, including the agnostic, Darwinian, and speculative ones, then dismissed them all in favor of Genesis. (The preacher's audience in rural Kentucky must have been severely taxed if he actually discussed these matters in a learned manner. The world was, he said, too mutable to be regarded as external. His second topic, the fall, he depicted in vivid terms, and at this point brought the audience into the act. As the minister cried 'Oh, brethren! What shall we do?' His auditors "began to sway to and fro on their seats and some of them groaned." With each, 'Oh, what shall we do?' the groaning grew louder. The sermon ended with a calm discussion of man's redemption. The lung power of the preacher Campbell found a little strong for his appreciation, but otherwise he was impressed with the sermon. It did credit to the minister and his teachers. Only when he spoke rapidly and excitedly did he err in his pronunciations; then he uttered such sounds as "fadder', mudder,' and Re Publican sinner.'"[12]

African American spirituals baffled the Reverend Mr. Campbell. To him they were in an unknown tongue, though later he heard and understood such familiar tunes as "Nearer, My God to Thee." To Lillie Wyman, on the other hand, it was when blacks attempted standard "congregational" hymns that they failed. When they resorted to the low murmur called moaning, they demonstrated clearly "the soul of savage people, upon whom its masters have imposed the religion of a civilized world."[13]

African American ministers at Savannah exhibited considerable ability in the opinion of the Reverend Timothy Harley, a Methodist minister from Great Britain. Even the older ones, though "lamentably ignorant," possessed a "natural eloquence" more effective than argument in dealing with the "emotional hearers whom they have to address." One of the worshippers stole a goose on Saturday and yet took communion on Sunday, apparently seeing nothing incongruous in the fact. Harley feared that the African American churches encouraged this type of behavior, and he denounced as dangerous that theology "which talks of 'mere morality.'"[14]

African Americans were much more devout in their worship than Euro-Americans, Dean Hole of Rochester observed. Hole was particularly interested in the hymns heard in a Richmond Church, "strange . . . and unsound in doctrine, quaint . . . in their language and in their association with common things," yet "stirring, pathetic, and harmonious." For example:

'De Gospel Train
'De Gospel Train's a-coming, I hear it just at hand, I hear dem car wheels movin',' and a rumblin' through the land . . .'

Chorus---
'Get on board, children; get on board, children; Get on board children, for dere's room for many more . . .'[15]

A somewhat different view of the Negro spirituals, approaching that of modern scholars, was held by Rossa Cooley, who heard them often on St. Helena Island.

My belief is that religion is the gift of the Negro to our American life . . . The spirituals are their one articulate contribution, echoing the history of a people who have come through the valley of the shadow. In their prayers no less than their music do we find poetic imagery and spiritual values.[16]

African American sermons, Du Bois felt, were "apt to be fervent repetitions of an orthodox Calvinism, in which, however, hell lost something of its terrors through endless repetition." In Farmville, Virginia at least, the African American ministry was improving educationally, and, unlike their illiterate counterparts, lashing out at immorality. Du Bois could not, however, agree with them that such pleasures as dancing were a "sin;" though even in the local church near Fisk University, they were denounced as such. For his part, this was nonsense, and he would continue dancing.[17]

The African American Church was more than a Sunday morning meetinghouse, most of the observers agreed. It was the social and often the political focus of the community, "the central clubhouse" in an even greater degree than "the country church in New England or the West." On St. Helena Island, for example, no decision of any importance was made without discussion in the churches.[18]

Financial support of African American churches came, as among Caucasians, from the congregations. Among blacks, however, the appeals were judged to be more fervent and more demanding. The black preacher at Jacksonville whom Abbie Brooks heard berate his congregation for saving their money rather than contributing it to the church was typical. The taking of the collection, Rossa Cooley observed, was a most important feature in African American services, for it gave *all* an opportunity to take part, and *all* were expected to do so. The deacons stood at the tables. Then the preacher lined out the hymn, and as the singing began the congregation marched to donate their money. If the offerings lagged a deacon would rise to lead a spiritual, and as a rule the money came faster. The African American congregation attended by the Reverend Campbell in Kentucky collected no money from white visitors, though they were given ice water at collection time.[19]

The baptisms which Laura Towne saw in South Carolina were apparently held out of doors even in winter. In January of 1877 an old black woman, said to be 120 years old, was immersed. She could not walk, so two elders took her to the water. In June of the same year a young black boy, one of Mrs. Towne's servants, was being prepared for the water. An African American baptism that Mary Allan-Olney saw took place in a pool formed from the widening of a little brook. "'Oh, Almighty God, we are here before thee this mornin', an we's poor mis'ble critters, an' we dunno nothin'" So began the baptism sermon. The preacher later led six women and a man into the pool, feeling with a big stick as he waded. The women were in

> very dirty dresses, dirty cloths round their heads and their skirts were tied tightly round them halfway down the leg. The man had a clean handkerchief round his head. I think he was barefoot; but the women stood in their stockings.

The first of them, a middle-aged, "yellow Negro" woman, "was dipped, head backwards, and went into the dirty water with her mouth wide open." The minister said: 'I baptize thee in the name of the Father, the Son, and the Holy Ghost.' As soon as she was on her feet again, she "gave a loud whoop, and threw her arms and legs about like one possessed."[20]

The fervid emotionalism associated with African American religion showed itself beyond the church door or the baptismal pool, particularly in times of crisis. During the Charleston earthquake of 1886, Jose Marti witnessed some of these manifestations. When the earthquake hit "fright sparked the Negroes' tempestuous imagination." For the first two days it was like "a religious jubilee, the arrogant whites, when fear grew, humbly joined the frantic Negroes in . . . improvised hymns; many a Negro girl hung to a white woman's skirt as she passed by and weepingly implored her to take her with her." Groups of blacks moved from city to country and back to city carrying tents, sitting awhile, then marching, then stopping and singing. They did not "seem to find a sure place for their rags and their fear."

The African, Marti felt, lived more than any other race in an intimate communion with nature, and thus seemed more capable than other people of "shuddering and rejoicing with her changes. In his fright . . . there is something supernatural and marvelous which cannot be found in other primitive races." During the Charleston quake the blacks, "having been taught the

Bible," uttered their fright in religious terms. "'Jesus, my Master,' 'my sweet Jesus,'" they called, "on their knees beating their heads and their thighs as spires and columns came crashing down." African American children rolled on the ground, frenzied, their eyes "bathed in tears." They saw, Marti concluded, their Jesus as "whipped and meek like themselves," and in this their most trying hour since emancipation they wanted Him to come and save them.[21]

Not all African Americans worshiped formally in churches, or were exclusively devoted to the Christian God. There were other spiritual and emotional forces at work among a large segment of the race, including many dutiful church members. For convenience sake we may speak of these forces as superstitions and fears though these labels do not really explain the wide variety of phenomena of a religious character prevalent among southern blacks of the late nineteenth century. Such names as voodooism, conjuration, and spooks are closer to the point. For the outside observer these matters were as interesting, or more interesting, than the African American's practice of Christianity.

Voodooism greatly intrigued the Irish-Greek journalist Lafcadio Hearn. The story of his association with a mulatto called Marie Laveau, reputedly a Voodoo Queen, is told by his biographer, Edward L. Tinker. Marie was about fifty years of age in 1879, although she looked younger. She had been free before the Civil War and had started life as a "coiffeuse." An early leader of the voodoo cult in New Orleans, she gained considerable control over superstitious blacks; indeed, many whites became her "victims."

On one occasion Marie took advantage of the African American fascination with death. She had a man pose as dead and requested money to bury him. Blacks by the score came to view the "body" and contributed. Marie sold charms for "good luck" in love, politics, or business, and amulets, such as snakeskin or teeth, to ward off "evil spirits." Many a black man or woman who discovered some voodoo sign on his or her doorstep, placed there obviously by Marie, would rush to her New Orleans residence to buy an antidote. Such a sign, unless nullified by an amulet, meant "bad luck" or even death.

Marie's principal activity was voodooism. She conducted her meetings mainly at midnight, in a swamp near one of the cottages she owned. To the traditional worship of a serpent, the sacrifices of a white cock or a goat, the drinking of "tafia," and orgiastic dancing, Marie added certain new features, as she sought to make the rites acceptable to Roman Catholics, of whom there were a good many among New Orleans' African Americans. She introduced the adoration of the Virgin Mary side by side with the worship of the serpent. Thus many Christian blacks joined the "pagans" in wild, drunken dancing, sometimes going into convulsions. Marie's practices so captured Hearn's "peculiar imagination" that the frequency of his visits to her grave led to "disagreeable gossip which has persisted to this day."[22]

Hearn was acquainted also with Jean Montanet, another noted New Orleans voodoo leader. Montanet's practices differed little from those of Marie, but his ideas were more extreme. He had apparently been exposed to voodooism in Africa and his "ideas of religion were primitive in the extreme." He always subordinated the Christian influences to the African. When Montanet died in August, 1885, aged nearly 100, "New Orleans lost . . . the most extraordinary African character that ever gained celebrity within her limits" and "the last of the voodoos." Later, at the end of 1886, Hearn could even say that "as a religion—an imported faith—Voodooism in Louisiana is really dead; the rites of its serpent worship are forgotten." What was left was "not an African cultus, but a curious class of Negro practices, some possibly derived from it, and others which bear resemblance to the magic of the Middle Ages." Voodooism rites were seen by Johannes Baumgarten during the Mardi Gras of 1880. He managed, however, to get participation in Mardi Gras confused with the voodoo worship, and concluded that all the African American celebrants were worshipping the "Voodoo Queen," Marie, whom he also designated their Mardi Gras queen. The blacks were dancing, clowning, screaming, and crying around a big fire. At the midnight hour men jumped into a pool of water, reemerged shortly thereafter, and continued dancing. Baumgarten was displeased with what he saw, and surprised that these practices of "fetichism," unlike their counterparts in Haiti, were not secretive in their behavior. Bryce also noted disapprovingly that in parts of Louisiana the blacks had "relapsed into the Obeah rites and serpent worship of African heathendom. How far this has gone no one can say." Similarly, Clowes said in 1891, that voodooism certainly existed in the South, "and especially in Louisiana." Whether either of them actually saw voodoo rites is doubtful.[23]

In Florida the older blacks experienced no uneasiness in the presence of serpents and other animals. One of Eunice White Beecher's servants had for a number of years walked at night two miles through the forest, unmolested and unafraid. Though somewhat apprehensive of large rattle snakes, she felt that even these could be "handled" with "a little caution." A younger Florida black man on the other hand confessed that if he came upon a rattlesnake, "I'ze leaves quick!"[24]

On St. Helena Island the regular churches had done a good deal by the end of the century to break down old superstitions. These had included the practice of keeping one door open, even in cold weather, so that the "good spirit" might readily enter. Other African Americans thought themselves "conjured," afflicted, or hexed by an enemy. One old man reported that spiders had to be taken from his arm and leg by a "conjure doctor," after which his whole physical condition improved. Rossa Cooley traced these phenomena "back to Africa and the East," and was glad to witness their passing.[25]

With their "bat's bones" and their "lucky horseshoes," the blacks of Washington were a very superstitious lot, Henry Loomis Nelson found. But the sight was so picturesque that he did not wish it to disappear. Few would have disputed the picturesqueness, but Nelson stood alone among observers in his desire for the perpetuation of superstitious practices.[26]

The African American's fascination with spooky tales might be seen in the adventure surrounding the Van Ness home in Washington, D. C. Legend told of a plot to abduct President Abraham Lincoln, hide him in the Van Ness cellar, and convey him across the Potomac, then demand a ransom for his life. Another story concerned the late Mayor Van Ness' six white horses. Hezekiah Butterworth, a New England author and traveler, accompanied a small group of students to the Van Ness residence in 1892 to learn details from the black servants, who were undoubtedly the source of the story. According to one black person the six white horses had dropped dead after returning from the Mayor's funeral. But at "'de midnight cock-crowin'" every Christmas they returned to haunt the mansion. Smoke came out of their "necks" and formed the face of the late Mayor. The storyteller later admitted that he had not actually seen any of this. "Aunt Marie," who supposedly had given a different version, saying that the horses had not fallen dead immediately after the funeral but had gone into the meadow and died of "broken hearts," there "'de riber rose, and covered 'em.'" Under questioning "Aunt Marie" became indignant, denounced the disbelievers "from up North," and terminated the interview.[27]

The emancipated nineteenth century African Americans were on the whole unlettered emotional persons. Like all such peoples, they were thus very susceptible to superstitious and other supernatural phenomena. As some observers suggested, time and education would be needed before they, and their ministers, developed a more sophisticated theology and the ability to discard unscientific beliefs and practices.

Yet African American worship in the 20th century differed little from that in the nineteenth. Consequently, outside views of black religion remained largely unchanged. Clifton Johnson's appraisal of black preachers, that they were "often blind leaders of the blind" and Charles Dyke's, that the illiterate among them bore much responsibility for black thriftlessness and indolence, were altogether typical of observer impressions.

The *Atlantic Monthly* carried in 1906 a colorful account by a novelist, John Bennett, of his attendance at a country church in Anderson County, presumably South Carolina. The building, formerly a gin house, had been bought by the blacks and converted into a sanctuary and a schoolhouse. A plantation bell, once used to summon cotton field gangs, occupied a "crude little belfry of boards" atop the church. The building, severely weather beaten, had taken on a "purple-gray and lichen-green" coloring. Illumination came from three kitchen lamps "with wrinkled tin reflectors" nailed against the wall. The doors, were "unpainted, whip-sawed plank," warped and cracked, and had no locks. The windows were also of plank. Wide cracks in the walls and floor let in both moonlight and wind. The women sat on one side, the men on the other, upon wooden benches which had been worn smooth by attrition.

Prior to the opening of the principal service an old black deacon led a prayer, with a "wonderfully soft, deep voice" that seemed to Bennett "a Laus Perennis [a continuous prayer], its melodious flow going steadily and musically on without a pause; like an old Ambrosian chant." The sermon at Little St. John's was a characteristic one, interrupted by the usual audience reaction. It struck Bennett as crude and child-like though eloquent. The African American revered spirituals he thought were stirring but barbaric in a way no musical score could convey. As far as he could make out the songs were "in the compass of a tetra chord," similar to medieval chants. Their harmonies were "wild and irregular, being for the greater part accidental or instinctive, except under direct white influence." The whole proceedings, sermon, music, prayers, shouting and all, seemed to border on the hysterical, if not the insane, combining a "half-Christian service "with" half-pagan frenzy."[28]

A degree of irreligion, something almost unheard of in nineteenth-century African American life, was beginning to appear, at least among the miners of Jefferson County, Alabama. The camp physician noted that many made no pretense of being religious. For them the lodges had become the principal social institution.[29]

That the irreligious were a very small minority among the blacks seemed to be confirmed by Albert Bushnell Hart's wider southern observations. Everywhere he went the Harvard historian encountered hordes of black Baptists and Methodists. He was somewhat puzzled to know why Roman Catholicism had not attracted a sizeable number of blacks. In his view (which most other commentators did not share) the "democratic" worship and the ritual of the Catholic Church should have appealed to "Negro nature." Urban black churches, he found, were quite prosperous, their members being "pertinacious about raising money for construction and other similar purposes;" buildings cost as much as twenty, thirty, or even fifty thousand dollars.

The intellectual and moral state of the African American ministry Hart thought pathetic, but "simply educating the minister" would not solve the problem. What the people desired was not intelligent theological discourses but an exhortation to "arouse them to pleasurable excitement." Before the situation could be improved, the type of piety prevailing among the blacks would have to undergo change. Their religion was in the state that the white frontiersman had passed half a century earlier, and that "backwoods" and "mountain" whites were slowly overcoming. Given time, Hart implied, blacks too would develop a more advanced theology. Meanwhile "a genuine colored service was extremely picturesque."[30]

Sir Harry Johnston took a more optimistic view of the status of African American religious characteristics. He thought "the whole set of influence amongst the leading pastors now is against religious hysteria." Revival meetings, to judge from the ones he saw, were "no longer to be characterized by the curious mixture of raving religious ecstasy and sexual laxity which was, no doubt, rightly attributed to them a few years ago."[31]

A decade later, when Thomas Jesse Jones completed a study of African Americans for the Phelps-Stokes Fund, he could not affirm Sir Harry's flattering view of the African American ministry. Though it was true that many black ministers, including some of the unlettered, were of high character and provided laudable leadership in spiritual, economic, and social affairs, the qualifications of the larger number were "very unsatisfactory." Jones urged "vigorous" action to increase the number of schools offering religious training. Unlike Hart, he felt that an educated ministry could have a positive effect.[32]

The superstitious and other pseudo-religious practices of African Americans attracted the attention of outsiders as much as, and often more, than their Christian worship. To reiterate these beliefs and practices were not confined to the unchurched segments of the race. It was common enough for a staunch black Baptist to visit the habitats of witch doctors, conjure women and voodoo queens.

The superstitions of North Carolina blacks so impressed African American novelist Charles Chestnutt, that he wrote a highly credible novel dealing with them. He felt the tales of ghosts and conjurers reflected in no small degree the simplicity of life among a largely ignorant people. One of Chestnutt's favorite tales was that of the "goophered" vineyard, in which a North Carolina grape plantation had mysteriously lost much of its produce. The plantation owner was forced eventually to call upon a "conjure woman" to help "keep de niggers offn de grapevines." Local blacks, upon learning that the vines had been "goophered" or "conjured," scrupulously stayed away. When a visiting black coachman ate from the cursed vine and soon met an untimely death, every one "knowed de goopher had b'en er wukkin!"[33]

African Americans on the Sea Islands had superstitions all their own. One of these was the enduring practice of giving "basket names" to infants so that "the Evil Spirit may not know the right name and so have greater power." Rossa Cooley noticed, approvingly, that many of the old superstitions were dying out by 1908, but this one seemed to have continuing appeal.[34]

The "fetishes" of the Sea Island blacks disgusted Sir Harry Johnston. With the possible exception of practices in the "remote swamps of southwest Louisiana" he thought the Sea Islanders' religion wilder and more primitively African than he had seen elsewhere in the country. It included witchcraft with "medicine men" or "guffer doctors." Their "fetish temples" were called "Praise Houses." It was there that their wild religious dances called "shouts" took place. In essence, these were the same dances performed by the adherents of Marie Laveau's brand of voodooism. The fact that the Islanders involved were all "pure Negroes, entirely without any infusion of white blood" had a distinct bearing on their behavior, Sir Harry believed.[35]

At New Orleans ordinances had been passed to control black "voodoo" and "voodoo" practices, Mildred Cram learned in 1917. The principal restraint was that all such activities had to be held behind closed doors. As a consequence, Mrs. Cram saw none. Julie Street, in the area at the same time, noted the removal of the voodoo ceremonies from "Congo Square" to "more secluded spots on the shores of Lake Pontchartrain," but he did not mention the ordinances which, to judge from Cram, were perhaps responsible. If anything the voodoos had won a wider appeal than before, "love powders were being sold in the drug stores in New Orleans." Street took a position with which many modern observers can agree: Voodooism was not "to be dignified by the name religion." It was rather "superstition founded upon charms and hoodoos," "witchcraft of the maddest kind, involving the most hideous performances." Street understood that "voodoo" had instilled fear among many of the blacks, particularly the French-speaking ones. Fear was, indeed, quite justifiable inasmuch as "the throwing of wager, or curse, may also involve the administering of subtle poisons made from herbs."[36]

Not only "voodoos" but also natural and "supernatural disturbances and phenomena continued to upset the emotional stability of some blacks. Several weeks after the great storm at Galveston, Texas, in the fall of 1900 which killed thousands of persons, Mrs. Alec Tweedie found the black population still "petrified." One "darky" only recently returned to the city told the Englishwoman that his escape had been "like getting out of hell!" Granting that the situation had been terrible, Mrs. Tweedie felt the blacks lingering fears were abnormal.[37]

A fear of ghosts, which possessed African Americans at Georgetown, South Carolina, evoked the sympathy of another Englishwoman, Lucy Soulsby, during the latter part of the First World War. On the whole Mrs. Soulsby was more interested in moral "purity" than in the African American, but her attention was drawn to "Plat Eye," the ghost who troubled local blacks, when an African American "kindling boy" named Nebuchadnezzar insisted that he be allowed to go home early in the afternoon rather than risk meeting "Plat Eye." The blacks fear of the ghost was, she thought, pathetic enough, but what amazed her most was that some local whites apparently accepted the blacks' stories. Whether motivated by fear, tradition, or devotion, African Americans had, it would appear, remained steadfast in singing praises to their God and gods.[38]

Having heard that the "funeral custom of Negroes" were "particularly curious," Jules Huret, the French editor, attended the funeral of two African Americans who died while he was visiting the "Alabama Plantation" in Louisiana. As it turned out, Huret attended not only the funeral but also the wake and the interment. The wake was held in what the blacks called a chapel but Huret would have designated a "hanger" since it bore little resemblance to a religious edifice. In this "chapel" the open coffins of the dead were exposed—a barbaric ritual, Huret felt—for the benefit of the congregation.

The funeral itself lasted two hours. The redwood, ornamented coffins occupied the front of the vast, gas-lighted room, along with the preacher and the choir. The preacher began the eulogy slowly and "sympathetically" then spoke "rapidly and vehemently," his mouth, filled with saliva. When cries of "O' Lord! O' God!" began to be heard, Huret found it difficult to understand the sermon. Following the eulogy, a series of prayers elicited more cries and shouts; the women in the audience "acting as if they were mad." Huret and his companions, the only Caucasians present, decided to leave at this point "lest this madness might reach us."

The next morning Huret returned for the burial. Many of the mourners had, he discovered, remained all night awaiting the event. The preacher, rejuvenated, began his interment remarks by telling the story of Job in a fashion, mostly incoherent, that had no relationship to the subject. He then related a conversation with the deceased women during their illnesses in which they had pardoned all, and wished all to forgive them. Now they were safely in Heaven, never to be seen again. This statement provoked "wild cries and sobs which come in floods." The daughters of the dead women beat the coffins, crying "Mother, Mother, "God, God" and then "Jesus, Jesus." The black girls eventually had to be led away, resisting "as though they were insane, shouting and crying." It was for Huret, "a frightening scene of sadness and mass confusion." Some people might call it an interment, but it was in reality a "grouping together of mad men," a "maddened hysteria."[39] What so appalled Huret was fairly typical of African Americans funeral rites not only at that time but before and since. The emotionalism of African American spiritual life, particularly among the masses, has held sway even to the grave.

Southern blacks in the first quarter of the 20th century were hardly less religious than their ancestors. The number of outsiders who took the time to comment on this phase of African American life steadily declined, but those who did reiterated the fact that black religion remained simple and emotional. Also virtually unchanged were the edifices in which services were held. At Charlotte, North Carolina, Jan and Cora Gordon attended service in a huge chapel "like an immense timber barn empty of timber. A hundred posts supported the roof which floated in darkness above the wide shades of the hanging lamps." "The floor was deeply bedded with sawdust. Members of the congregation were shouting to 'de Glory of de Lord!" The Gordons noticed that the ushers discouraged men from participating in this "growing religious ecstasy." It included dancing "of a curious and savage nature . . . necessary to elicit moans and shouts from the audience. Some even had a kind of cataleptic fit and rolled stiffened to the floor." Often a song or a prayer would do so, and even a lay sermon or a spirited address could awaken the "Amen Comer." On an occasion when Amy Garvey spoke in Baton Rouge on the night following a lynching, she sensed that the blacks needed "comfort and cheer" and used verses from Isaiah, "'comfort ye my people,'" as her theme. "By the moans . . . and, expressions such as 'Tell it Sister, tell it! Hallelujah!' I felt that they were indeed comforted."[40]

During an automobile trip through the Shenandoah Valley, Ernst Prossinagg was fortunate enough to witness the rite of baptism being conducted by a black Baptist congregation. The blacks had dammed up a small stream as a pond. A crowd of them, men, women and children, stood around the edge of the pond praying loudly in unison. Suddenly, Prossinagg saw the black preacher wade in the water and then seize, one by one, a number of the blacks whom he fully submerged for a moment. The newly saved, dripping wet, then emerged and resumed the prayer. Both the way in which the blacks had constructed their baptismal pool and the fervor of their ceremony impressed Prosssinagg as unusual features of this ancient rite.[41]

NOTES

1. Benjamin Elijah Mays and Joseph William Nicholson, *The Negro's Church* (New York: Institute of Social and Religious Research 1933), 1–2.

2. *Outlook*, XC.

3. Mays and Nicholson, *The Negro's Church*, 1–2; E. Franklin Frazier, *The Negro Church in America* (New York: Schocken Books, 1963), 1–6, 82–83. Mays and Nicholson, *The Negro's Church*, 1–3. Professor E. Franklin Frazier vigorously dissents from these views, and questions the American origin of the songs. He does, however, see some continuity between the spirituals, especially as song of the Sea Islands, and the African background, and does give some credence to the contention that they partly reflect the oppressed condition of the slaves. *The Negro Church in America*, 12–13.

4. Brown, *My Southern Home*, 195–196. Rossa B. Cooley, *School Acres: An Adventure in Rural Education* (New Haven: Yale University Press, 1930), 154–157. Rossa Belle Cooley, northern philanthropist and educator taught for several years at Penn School on St. Helena Island, South Carolina, before succeeding Laura M. Towne as principal of the school, a position she held for some twenty years. *Outlook*, XC 432.

5. Campbell, *White and Black*, 132–133, 307.

6. Fletcher M. Green in Caerk, ed., *Travels in the New South*, I, 25: Abbie M. Brooks, *Petals Plucked From Sunny Climes* (Nashville: Southern Methodist Publishing House, 1880), title page, 40.

7. Saunders, *Through the Light Continent*, 77.

8. Allan-Olney, The New Virginians, I, 239–246; W. H. S. Aubrey, "Social Problems in America," *Fortnightly Review*, (b. 1848), edited a number of English newspapers and magazines, including Capital and Labour (1874–1882), and was an unsuccessful liberal candidate for Parliament in 1886 and 1892. He visited Kentucky and other parts of the South in 1888. *Who's Who*, 1904, pp. 56–57.

9. Brown, *My Southern Home*, 190–191, 195–197: Bryce, *American Commonwealth*, II, 521.

10. Freeman, *Some Impressions of the United States*, 170–171.

11. Wyman, *New England Magazine*, III, 786–787.

12. John Kerr Campbell, Through *the United States and Canada: Being a Record of Holiday Rambles and Experiences* (London: S.W. Partridge and C., 1886), title page, 151–154. Campbell, a fellow of the Royal Physical Society, Edinburgh, published an account of his "rambles" in the Middle East, entitled Through Egypt, Palestine and Syria.

13. Wyman, *New England Magazine*, III, 787.

14. Timothy Harley, *Southward Ho! Notes of a Tour to and through the State of Georgia*, in the winger of 1885–6 (London: Sampson Low, Marston, Searle, and Rivington Co., nomical Society, and author of *Moon Lore*, toured the South, mostly Georgia, during the winter of 1885–1886. He stopped at several places between Atlanta and Savannah.

15. Hole, *A Little Tour in America*, 298.

16. Cooley, *School Acres*, 157.

17. Du Bois, *United States Department of Labor Bulletin*, III, No. 14 , pp. 35–36, and Du Bois, *Dusk of Dawn*, 33.

18. Du Bois, *United States Department of Labor Bulletin*, III, No. 14, pp. 34–35: Campbell, *White and Black*, 132–133: Nelson, *Harper's Weekly*, XXXVI, 654.

19. Cooley, *School Acres*, 155–156.

20. Towne, *Letters and Diary*, 258, 367: Allan-Olney, *The New Virginians*, I, 240: II, 235, 239–244.

21. Marti on the *U. S. A.*, ed., and trans. by Luis A. Baralt (Varbondale, Illinois: Southern Illinois University Press, 1966), xi–xxvii, 95, 98–104, Marti (1835–1895). Cuban poet, essayist, dramatist, and patriot, has been considered one of his country's greatest heroes, and, like Simon Bolivar, is a symbol of liberty throughout Latin

America. The son of a Spanish sergeant stationed in Cuba, Marti sympathized with the cause of the Cuban patriots. For this he served six months of hard labor and was finally deported to Spain in January, 1871. On his third return to Cuba in 1895 he was killed fighting among the rebels. Encyclopedia *Britannica*, XIV, 1965 ed., 974–975.

22. Edward Laroque Tiniser, *Lafcadio Hearn's American Days* (2nd ed.; New York Dodd, Mead and Co., 1925), Santa Maura. His father was surgeon-major of a British infantry regiment stationed there. His mother was Greek. Hearn came to the United States in 1869 and by 1877 was a newspaperman in New Orleans. He achieved some fame as an editorial writer and actually much more as an author. Hearn left the United States in 1887 for the French West Indies and finally Japan. Tinker, Hearn, 1–4m 11: *Who's Who*, 1904, p. 699.

23. Lafcadio Hearn, *Miscellanies* (2 vols.; London: William Heinemann, Ltd., 1924), I, 201–202, 206, 209.

24. Mrs. H. W. Beecher, *Letters From Florida* (New York: D. Appleton and Co., 1879), 61–62. Eunice White Bullard (1812–1897), New England-born, was the wife of Henry Ward Beecher and an author of sorts. Her works included From *Dawn to Daylight* (1859), and *Motherly Talks With Young Housekeepers* (1875). *Who Was Who in America*, 1607–1896, Historical Volume (Chicago: A. N. Marquis Co., 1963), 49.

25. Cooley, *School Acres*, 155–157.

26. Nelson, *Harper's Weekly*, XXXXVI, 654.

27. Hezekiah Butterworth, *Zig-Zag Journeys on the Mississippi: From Chicago to the Islands of Discovery* (Boston: Estes and Lauriat, 1892), 124–127. Butterworth (1839–1905), born at Warren, Rhode Island, was assistant editor of Youth's companion for 1870 until 1894. He traveled extensively in the United States, Europe, Canada, and Latin America, and published numberous volumes of *Zig-Zag Journeys* and other works. He was conducting a private Spanish class for New Englanders in 1892 when he visited Washington, Louisiana, and Missouri. *Who Was Who in America*, I, 178.

28. John Bennett, "Revival Sermon at Little St. John's," *Atlantic Monthly*, XCVIII (August, 1906), 256–267. Born at Chillicothe, Ohio, in 1865, Bennett was educated in the town's public schools, and at the Art Students League of New York. Having married a South Carolina, he took up residence at Charleston in 1902. His novels included Master Skylark (1897) and The Treasure of Peyre Gaillard (1906). *Who's Who in America*, 1910–1911, VI, 141.

29. A Camp Physician (pseudo.), *Independent*, LXIII, 791.

30. Hart, *The Southern South*, 117–118.

31. Johnston, *The Negro in the New World*, 430.

32. Jones, *Educational Adaptations*, 65.

33. Charles W. Chesnutt, *The Conjure Woman* (Boston: Houglin-Mifflin Co., 1899) vi, 3–17. This novel, the only one employed in the present study, is demonstrably based upon the observations of an outsider with special credentials for obtaining valid information and impressions.

34. Cooley, *Outlook*, XCVIII, 425.

35. Johnston, The Negro in the New World, 470–471.

36. Cram, Old Seaport *Towns of the South*, 315. Street, *American Adventures*, 649–650.

37. Tweedie, America As I Saw It, 372.

38. L. H. M. Soulsby, *The America I Saw in 1916–1918* (London: Longmans, Green and Co., 1920), 156. Lucy Helen Muriel Soulsby, who died shortly after her return to England in 1918, was an author of pious works and former headmistress of the Manor House School, Brandesbury. She came to the United States to attend the world Purity Conference at Louisville as delegate of the British Mothers' Union. Rupert B. Vance in Clark, ed., *Travels in the New South,* II, 92.

39. Huret, *En Amerique,* 360–366.

40. Gordon, *On Wandering Wheels,* 289–290, 293–297; Garvey, *Garvey and Garveyism,* 157.

41. Prossinagg, *Das Antlitz Amerikas,* 222.

Chapter Four

Pedagogs and Pupils

Prior to Reconstruction the educability of African Americans had been a question pondered by northerners as well as southerners, with many concluding that it was an impossibility. The experience of Freedmen's Bureau schools, and the rise of black colleges in the South, convinced many in both regions that the race could absorb formal academic training. Many remained doubtful, however, and opposition to African American education continued widespread, especially since scientific studies purported to show the brain of Africans smaller than that of Caucasians and their mental capacity more limited. Almost all outside observers wanted, therefore, to see for themselves how the blacks were doing in school.

Most outsiders took a pessimistic view of the educability or capability of African Americans while applauding their zeal for learning. Mary Allan-Olney remarked that black students had a faculty for learning by rote, but "so has a monkey." She had heard of "the wonderful progress of the negro race, so vaunted by the supporters of the Hampton Institute," but thought it began and ended there. Allan-Olney's impressions were apparently not obtained from observing black children in classrooms, though she expressed a wish to have "a few young negroes to bring up as an experiment, quite away from any Negro or mean white influences." She did try to teach one or two relatives of her servants in rural Virginia. One boy, recommended as "right smart," was given some religious training and an opportunity to learn reading, writing and arithmetic. He failed, not because he was stupid, but because he was "incorrigibly lazy." He had heard of God, but not of Jesus. As to faith, hope, and charity, "never heard nothin' 'bout 'em." What most disturbed Miss Allan-Olney concerning the whole venture was that this "right smart" black, superior despite his shortcomings to most of his kind, would become an elector.

"With less intelligence . . . than a well-bred English dog, he will actually vote for a presidential candidate." Miss Allan-Olney must have applauded the measures to disfranchise African Americans later adopted throughout the South.[1]

The great difficulty in educating African Americans, as Abbie Brooks saw it, was bringing them up to "the standard of appreciation, "by which she evidently meant appreciation of European cultural values. The few blacks going to school in Florida were mostly "numbskulls whose heads are so thick that an idea could not get into their minds unless it was shot there "with the force of a bullet." Edward Hogan noted that in South Carolina not many African Americans attended the schools, which were distant from their homes, and he expressed doubt whether the blacks could "grasp" education. The Oxford historian, Edward Freeman, was also pessimistic. "Education cannot wipe out the eternal distinction that has been drawn by the hand of nature. No teaching can turn a black man into a white one." Dean Hole of Rochester was similarly convinced, after his short tour of the South, that there was no hope that the African American's intellectual capacity could be substantially improved on any level.[2]

A majority of the students in the black school visited by William Saunders, the English journalist, were more or less white; "the nearer the mulattoes are to white the brighter as children they seem to be." Yet teachers at Atlanta insisted that black children equaled whites in intellectual capacity. It was too early in 1880, George Sala thought, to say whether "full-blooded" African Americans could meet the demands of academic training. Undoubtedly the "mixed-bloods" could become as intellectually distinguished as Alexander Dumas. Certain of the black youngsters at Richmond impressed the French politician D'Haussonville as being "very precocious and intelligent." They seemed to learn faster than white children, but he understood that their learning stopped toward the age of twelve and they remained children for the rest of their lives. Even so, D'Haussonville hoped that the influences of education would prevent the total degradation of the race.[3]

The African Americans' eagerness for knowledge evoked mixed feelings among observers. Saunders admired the blacks' perseverance in sending their children to school even when the family could "ill afford to lose their services." Sir George Campbell also found zeal for education on all levels and felt that as much had "been done as could be expected under the circumstances." George Sala noted that blacks were grasping the opportunities for education at New Orleans in 1880. Wherever found Barbour observed, the blacks were "always solid friends to all educational improvements." Even in the camps of railroad construction workers in Florida blacks strove diligently to learn to write letters and to read newspapers. Newspapers were read aloud to those who had not yet mastered reading. But James Bryce felt that there was something pathetic about this zeal for knowledge because "book learning" would not necessarily raise the African American "in the industrial scale." William Chauncy Langdon disapproved the blacks' ambition to remedy their gross ignorance because he attributed it to a base motive, i.e., their desire to reduce the advantages which the whites had over them. Even if blacks gained education, they would remain inferior to whites because of their lack of moral character.[4]

Partly to see how the African American was faring in the hands of "the intelligent" white people of the South, President Rutherford Hayes in September, 1877 made a "goodwill" tour to Alabama, Georgia, Kentucky, and Tennessee. At the Central Colored School in Louisville he was greeted by a white trustee and a black "leader" and the black children sang for him. Afterwards he acknowledged the progress which the African American was making in education, and praised the people of Louisville for their "liberal and just sentiments on the subject of education for all classes." The President believed that "the schoolmaster alone can abolish the evils which slavery has left in the South."[5]

African American public schools in Pensacola in 1877 left much to be desired in terms of pedagogs and pupils, Abbie Brooks found, despite the fact that they were "light, airy and roomy—more provision being made for the education of the colored race, all over the State of Florida, than for the white." The black teachers excelled only in the maintenance of order, relying for that purpose upon "a huge leather strap—that relic of barbarism revived—and a piece of plank for the more incorrigible cases."[6]

Farmville, Virginia—a town conspicuous in a later generation for opposition to racially integrated schools—maintained no school of any kind for African Americans in 1897. The school black children attended was located just outside the corporation limits in a large frame building of four rooms. There were five teachers counting the principal, three of them female. By the general testimony of the townspeople the school was not very successful. Average daily attendance was unbelievably good (eighty to ninety percent according to Du Bois' figures), but the school-term lasted only six months (September 15 to April 1) and the teachers were "not particularly well-equipped," a salary of thirty dollars per month being insufficient to attract outsiders of ability into the area.[7]

Meager as was the educational effort at Farmville, it was superior to that experienced by Du Bois in rural Tennessee. There he had taught in a log hut with an entrance not deserving to be called a door; a fireplace within, and great chinks between the logs that served as windows. Accommodations for the teacher were a desk composed of three boards and a borrowed chair. The pupils sat on rough plank benches, without backs and sometimes without supporting logs, an arrangement which had "the one virtue of making naps dangerous—possibly fatal—for the floor was not to be trusted." At times attendance dropped radically, partly because of the doubts of the old folk concerning "book learning," and when Du Bois traveled through the countryside he found his pupils plowing crops or "minding the baby." Du Bois tried going into the cabins and putting Cicero "into the simplest English with local applications." This usually served to convince the skeptics "for a week or so."[8]

Even with public schools in existence many African Americans continued to send their children to private schools organized by them or more commonly by northern missionaries and philanthropists during and after the Civil War. Laura Towne, who spent many years of her life at one such school on the Sea Islands, recorded that commencement in June, 1877, called for a large celebration. Graduates and ex-students came from as far as Charleston and Savannah to witness the recitations, singing, and skits. Prizes were awarded, and a good time was had by all. On another occasion Mrs. Towne said that the Penn School was "a delight" and the student's eager learners. They walked as much as twelve miles round trip a day to attend school "besides doing their task of cotton picking." They regarded being deprived of a lesson as "a severe punishment." All of this convinced Mrs. Towne that their race was "going to rise."[9]

Work at Penn School on St. Helena Island was in the beginning almost exclusively academic. Later, however, partly because of practical needs, and more because of white opposition to non-vocational training for blacks, agricultural education became a prime part of the curriculum. Following three weeks of "book learning" the children were turned out into the fields. There they cultivated mostly sweet potatoes. The teachers supervised their work and threw in a little "book learning" here and there. The potatoes were eventually placed in pyramids beside the houses or barns to await the winter. Parents worked alongside the children in these endeavors, thus giving their experience to the project and at the same time learning new methods from the teachers, some of whom were Hampton graduates. According to Rossa Cooley, head of the school, all of this was done in an orderly and efficient manner.[10]

Mrs. Lillie Wyman visited schools in the "Black Belt" to see what, if anything, was being done about the urgent need for African American literacy. In one town, she found a black couple, both ex-slaves educated at Atlanta University, trying to teach about 100 children in a warehouse. A schoolhouse was being built with the African Americans of the town assisting in the process. Pupils of all ages attended the school, including a Baptist minister and a hotel night watchman. As a rule the younger children were neatly dressed.

They gave the impression that they possessed some intelligence, and were in perfect order, a sharp contrast to the "wiggling of juvenile Yankees." The teachers were quite satisfied with the progress of their students, regretting only that "industrial training" could not be provided.[11]

Important as the grammar schools were, it was the fledgling black colleges that constituted the core of the African American educational system. Many expected that they would someway, somehow, work miracles, that they would take the recently emancipated race and from it produce immediately scientific farmers, skilled craftsmen, teachers, doctors, nurses, and lawyers. Outside observers were eager to see how this Herculean task was being performed.[12]

The "big five" among southern black colleges prior to 1900 were Hampton Institute, Tuskegee Institute, Howard University, Fisk University, and Atlanta University. It was upon them that the attention of most outside observers was focused.

Hampton Institute Sir George Campbell found to be principally a teacher-training institution instead of the major agricultural and industrial school he had expected. Several trades were taught there, however, and he understood, probably erroneously, that it was the only place "in the southern states where black printers are educated." Campbell himself was more interested in the western Native Americans sent to Hampton by the United States government than he was in the African Americans there. The Native Americans were yellow rather than red, not "unlike some of the Indo-Chinese tribes to the east of Bengal." General Samuel Armstrong, the Euro-American head of Hampton, thought both Caucasian and Native Americans stronger than blacks in intellect, but the blacks were improvable, and the Native Americans "much more difficult to manage." James Bryce visited Hampton as well as the newly founded Tuskegee Institute and praised their work, though they were, like other black colleges, on "a comparatively humble scale and . . . might rather be called secondary schools than colleges'.[13]

By 1890 Tuskegee had become famous. More than half of the fourteen buildings had been erected by the students. Samuel Barrows found that, contrary to the practice elsewhere, all the teachers were blacks. They taught "the dignity of labor, and how to get out of debt," and the influence of the Institute was being felt all through the Black Belt. Professor Booker Washington related how a black girl trained at Tuskegee had influenced her father to rebuild his entire home. Barrows noted similar occurrences at and around Hampton Institute.[14]

During a southern tour in the winter of 1898 President William McKinley stopped at Tuskegee. A parade and exhibit were held in his honor, and he saw the wheelwright, blacksmith, and harness shops as well as buggies and wagons constructed by the students. When the President spoke he praised Tuskegee for its "generous and progressive" policy, for not being over ambitious, and for fostering "an amicable relationship between the two races." Alluding to the influence of the institution upon blacks, he counseled them to follow the moderate principles of that "accomplished educator," "great orator," and "true philanthropist, "Booker T. Washington.[15]

A visit to Atlanta University convinced the Reverend Timothy Harley that the "coloured student is capable of liberal education and that the white southerner is as ready as any man to acknowledge and rejoice in it." Harley asked one of the professors whether or not he had detected any considerable difference of intellectual capacity between the "pure" black and the mulatto. The teacher reported that no great differences existed. Harley was not wholly convinced on this point, however. William Saunders, who visited Atlanta as the guest of the institution, reported that about 75 of the 175 students were girls. Their progress was regarded "as universally satisfactory."[16]

The African American politician, Mifflin Gibbs, a friend and supporter of Booker Washington, found much to applaud in the work of Howard University at Washington. Situated on one of the most beautiful sites in the city, it had, he said, splendid departments of law, medicine, theology, and arts and sciences, and its graduates numbered some of "the most distinguished men of the Negro race in America."[17]

Following the founding of Tuskegee Institute in 1881, and the rise to prominence of its principal, Booker T. Washington, African Americans started to debate loudly among themselves (with words tossed in here and there by their white "friends") the virtues of the "agricultural-industrial" education represented by Hampton and Tuskegee as opposed to the Atlanta-Fisk-Howard variety of "classical" learning. Mifflin Gibbs supported the classical program at Howard University but T. Thomas Fortune, African American journalist and friend of Booker Washington, was much more vociferous on the other side. After visiting Hampton he was convinced that its success and the favorable attitude of both white and black toward it justified those who advocated industrial education. Fortune denounced the multiplication of institutions which emphasized traditional subjects as if those

> were the things best suited to and most urgently needed by a class of persons
> unprepared in rudimentary education, and whose immediate aim must be that of
> the mechanic and farmer — to whom the classics, theology, and the sciences, in
> their extremely impecunious state are unequivocally [sic] abstractions.[18]

White control of black colleges and their dependence upon white support, both almost universal in the South of 1880, were denounced by William

Wells Brown. The education of the southern African American, which Brown believed the most important matter facing the country at the time, could not be left entirely in the hands of Caucasian men whose "principles of thought" often differed from those of the African American. He deplored the common failure to hire black teachers and the tendency of white teachers to ignore their black pupils outside the classroom. He applauded schools, such as Storer College at Harper's Ferry, that were owned and managed exclusively by African Americans. William Aubrey, unlike Brown, applauded the support of black colleges by whites (usually northern).Yet he felt this was insufficient to meet the African Americans' pressing need for education. Federal assistance was as essential in the area of higher learning as in primary and secondary education.[19]

The President of Atlanta University, who was, like all the early presidents of that institution, a white man, told Samuel Barrows in 1891 that much of the financial support for black colleges came from African Americans. They contributed at least a half million dollars, for every million contributed by northern whites.[20]

What judgment was to be passed upon the education of African Americans thus far? A New York journalist, D. Allen Willey at the close of the century, warned that "glowing descriptions" of the black colleges were apt to cause readers "to overlook the great field still untouched by them, and the millions of people still unaffected by their influence." Edward Hogan, Edward Freeman, and William Edwin Adams, who derived their opinions mainly from observations of grammar school children in the early 'eighties, concluded that little improvement had taken place in the life of the African Americans as a result of education. On the other hand, William Wells Brown, the black historian, remarked judiciously that "nations are not educated in twenty years," and pointed to the improvement already made, and suggested that one might "predict from it a very satisfactory future."[21]

In Atlanta in 1895 Booker T. Washington begged the white people in his audience to help and encourage southern blacks in the education of their heads, hands, and hearts. In the controversy that followed the address many quoted him erroneously as advocating training of hands over heads. This added heat to the debate over educational goals for the freedmen and their descendants. The "Atlanta Compromise" speech did, it was true, emphasize agriculture and mechanical pursuits rather than the professions, assigning as much dignity to tilling the soil as to writing a poem; and Washington stressed the same things in his policies at Tuskegee. He did not, however, condemn academic education, nor advocate its exclusion from curriculums for African Americans. Nevertheless many of those who discussed African American education including both supporters and detractors of Washington, spoke as if it were conveniently divided, at all levels, into two warring camps—one exclusively training the head, the other the hand. Outsiders naturally wanted to see which was winning.

On the grammar school level W. E. B. Du Bois, himself, a leading figure in the educational debate, was convinced by 1901 that the whole tedious structure of "common school training" was in danger of collapse, regardless of curricular emphasis. He believed that only massive federal aid could save it. (George Howard and Julian Street, who observed educational conditions among blacks some fifteen years later shared this view.)[22]

On the basis of his observations in South Carolina, Charles Francis Adams differed somewhat from Du Bois. Local whites there had made "both honest and strenuous" efforts "to educate the African[s]," but "in spite of expensive schooling" the outlook, as far as Adams could observe was not "propitious." It seemed that no amount of aid, from whatever source, could raise the blacks' educational level.[23]

Another who felt little optimism about the general educational situation was Professor Kelsey. The poor home environment of the children seemed to him enough in itself to discourage obedience, neatness, and punctuality in the schools, and the incompetence of teachers, plus poor equipment, made adequate learning almost an impossibility. Many teachers, Kelsey discovered, received their positions on grounds other than ability to teach. And even the fairly well trained lacked books and maps to aid them.

One notable exception to the dismal picture was the work, which Kelsey saw at the Penn School on St. Helena Island. There the blacks, enjoying the benefit of contact with "a good class of whites," were making substantial improvements. Even the older generation had become more "industrious" through the long-standing social and intellectual influences of the school.[24]

Progressive editor Ray Stannard Baker did not find large sums being spent for African American education by local authorities, as Adams had in South Carolina. In Atlanta blacks were eager for education, and willing to make great sacrifices in order to obtain it for themselves and their children, but the city had not seen fit to provide room enough for all in the public schools. The black "colleges" and "universities" carried a disproportionate share of the load. The largest of these, Morris Brown, called a college but "in reality a grammar school," enrolled nearly 1,000 pupils from age seven and up. Julian Street, observing the Atlanta situation during the World War, shared Baker's opinion. Atlanta also lagged in the institution of industrial training in the public schools.[25]

Educational conditions for blacks of Albany, Georgia, and Oak Grove, Alabama, were enough, Albert Bushnell Hart thought, to discourage any would-be scholar. At Albany the building was a "wretched structure" with six windows, mostly broken, and the sky was visible between the weatherboards. The one desk, of rough plank, belonged to the teacher. The school enrolled forty-four pupils, some living as far as three miles away; thirty-two, including six mulattoes, were present the day Hart visited. All were neatly dressed and well behaved as they sat in the midst of dirt on dirty benches. The teacher, an "apparently untrained" black woman, said she made $35 a month, and that this was the first school ever opened for blacks in the area. It had been established in 1906. Some of the conditions found at Albany existed also, though to a lesser extent, in southern white schools, Hart noted. Occasionally, as at Calhoun, Alabama, one came upon a prosperous black school, but even here the influence of the school was more moral than intellectual.[26]

The grammar schools conducted as preparatory branches at Hampton and Tuskegee were highly creditable institutions, and could well serve as models for the entire South, Sir Harry Johnston thought. Neat and alert, the students at the Hampton adjunct marched to their seats singing: "'An' before' Ah'll be a slave, Ah'll be buried in ma grave, and ma spirit shall ascend to God on high." Apparently neither the faulty English nor the neo-abolitionist tone, more in the "academic-classical" than the agricultural-industrial tradition, struck Sir Harry as significant.

Hampton graduates constituted most of the teachers in another creditable institution for African Americans, the Penn School. They were trying to introduce scientific farming as a means of improving St. Helena Island's poor crops, and to give such skills as carpentering and blacksmithing to the school's 275 pupils. Their work, Sir Harry believed, was both practical and urgent. About 1912 the blacks of St. Helena Island constructed an oyster shell concrete industrial building at the school to mark its fiftieth anniversary. They sang and laughed in the process, and Rossa Cooley, then celebrating more than twenty years of service to the blacks, shared their pride.[27]

Among African American institutions of higher education Tuskegee and Hampton continued to attract the largest number of observers. Jules Huret, an editor from Paris, was a guest in the home of Booker Washington at Tuskegee. An edifice of brick and wood with climbing plants between the columns, it was simply furnished and decorated. There was a piano, "rather average" photographs and paints (including Raphael's "Virgins"), a plaque of Napoleon, and books by Theodore Roosevelt and others. Washington, then forty-four years old, was of medium height and weight, clean shaven, with a golden complexion like "smoked lemon," bluish-grey eyes, large nostrils, and short, curly hair. His general expression was "very energetic."

From Washington Huret heard much about his educational and racial philosophies. Manual labor was required at Tuskegee because, Washington felt, it "ennobled and elevated." African Americans, though a distinct race, were not inferior to whites, and given help and opportunity could progress "up to the level of whites." Washington held no bitterness against his supposedly white father, regarding him as a product of the morals of his time. Huret left Tuskegee with the highest respect for the institution and its head. Baron D'Estournelles De Constant, who visited both Hampton and Tuskegee and was pleasantly surprised at their work and their influence, formed a similar estimate. He predicted that they would transform the African race, indeed; they had already "raised the Negro level beyond all expectations." Washington himself was an "example for the high culture of which a Negro is capable and of the eminent services he can render the country." Professor Kelsey also praised the work of Hampton and Tuskegee as far as it went, but thought their influence not widespread beyond the few who benefited directly from their efforts. The African American needed much more. Professor Munsterberg, while unable to echo the praises of Booker Washington—"it is to be admitted that Booker Washington himself is not a really great, independent and commanding personality"—did grant, however, that Washington's Tuskegee Institute set the most admirable example of the manual training which African Americans needed.[28]

After a tour of Hampton, Sir Harry Johnston spent ten days at Tuskegee together with James Bryce and his wife and Robert C. Ogden, a Tuskegee-Hampton trustee. The students at both schools included a good many mulattoes and a sprinkling of West Indians, Filipinos, Cubans, Africans, Puerto Ricans, and Native Americans (The latter were seen at Hampton only.) Sir Harry was amazed at the extensive agricultural and industrial projects conducted at Tuskegee, especially in the divisions of horticulture, veterinary science, botany, and shoemaking. In "bee culture" the work of John H. Washington, brother of Booker T. Washington was "almost as remarkable as that of his better-known brother." George Washington Carver, the noted Tuskegee scientist, proved to be an "absolute Negro," but articulate, and well-dressed. From "the soundness of his science" one might think him "professor of Botany not at Tuskegee, but at Oxford or Cambridge."

Sir Harry was much impressed by the quality of the faculty not only at Tuskegee but at other African American schools also. Like Huret, he denounced as "nonsense" the discriminatory system in the South, which branded such men as Carver, Washington, and Du Bois as "untouchables." Washington made him aware, however, that such grievances should not cause excitement. The Tuskegee principal stated his main objective as getting "the Negro to work, and to stop talking."[29]

William Archer visited Tuskegee after leaving the fledging State College for Negroes in Montgomery. The State College was spacious and enjoyed an excellent system of industrial training under a "Yankee" professor who had been in the South since Reconstruction. Though it was a state school, the authorities evidently allowed a great deal of academic freedom, for Archer noted discussion of the Brownsville, Texas) riot of 1906, an extremely touchy subject.

Archer found Tuskegee a "wonderful place, full of energy and evidently imbued with singleness of purpose." A black senior escorted the English visitor around the campus with the same enthusiasm for his alma mater as a "Princeton or Cornell" boy might have shown. Everywhere Archer saw earnest work, order, discipline, and "thorough scientific method." He did not meet Washington there (He had talked with him earlier in New York), but met Emmett J. Scott, Washington's secretary, Warren Logan, the school's treasurer and Mrs. Washington, "a lady with the mind and manners of a somewhat dusky Duchess." All of them "were far more Caucasian than African in features and very light in colour"; indeed, Archer saw no one in a high position at Tuskegee who was not nearly white. He did not, however, regard this as signifying any intellectual superiority of the "mulatto" over the "pure Negro."

Though Booker Washington's work was "wise and salutary," Archer doubted whether it and/or "the Atlanta Compromise" could reduce racial conflict in the South. Washington's program implied that the key to the conflict lay in the defects of the African race; improve that race, materially and morally, and the conflict was on its way toward alleviation. Archer feared that the conflict was larger than the qualities or defects of either race, lying perhaps in instincts beyond the control of either or both.

From Tuskegee, "the daughter" Archer moved on to Hampton Institute, "the mother." He found three major differences between mother and daughter. First, the Hampton campus, on the edge of Hampton Creek, was the more beautiful; second, at Tuskegee, the staff was all black, at Hampton, all white; and third, Hampton had Native American as well as African American students. The blacks and Indians seemed to get along well together, yet seldom dined at the same tables while the visitor was present. None of the white instructors ate with the blacks. Most of the day light hours at Hampton were devoted to agricultural and vocational training, the academic work being done at night.

Atlanta University lacked "the cheerful energy and optimism" of Tuskegee, in Archer's view. It was a "home of intellectual culture; and intellectual culture, however, necessary, can scarcely be exhilarating to the Negro race at this stage of its history." The highlight of the visit was a talk with Du Bois. Were it not for racial injustice and prejudice, Archer felt, Du Bois might well teach in Europe or at some major northern university, instead of in the world's largest center for African American higher education. He seemed to Archer an unhappy man.

> With perfect simplicity, without an
> atom of pose, he is and remains a
> singularly tragic figure. Beneath
> his calm one is conscious of a profound
> bitterness of spirit. If he is hopeful at all,
> it is for a day that he will never see; and
> in a man still in the prime of life, such hope
> is not very different from despair.

Du Bois viewed the race problem not in terms of physical characteristics but in terms of attitudes. The older generation of African Americans had friends among the white people of their own age, but the youth of his time had no white friends. "The younger white people have no feeling towards the Negro but dislike, founded on utter lack of comprehension." Archer differed sharply with Du Bois, although not openly, over the gist of the race problem. He saw it mainly in terms of color. "If the Negro could but change his skin, how trifling would be the problem raised by his ignorance, shiftlessness, poverty and crime!"[30]

Before Du Bois left Atlanta, after some fifteen years there, to join the NAACP in 1910, he had visited Hampton and had some contact with Tuskegee. He regarded both as "great institutions," and had considered teaching for them. But he had a still higher regard for Atlanta, looking upon its "college department" as "perhaps the largest and best in the South at the time." Even industrial training in the South, he observed, was often in the hands of Atlanta graduates, who comprised many of the faculty at Tuskegee and other institutions.

Du Bois had, of course, already become a central figure in the debate over African American educational and racial goals. As the controversy between him and Washington grew "more personal and bitter" than Du Bois had ever dreamed it would, Atlanta University was "necessarily dragged" in. This Du Bois deeply regretted, for his being *persona non grata* to "powerful interests" cost the University important financial support. Du Bois thought, at least in retrospect, that the division between Atlanta and Tuskegee was carried much further than the situation demanded, an extremely unfortunate development because Atlanta had done, and was doing, work of much importance in education and research relating to the "Negro problem."[31]

During the heat of the African American educational debate Edward T. Ware, a white man, was President of Atlanta University. He saw early what most enlightened observers now concede.

> The question of the relative importance of
> Industrial and higher education for the
> Negroes has led to much fruitless discussion.
> The truth is that both types of training are
> Indispensable for the proper education of the
> People, and neither can fulfill its mission
> Without cooperation with the other.

He noted, as had Du Bois, that Atlanta graduates were teaching at Tuskegee, and also that Tuskegee graduates were among Atlanta's better students. Industrial training and academic training were conducted at both places. The educated African American, whether a product of the Hampton-Tuskegee system or the Atlanta-Howard-Fisk school, would present serious challenges to the South. This type black had, Ware warned, become increasingly restless amid the discriminations placed upon them, and they did not possess the patience of Job.[32]

Views differing from those of Ware (and presumably far less informed), particularly in the prediction of African American attitudes, had been presented in the London *Times* by its Washington correspondent in 1910. Most black leaders in the United States were said to have abandoned the idea of "social equality," adopting instead the formula of Booker Washington. They aimed at industrial efficiency and a stable social organization of their own. Applauding this development and the work of Tuskegee Institute, which he had visited earlier, the English journalist saw the Washington philosophy, matched by an equal degree of tolerance and reason from southern whites, as the solution to the "American colour problem."[33]

Ray Stannard Baker, Albert Bushnell Hart, and Thomas Jesse Jones also assessed African American colleges of both the agricultural and the academic persuasions. Baker visited Hampton, Tuskegee, Atlanta, and Fisk. He was struck by the prevalence of mulattoes in all the student bodies. Many of them were, he learned, being educated by their Caucasian fathers. Upon reflection, Baker saw a relationship between skin color, education, and achievement among the blacks, for "most of the leading men of the race today in every line of activity are mulattoes." He cited Washington, Du Bois, Frederick Douglass, and the jurist, Robert H. Terrell of Washington, D.C. One of the exceptions was Paul Laurence Dunbar, the poet.

In the Washington-Du Bois controversy, Baker sided with the Tuskegeean. Granting that there "must always be men like Dr. Du Bois who agitate for rights," yet "at the present time it would seem that the thing most needed was the teaching of such men as Dr. Washington emphasizing duties and responsibilities, urging the Negro to prepare himself for his rights." Wherever Baker went among African Americans, a picture of Booker Washington was almost sure to be prominently displayed. Washington was "one of the great men of this country," and would in the future be so honored.

Even though Hampton and Tuskegee were prosperous and apparently successful, at least in preaching "a gospel of work" and holding up "a standard of practicality," Albert Bushnell Hart believed that the African American colleges were in many respects "the weakest part of Negro education." Housed as a rule in only "tolerable buildings," few had "adequate libraries, laboratories, or staff of specialist instructors." The state colleges were inferior in quality to the church-supported ones, and even the latter were "low in standards," emphasizing normal or industrial training and affording little inducement to academic achievement. One bright spot in an otherwise dismal picture presented by these schools was the work of the black members of the faculties, many of whom had been trained in the best northern universities and tried to imitate their methods.

Thomas Jesse Jones, a sociologist, conducted far reaching studies of African American education in the South between 1913 and 1920. He discovered very early that the terms "academy," "college," and "university" were quite misleading in application to black schools, for more than seventy-five per cent of their students were elementary. Moreover, the phrase, "industrial education" among African American institutions was largely a misnomer. Despite the "genuine efforts" of such schools as Hampton and Tuskegee to impart industrial training, the "fundamental purpose" in all of the institutions was "much broader than vocational efficiency," and all training was aimed at the head, hand, and heart. Rather than over emphasizing agricultural-industrial training, Jones found "an almost fatalistic belief . . . in the Latin and Greek features of the course. The majority of them [black colleges] seem to have more interest in traditional forms of education than in the adaptation to the needs of their pupils and their community." Such adaptation, he thought, would mean more work of the agricultural-industrial variety.

Jones was especially unhappy over the physical and financial conditions of black schools. Inadequate support from state funds was largely to blame, but poor management, "unfortunate location," and "fraud" hurt also. In physical plant, finance, and administration, as well as in academic areas, there was still need for vigorous efforts by African Americans and their "friends."

One of the black "universities" whose physical and financial condition, not to mention its management, had caused concern was Latta University, near Raleigh, North Carolina. When Julian Street was there it consisted "of a few flimsy shacks in the Negro village of Oberlin." Its founder and president, "Professor" Latta, was "one of the rare Negroes" who combined the manner of "the old fashioned southern darky" in his relations with whites "and the astuteness of the 'new issues' in high finance." Latta had traveled to New England and Europe seeking funds for his fledging school, and had published *The History of My Life and Work* to aid his financial condition. What success he had enjoyed was embodied in the best building on the campus, the residence of the president. Around Raleigh he and his "university" were sources of amusement, and Street could not help but share the view.[34]

At Atlanta, Street came to African American higher education of a different order. Besides Atlanta University there were Spelman, "Seminary" for black women, Morehouse College for men, and Morris Brown "University," sponsored by the African Methodist Church. All of these institutions were said to carry on creditable work of the academic-classical variety. Street felt, however, that they could do even better if they combined. It was unfortunate that white citizens did not take more interest in them, but "most southerners do not believe in higher education for Negroes."[35]

As late as 1917 the African American educational debate continued. By this time a good many observers such as Edward T. Ware and George E. Howard had come to agree that it was not a question of head or hand, but, as Howard put it, of "hand and mind." Howard saw "excellent models" of black achievement in the work of the late Booker T. Washington and of R.R. Wright.[36]

Increased opportunities for education, whether at "agricultural-industrial" or "classical" institutions, had apparently done much to improve the speech of southern blacks by the early 1900's. No outsiders reported any difficulty comprehending the utterances of the literate, though the dialect of unlettered, mostly rural blacks might impose serious strains upon the ears of non-southerners. Not so troubled was the African American novelist Charles Waddell Chesnutt, who denied that there was such a thing as a Negro dialect. The speech pattern presented under this name was really an "attempt to express, with such a degree of phonetic correctness as to suggest the sound, English pronounced as an ignorant old southern Negro would be supposed to speak it," and "to preserve a sufficient approximation to the correct spelling to make it easy reading."[37]

The educated blacks encountered by Sir Harry Johnston at places like Hampton and Tuskegee had been taught to articulate as clearly as possible, and to be particularly careful of their pronunciation. Sir Harry learned that they had been advised to speak from the chest, not through the nose. Their voices were in fact "pleasant," "deep-toned, and "melodious" to English ears. The "nasality in the pronunciation" of illiterate blacks still remained, however, especially on the East Coast. One of the principal reasons for this, according to Sir Harry, was that many of these blacks came from the "Guinea Coast region where the native languages are extremely nasal."[38]

A Chicago-born actress and author who toured Virginia and Maryland in 1915–1916 was surprised to learn that "darky dialect was difficult to understand." She stopped on one occasion at Farmville where she tried unsuccessfully to learn where an African American ox cart driver lived. Eventually a southern white woman translated for her. The actress took the ox cart driver's speech to be fairly typical of the town's blacks. Apparently she did not meet the scores of literate African Americans earlier described by Du Bois.[39]

Another Chicago-born author, Julian Street, was particularly interested in the "gulla" or "gullah" dialect prevalent among the rice plantation blacks of the Sea Island and the South Carolina coast. He understood that the Charleston area was "headquarters for 'gulla niggers,'" though he had heard the "argot" spoken as far south as Sapelo Island, which he rather inaccurately placed "off the town of Darien, Georgia, near the Florida line." Street thought gulla almost a language in itself, a combination of English with "the primitive tongues of African tribes, just as the dialect of old Creole negroes, in Louisiana, is a combination of African tribal tongues with French." He admitted his inability to comprehend most of it, especially the "thick gulla." With the help of local whites he was able, however, to devise a working vocabulary. The Gullah word 'shum," for example, meant all kinds of things having to do with seeing—*to see_her, to see him, to see it*. Gullah was without genders or tenses. "Enty' might mean: *Aren't you? Didn't you?* or even *Isn't it?* Another common Gullah word was "Buckra,' meaning an upper class white man. To master the complete language would take quite a long time, Street supposed, though numbers of whites in the area had done so, as indeed they must communicate with many of these blacks.[40]

African Americans were advancing in education in 1917, George Howard believed, but he saw, too, a need for greater educational efforts with respect to race relations among whites. The White South urgently needed to learn that "mutual respect" and "common ideals" among people of all colors could lead to "the speedy mastery of her splendid resources," and presumably to a better life for all. In a sense, Howard was echoing a part of the Washington formula; and, in a sense, he was far ahead of Washington, for he seemed to perceive that there could be no solution of the "Negro problem" as long as there was a white problem.[41]

After the war the question of head or hand, with respect to African American education, faded into the background. Most seemed to sense that the urgent need of the race was for leaders in the cause of civil rights. It mattered little whether they were educated at Tuskegee or Hampton, at Fisk, Howard or Atlanta, or even at Harvard. The emphasis on civil rights led to the beginning of an ascendancy for the Du Bois School of African American leadership. A so-called "New Negro" appeared, spearheaded by a group of Harlem intellectuals, but including southern college personnel. The outsiders who were in the South during the twenties thus saw African American cultural and higher education activities under relatively new management, even though many of them were unaware of it.

In higher education African Americans were making "considerable spiritual advance," Felix Graf von Luckner concluded, apparently on the basis of observations of Howard University. He felt that black colleges had opened to blacks "the riches of European culture," and applauded their doing so. On the other hand, President Warren Harding's "separate-but-equal" speech at Birmingham declared that the training of blacks should not emphasize "the riches of European culture." Harding had no sympathy with attempts "to educate people . . . into something they are not fitted to be," nor with the "half-baked altruism" that "would overstock us with doctors and lawyers of whatever color, and leave us in a need of people fit and willing to do the manual work of a work-a-day world." African Americans did need education for leadership, leadership which would "inspire the race with proper ideals of race pride," of national pride, and of "an honorable destiny."[42]

Odd as it might seem, Marcus Garvey, Jamaican-born black nationalist, shared to a large degree Harding's view on higher education for blacks, and telegraphed his congratulations on Harding's Birmingham speech. In 1923, Garvey and his wife Amy stopped at Tuskegee Institute for two days "primarily to pay homage to the late Booker T. Washington." At the Institute, which owned about 115 buildings and more than 2,000 acres of land, Garvey was much impressed by the work of Washington's successors, especially "the Scientific Wizard," George Washington Carver. Carver proved to be an excellent conversationalist, and notwithstanding his "marvelous discoveries," he was humble, gracious and charming.[43]

A special correspondent for the *Pittsburgh Courier*, a leading African American weekly, witnessed commencements at two important black schools in Nashville in 1924. Fisk University, in its fifty-fourth year, had just secured a million dollar grant from the Carnegie Foundation and the Southern Education Board. A matching contribution of fifty thousand dollars had been secured from sources that were mostly southern and white. This "enormous feat" demonstrated the changing attitude of the South toward the higher education of African Americans. Fisk was one of the leading "New Negro" institutions, numbering a daughter of W. E. B. Du Bois among the forty-two current recipients of bachelor's degrees and having Du Bois himself as the principal speaker at the annual alumni banquet. The most notable achievement of Fisk during the preceding year, the correspondent felt, had been a reorganization of the curriculum bringing it up to "the recognized standard of Northern colleges." Meharry Medical College had attained recognition "as a Class A medical school," and recent improvements in laboratories would soon bring the Dental College similar status.[44]

In Atlanta the Gordons stopped at Spelman, a college for women, and Morehouse, a college for men. They arrived in time to witness the inauguration of a white woman, Florence Matilda Read, as Spelman's new president. The inauguration parade was, "considering the poverty of the homes from which the girls came . . . a tribute to what can be done on very little." At Spelman the English couple noticed both a good deal of religious fervor and strict standards of behavior including disapproval of "ostentation in dress." The women excelled in rendering such melodies as:

> There's a li'll wheel a turning in my heart,
> O'Lord
> A li'll wheel a turning in my heart . . .

The Gordons were not impressed, however, with the school's intellectual atmosphere.

At neighboring Morehouse College the president was John Hope, a blonde mulatto. A staunch civil rights supporter, Hope voluntarily rode in Jim Crow railroad cars because he wished to identify with his race. He told the Gordons that he took pains, when greeting white men, to avoid any appearance of inviting a handshake, preferring to let the whites make the move if they chose to do so. Morehouse students like those at Spelman seemed to enjoy music and sports better than studies, but the Gordons judged them to be "almost fifty percent brighter" than the Spelman girls.

At a "new management" black school in North Carolina the Gordons learned that the students themselves made the rules for their behavior and enforced them. According to the college president they were more severe with themselves than the college authorities would have been. The Gordons concluded that the sorely needed progress of the African American colleges was rendered doubtful by an "expressed belief' in educated black circles in the South that the African race would in the course of time "be absorbed." After observing the large numbers of mulattoes in the student bodies and on the faculties of black schools, the Gordons were inclined to agree.[45]

The condition of rural schools for African Americans, especially in Virginia, was carefully examined in 1927 by Lance G.E. Jones, a British scholar who received a grant from Oxford University to assess the work of the Jeanes Fund in the South. Founded in 1900 by a Philadelphia Quaker, Anna T. Jeanes, the Fund was actually the first to be strictly confined to rural public school for blacks. It provided African American teachers and "Jeanes Supervisors" for the schools. Expenditures for this work in twelve southern states from 1915 to 1920 totaled $246,000.

The Jeanes teachers were almost all women, often married or widowed, some as old as sixty, the majority over thirty-five. In almost all cases, Jones learned, the supervisors had previous experience as teachers, and about half had been educated, '.either wholly or in part, at state normal schools or at private schools like Hampton or Tuskegee." The role of the Jeanes Supervisor was to help teachers, by means of faculty meetings or "demonstration lessons," to plan their work and improve their methods. The first Jeanes teacher in the South, supervisor for Henrico County, Virginia was Virginia Estelle Randolph. Jones was very much impressed with the patience, faith, tact, kindliness, good humor, and humility of the black woman, who was known after nearly twenty years of service "not merely in her own country, but in other parts of the world."

Jones found great unevenness in the schools for African Americans. In one community the school building, whether old or new, might be in decent repair and well cared for; in another the building would show every sign of local indifference and neglect, sometimes of willful destruction. In one school the pupils might be carefully classified and "reasonably well taught;" in another attendance would be irregular, teaching poor, and retarded pupils numerous. Of teaching equipment there might in some cases be a "reasonable sufficiency;" in many others, little or none.

Assessing the Jeanes program, Jones concluded that "without leaders whom they could understand the coloured people would have remained uninformed and undirected, and as leaders in the cause of education and social improvement the Jeanes Teachers have played their part well."[46]

One of the oldest black rural schools in the South, the Penn School on St. Helena Island, South Carolina remained largely unchanged after the First World War. The most noticeable advance was the summer school, which ran all summer, and had been appropriately dubbed the "Sunrise School," since the pupils were in their seats at six-thirty a.m. to catch "the cool of the day." As one African American student put it: "I like this school for it comes at the waking of the brains." Whether in fall or summer, Rossa Cooley observed, blacks remained zealous in their desire to learn.[47]

Racial segregation and discrimination in public schools drew the attention of at least two post-war observers. President Warren Harding in a speech at Birmingham insisted upon "equal educational opportunity for both [black and white]." He had no quarrel with the separate schools, but felt there was still a good deal to be done toward improving the quality of African American education. In Washington, Prossinagg, who daily passed a black school on the way to his office, noted the differing standards for white and for black schools. Apparently he found nothing objectionable in segregated schools, but he did disapprove the obvious discrimination against the schools for blacks.[48]

Culturally, President Harding believed, "the black man should seek to be, and should be encouraged to be, the best possible black man and not the best possible imitation of a white man." Prossinagg also expressed appreciation for the African American's cultural potential. He felt that their most significant cultural contribution could best be seen in the Negro spirituals, which were "partly deeply melancholy, partly burlesque" in character. The spirituals had attracted the attention even of white intellectuals. On St. Helena Island a local folklore society attempted to preserve Negro spirituals and folk songs "in the midst of a faster life epitomized by the automobiles and tractors." This was a noble task, Rossa Cooley believed, because one could hardly claim to have heard music unless he had attended a concert of "Negro hymns." The spirituals were, to paraphrase President Harding, at least one element in African American culture that was not an imitation of the white man.[49]

NOTES

1. Alan-Olney, *The New Virginians*, II, 262; I, 246, 231–234.

2. Brooks, *Petals Plucked From Sunny Climes*, 374–376; Hogan, *International Review*, VIII, 111; Freeman, *Some Impressions of the United States*; Hole, *A Little Tour in America*, 286.

3. Saunders, *Through the Light Continent*, 79, 83–85; Sala, *American Revisited*, 191; D'Haussonville, *A Travers, Les Stas-Unis*, 158; Wiley, Arena, XXIII, 555.

4. Saunders, *Through the Light Continent*, 79, 83–85; Campbell, *White and Black*, 131, Sala, *America Revisited*, 191; *Barbour, Florida for Tourist*, 237; Langdon, *Political Science Quarterly*, VI, 35; Bryce, *American Commonwealth*, 521.

5. In this connection it is ironic that Hayes should have been the architect of the policy, which, if Professor Logan's estimate is correct, helped to send the Negroes to their nadir; *Ibid.*, 24–25; *Diary and Letters of Rutherford Birchard Hayes, Nineteenth President of the United States*, (ed. By Charles Richard Williams; Columbus, Ohio: The Ohio State Archaeological and Historical Society, 1924), III, 621.

6. Brooks, *Petals Plucked from Sunny Climes*, 374–376.

7. Du Bois, *United States Department of Labor Bulletin*, III, No. 14, pp. 12–13.

8. Du Bois, "A Negro Schoolmaster in the New South," *Atlantic Monthly*, LXXXIII, 100–101.

9. Towne, *Letters and Diary*, 281, 295–297.

10. Cooley, *School Acres*, 69.

11. Wyman, *New England Magazine*, III, 793–794.

12. One should not allow the designations "college" and "university" obscure the fact that most African American institutions attempted to offer work on the "secondary level" and almost all had "normal" departments.

13. Campbell, *White and Black*, 275–276; Bryce, *American Commonwealth*, II, 519.

14. Barrows, *Atlantic Monthly*, LXVIII, 811–812.

15. Thomas J. Callaway, "The President at Atlanta and Tuskegee," *Harper's Weekly*, XLII (December, 1898), 1300.

16. Saunders, *Through the Light Continent*, 86–87; Harley, *Southward Ho!*, 130.

17. Gibbs, *Shadow and Light*, 369.

18. Fortune, *Black and White*, 81, 86–87; Gibbs, *Shadow and Light*, 369.

19. Brown, *My Southern Home*, 213–217; Aubrey, *Fortnightly Review*, XLIII, n. s., 861.

20. Barrows, *Atlantic Monthly*, LXVII, 811–812.

21. Freeman, *Some Impressions of the United States*, 141–146; Hogan, *International Review*, VIII, III; Brown, *My Southern Home*, 212; William Edwin Adams, Our *American Cousins: Being Personal Impressions of the People and Institutions of the United States* (London: Walter Scott, 1883), 290. Adams, a writer for the New Castle *Weekly Chronicle*, was in the South during 1881–1882. Thomas D. Clark in Clark, ed. *Travels in the New South*, I, 137.

22. W. E. B. Du Bois, "The Relation of the Negroes to the Whites in the South," *Annals of the American Academy of Political and Social Sciences*, XVIII (July, 1901), 134.

23. Adams, Studies, *Military and Diplomatic*, 230–231.

24. Kelsey, *The Negro Farmer*, 42, 61–62.

25. Baker, *Following the Color Line*, 53–54.

26. Hart, *The Southern South*, 311–314, 317–318.

27. Johnston, *The Negro in the New World*, 396, 399, 409; Cooley, *School Acres*, 53.

28. Huret, En Amerique, 385–407.

29. D'Estournelles de Constant, *America and Her Problems*, 364–367; Kelsey, *The Negro Farm*, 731; Munsterberg, *The Americans*, 170–172, 181–182. Johnston, *The Negro in the New World*, 404–419.

30. Archer, *Through Afro-America*, 47, 106, 108–110, 112–113, 117–125.

31. Du Bois, *Dusk of Dawn*, 69, 77, 93.

32. Edward T. Ware, "Higher Education of Negroes in the United States," *Annals of the American Academy of Social and Political Science,* XLIX (September, 1913), 213–218. Edward Twichell Ware (1874–1927), son of one of the founders and the

first president of Atlanta University was born in Atlanta. He went to high school at Hartford, Connecticut, to Yale, and to Union Theological Seminary. A member of the Congregational Church, he was successively chaplain (1901–1907), president (1907–1922), and president emeritus and trustee (1922–1927), of Atlanta University. *Who Was Who in America*, I, 1299.

33. London *Times*, July 21, 1910, p. 5.

34. Baker, *Following the Color Line*, 170–173, 222, 304, 307. Hart, *The Southern South*, 130, 317–318. Thomas Jesse Jones, *Educational Adaptations; Report of Ten Years' Work of the Phelps-Stokes fund, 1910–1920* (New York: Phelps-Stokes Fund, 1920), 4, 31–65. See also by the same author, *Negro Education*, U. S. Bureau of Education *Bulletin*, I, 1916. Born in Wales in 1873, Jones came to the United States in 1884 and presently attended Washington and Lee University in Virginia, Marietta and Ohio, Union Theological Seminary, and Columbia University, where he received the Ph.D. in 1904. He was a member of the faculty at Hampton Institute, 1902–1909; a specialist in education for the United States Bureau of Education, 1912–1919; and director of research, Phelps-Stokes Fund, beginning in 1913. His studies of black education for the Phelps-Stokes Funds and the U. S. Bureau of Education won him wide recognition. *Who's Who in America*, 1920–1921, 1535.

35. Street, *American Adventures*, 290–292, 295.

36. A similar recommendation had been made by Thomas Jesse Jones in 1916. Beginning in 1929 the six black colleges in Atlanta formed a rather loose consortium, which became known as the Atlanta University Center—the world's largest aggregation of African American higher education.

37. Street, *American Adventures*, 385–386; Howard, *American Journal of Sociology*, XXII, 577, 591–592.

38. Quoted in Logan, *The Negro in American Life and Thought*, 241. Chesnutt, perhaps "the most eminent colored novelist," was born in Cleveland, where he attended public schools until his father, a veteran of four years in the Union Army, returned to the South. Chesnutt taught at, and then was principal of, the State Colored Normal School at Fayetteville, North Carolina. In 1863 he returned to the North. Admitted to the Ohio bar in 1887, he never practiced actively but was a court reporter. He published his most famous work, *The Conjure Woman* in 1889. Chesnutt returned to the South in 1901, visiting North Carolina, Alabama, Georgia, and Maryland. Considering his northern birth, and his eighteen year absence from the region, he may be classified as an outsider. Helen M. Chesnutt, *Charles Waddell Chesnutt: Pioneer of the Color Line* (Chapel Hill: The University of North Carolina Press, 1952); *The National Cyclopedia of the Colored Race* (2 vols.; Montgomery, Ala.: National Publishing Co., 1919), 347.

39. Johnston, *The Negro in the New World*, 396.

40. Louise Closser Hale, *We Discover the Old Dominions*, 243.

41. Street, *American Adventures*, 338–339.

42. Howard, *American Journal of Sociology*, XXIII, 577, 591–592.

43. Amy Jacques Garvey, *Garvey and Garveyism* (Kingston, Jamacia: Amy J. Garvey, 1963), 123–124.

44. *Pittsburgh Courier*. June 7, 1924, p. 14.

45. Gordon, *On Wandering Wheels*, 243–246, 248, 312–313.

46. Anna T. Jeanes Foundation, *The Negro Rural School Fund* (New York: The Anna T. Jeanes Foundation, 1907, 1933), pp. 7–9.

47. Cooley, *Outlook*; CXXI, 740.

48. *New York Times*, October 27, 1921, p. 11; Prossinagg, *Das Antlitz Amerikas*, 121.

49. *New York Times,* October 27, 1921, p. 11; Prossinagg, *Das Antlitz Amerikas*, 109–11; Cooley, *School Acres*, 140–141; Cooley, *Outlook*, CXXI, 741.

Chapter Five

"In All Things Social"

According to southern legend the happy, grinning "African American" chose to spend the bulk of their earnings on liquor and to "have a good time." Their material wants and needs, including food, dress, and housing, were meager, and they paid little attention to their health and safety. Yet they were doing well and had no complaints to make. Outside observers judged for themselves the validity of the tale.

Emancipated African Americans were housed mainly in cabins of one or two rooms, void of bathing facilities and without any hint of cleanliness or sanitation. The cabins were ordinarily constructed of wood, though logs plastered with mud were mentioned in Kentucky and Tennessee, and tin, domed-like facilities in Alabama. The disorder and uncleanliness of black cabins in Florida and Louisiana astonished Julian Ralph, the New York author. He had never seen "worse habitations, except the tepees of Wild Indians." The squalor of blacks living in the "Black Belt" also profoundly distressed Lillie Wyman. Their condition was alien to American hopes and ideals and a serious problem for the "patriot and the Christian." Samuel Barrows, another observer who presented a favorable picture of blacks, conceded that the typical Black Belt African American home was poorly constructed and poorly furnished. He saw windowless one-and two-room cabins which he understood were occupied by as many as twenty-five persons. In Florida, Iza Duffus Hardy observed that many of these "ramshackle shanties" were without facilities for heating. Thus, in winter, many blacks would congregate around a community bonfire to warm themselves until time for bed.[1]

The African Americans whom Du Bois studied at Farmville lived fairly comfortable in comparison with members of their race elsewhere. Though Farmville had a crowded slum section, Du Bois would have us believe that slum dwellers were a minority. In fact he reported among the black middle class of Farmville a set quite fashionable in both dress and homes. This was not, however, what most other observers saw in the agricultural South and it differed radically from what Du Bois himself had experienced in rural Tennessee. As a young teacher he had often gone home with students for the weekend, usually to a cabin of one or one-and-a-half rooms filled with "great, fat white beds, scrupulously neat . . . and a tired centre-table." If there was a kitchen, it was often aromatically filled with the smell of fried chicken, wheat biscuits, corn pone, and string beans. When a guest like Du Bois was present, berries or some other "delicacy" might be added to the menu. At bedtime the hosts discreetly stepped into the kitchen or out of doors until the guest was tucked away in bed. For two summers Du Bois lived in "this little world" finding it "dull and humdrum."[2]

"Tastefully furnished" homes, such as those of the black professional people at Montgomery, where there were said to be 250 to 300 pianos and organs in "colored" homes, struck Samuel Barrows. Prosperous African Americans there, and in other places such as Pensacola, were eating "as fine food as millionaires." In Washington a group of "the thriftier Negroes" lived fashionably on Massachusetts Avenue and on Sixteenth Street. Wooden or brick tenements were often seen in the cities. Differing with Barrows, the black living area in Washington, D.C. shocked the French traveler, Albert Tissandier, who contrasted the neglect and uncleanliness and mud and dust there with the "rich residences of the rest of the city."[3]

Living conditions among African Americans were judged by outsiders as mostly poor, this environment could not but adversely affect the mental and physical condition of the race. When James Bryce toured the South in 1881, he understood that insanity was increasing among blacks. He regretted and deplored the fact but blamed it upon the "increased facilities which freedom has given for obtaining liquor and to the stress which independence and education have imposed on the underdeveloped brain of a backward race" rather than upon the adverse conditions of African American life. This view was shared by Professor Cesare Lombroso, who was in the South almost twenty years later.[4]

Laura Towne, looking at the African American's physical condition on St. Helena Island, represented a different point of view. She lived in constant fear of a smallpox epidemic on St. Helena. A "terrible smallpox scourge" had swept the island in 1863, yet fourteen years later none of the black children on the island was vaccinated. She had seen also the effects of anemia and poor diet on the island's black children. Once three "little skeleton babies" were brought to her near death. One of the mothers told Mrs. Towne, an ex-medical student, that "Me been-a-pray day and night for you to come and save my baby." Mrs. Towne gave the mother medicine and advice, but she feared that one of the babies would die before the mother could get it home. With increasing frequency Mrs. Towne had to note the death of some of the island's blacks, especially the old people who "do not need our care long. They seem to drop off very fast." In the case of old women, they would often leave behind a helpless old Uncle (husband) and a tribe of grandchildren." Mrs. Towne, of course, grieved at the loss of these old stalwarts of the race.[5]

Efforts were being made at the time to cope with the African American's physical ills. A black doctor, nurse, and a staff of midwives served St. Helena Island by the close of the century, and they literally had their hands full. Yet Rossa Cooley noted that they did their work with unblemished pride. As one nurse put it, "I walk an' walk dis day, an' yet I ain't tire . . . I see de Greater Day a-comin."[6]

At Montgomery a "leading" African American, Joseph Hale, and his son had founded the Hale Infirmary for the treatment and care of the city's blacks. Housed in a large two story structure quite adequate to the purpose, the infirmary inspired Samuel Barrows to remark that in charging the African American with imitating the vices of the white "it is often over looked that he also imitates his virtues."[7]

Even in the Southern Highlands the rate of tuberculosis was high in the late nineteenth century. John Campbell attributed the frequency of the disease there, as in the rest of the South, to the "well known fact" that African Americans were "peculiarly susceptible" to it. Not being a physician, he wisely suggested no census and no cures.[8]

William Wells Brown, a physician as well as novelist and historian, thought the African Americans' diet contributed to their serious health problems. "The most inveterate eaters in the world," the southern blacks knew not what to eat. Hog, hominy, corn bread, cabbage, coffee, and sweet potatoes were the standard items. This diet, in Brown's view, lacked sufficient vegetables. A knowledge of "the laws of health," he thought, was urgently needed by the race.[9]

If one judged African Americans by their dress, they were still not well off. The older women generally dressed in about the same manner of "old slave pictures." From observations in North Carolina Charles Dudley Warner concluded the African American was a conservative element in the population, manifesting little inclination "to change his clothes or his cabin." His "swarming presence" gave "a ragged aspect to the new civilization" of the South. On Sunday the men might wear starched shirts, bright ties, and tall hats or "deck out" at Easter in Prince Albert coats with flowers in their button-holes, but most often they were clad in rags. Black children sometimes lacked even rags, so that nudity by necessity was common. Hesse-Wartegg saw two "pitch-black, fine" African American boys fishing in such a state.

The Edinburgh engineer, Archibald Sutter, remarking upon "half-naked" black children in Memphis, felt they were to be envied, rather than pitied, "for clothes feel an abomination now."[10]

To be sure, the younger women generally dressed adequately, many showing a preference for fiery red which they sometimes spotted with tobacco juice. Some even purchased "broadcloth" coats from their employers, and sought to buy Paris or London fabrics whenever feasible. William Wells Brown felt that many of the black women who came to market at Huntsville, Alabama were overdressed. The average black man was poorly outfitted, most often wearing patched garments, but the women wore "finery of every conceivable fashion," including "bright, colored dresses" and "flimsy" bonnets. Brown had seen one woman spend up to thirty dollars on "millinery goods" alone.[11]

Observers believed that African Americans trailed all other ethnic groups in mastering the English language. Such was the opinion of Theodor Kirchhoff, who had heard Irish, French, Germans, Chinese, Mexicans, Indians, and "half-breeds" speak English. As between Native Americans and African Americans specifically, he found the red man's speech "elegant" while that of the blacks was set. Mary Allan-Olney did attribute to the African American speech" in another sense. "I have never heard a Negro say 'begin.' It is always 'commence,' with a great emphasis on the first syllable."[12]

During one of his boat rides on the lower Mississippi, Hesse-Wartegg encountered in the ladies compartment a group of "old, decadent," pipe-smoking, whiskey-drinking, "cackling" black women in lively conversation. They were supposedly speaking French but Hesse-Wartegg could not follow them. The captain explained that Louisiana plantation French demanded "black ears in order to be understood." Hesse-Wartegg described it as "a curious dialect which has lost complete touch with the original language." Perhaps half of the blacks in southern Louisiana spoke this dialect, and hardly understood a word of English.[13]

Chaplain Cowan, who talked with African Americans wherever he went in the South, heard such statements or questions as "Dey is Yank hossifers" and "Is dey hard times in de North?" Professor Freeman, in the region at the same time, found African American speech difficult. What he heard was not "the racy dialect of Uncle Remus, nor the speech of foreigners troubled by English but fluent in another tongue, rather of beings to whom the art of speech in any shape was not altogether familiar." Seemingly blacks had "lost their own tongue without having fully found ours." The African Americans heard by Charles Beadle in Charleston spoke "fair" English, as did those encountered by William Smith in Washington, by Charles Dudley Warner in Virginia, and by Du Bois in Tennessee and Virginia. Almost all agreed, however, that they talked too much and too loudly.[14]

Only Lillie Wyman, among nineteenth century observers, sought to analyze critically the typical African American speech pattern. She concluded that it was at its best an "exaggeration of the peculiarities of accent and pronunciation observable among the [southern] whites." From that point it degenerated into a sort of dialect "in which the tendency to sound *th* like *d* after some and *n* like *b* is confirmed." After some vowels *ing* was rendered simply as *R*, after consonants it was turned into *un* or *en*. A general habit prevailed of reducing words to mono-syllables. Mrs. Wyman speculated that the moving about of blacks by sale in slavery, and their voluntary migrations since emancipation, along with the influences provided by whites of various backgrounds, had caused their speech to become so modified that in any given case it was largely a question of the individual's personal history, not merely of local dialect. African Americans spoke by ear rather than "by rule or according to confirmed customs." In tone, their voices were generally softer than those of Euro-Americans, and "persuasive."[15]

A black amusement that whites relished was story telling. Old uncle Gabriel of Virginia entertained Arthur Granville Bradley with a tale concerning hounds and a fox.

> Yes, suh, for Gawd I's tellin' you de solemn troof.
> Dem ar dawgs run data r ole fox fur two days an'
> Two nights . . . It was de day befo' Christmas . . . and
> When de ole man quit off huntin' at sundown he done
> Tell me ter foller dem hounds and see whar they's
> Gwine ter . . . I follered 'em all Christmas day and all
> Dat night too, and when I caught up wid 'em jes as
> Sho' as yo' born, suh, . . . and fo' de Lawd de fox was
> Walkin'; and de hounds was walkin', dey was all
> Walkin' wid en a few yards of one nur's.[16]

At Union, Tennessee, Charles Dudley Warner sought out a black woman reputedly 100 years old to hear her tell of her life as a black person. She had been sold separately in slavery from her husband at a sheriff's sale, had never seen him again, and had never remarried. She was appalled by the lack of decency and morality among young blacks at the present time. The whites were not much better, certainly nothing like they used to be. As for slavery, she confessed that it had been bad—she had seen on one occasion "five hundred niggers in handcuffs, all together in a field, sold to be sent South." Warner admired the spunk of this limber-tongued old woman.[17]

When one of Hezekiah Butterworth's party on board a steamboat from St. Louis to New Orleans besought a group of young blacks to sing for her he was met by a counter request, that they be told of "'the captains of the Nof--- them who made us free.'" She confessed that she had not known Lincoln, nor John Brown, nor William Lloyd Garrison, but she did remember the funeral of Charles Sumner, and to hear about that the blacks gathered around in intense interest. Most were not familiar with Sumner's life, but they enjoyed his death, or at least the story of it. To "the mind of the Negro," Butterworth learned death and burial were the most interesting of events.[18]

In Virginia the old plantation songs were a source of great entertainment to all who heard them. When African Americans gathered to eat hot cakes—"the Ethiopian's staff of life," according to Bradley—a lusty voice might suddenly roar:

> 'O-O my lovely Lemma,
> I-I do love you so'
> 'I-I love you better tha-a-n
> I ever did befo'
> O-oh-O-oh'

Similarly at "corn-shucking time" in November, the great social event of the agricultural year in Virginia, tongues were loosened and songs stimulated by food and whiskey passed out among the blacks to climax the day's work. Such melodies as 'O my lovely Lemma' filled the air until long after midnight.[19]

African American boys fishing in a ditch caught the attention of Hesse-Wartegg during his journey through the sugar country. The tackle of the naked fishermen consisted of a string with a little piece of meat tied onto it. On this occasion a crab took the bait and the boys quickly pulled him out of the slimy water. They would spend their childhood in such ways until big enough to go onto the cane field, then pass their "juvenile leisures" onto their younger brothers.[20]

Fishing among southern blacks was in the eyes of Julian Ralph "'idle time not idly spent.'" The entire family seemed to be eternally at it wherever "they and any piece of water, no matter how small, [were] thrown together." The picture was idyllic; "after one has seen a few darkies putting their whole souls into fishing, it is painful to see a white man with a rod and line. The white man always looks like an imitation and a fraud."[21]

Going to town on market day, Saturday, was a great source of entertainment and recreation. Many blacks came from such a distance that they started on Friday and camped by the roadside all night. Their tendency to flock into town caused Saturday to become known as "nigger day" in most of the South. It was not uncommon, as William Wells Brown observed, for an African American to bring "two jugs, one for the molasses, the other for the whiskey." The street life of a town in Georgia or Alabama observed by Lillie Wyman became on Saturday "nearly as unique as that of Naples." Though the whites abandoned an entire sidewalk on the main street to the blacks, that boundary was overflowed. The men gossiped about bargains and other business matters, the women about sunbonnets, clothes and the like. It was also a time for boys and girls to flirt. Most of the selling, in the town, mainly of "small game," was done in the morning. At noon the blacks, leaning against the walls of buildings, ate their lunch "with unabashed frankness, and in a manner suggestive of primitive customs as to the use of fingers and teeth." By night fall those whose energy was spent headed home while others stayed for more revelry.[22]

The circus attracted large crowds of blacks into southern towns. If they were too poor, as they often were, to pay the entrance fee to the tents, their joy was "found in watching the procession of the sorry little shows through the streets, and in mingling with the crowd outside the canvass walls." The more thrifty blacks might bring wood with them, hoping to sell it during the day to pay for admission to the circus. On circus night the country blacks returned home, but the town blacks generally lingered on the corners, often clustering around a fire in the middle of the street, gossiping and sucking stalks of sugar cane.[23]

The cakewalk was a favorite source of entertainment among African Americans both rural and urban. As performed by a church group in North Carolina the couples marched around the room singing a hymn to "a good marching tune" while the matrons and married men looked on to criticize. A large cake was awarded to the "most graceful couple" in this "promenade." A supper closed the entertainment, which was likely to be a topic of conversation for days thereafter.[24]

Sports such as baseball and something called football did not escape the attention of the blacks. At Dalton, Georgia, Sir George Campbell witnessed a group "of very tidy, well set-up looking blacks playing baseball, in a very vigorous way, with one or two whites mixed with them." Fraternization between whites and blacks in this manner Campbell thought was not uncommon.[25]

Croquet was engaged in regularly by the refined African Americans of Farmville, Du Bois tells us. The games generally followed luncheons, and preceded dances. Henry Nelson noted luncheons, receptions, and the like among the black middleclass in Washington, but no croquet.[26]

Fairs and exhibitions afforded African Americans not only entertainment and recreation but also an opportunity to demonstrate creative or artistic

skills, whether in grooming a prize pig or carving a piece of sculpture. The
Penn School on St. Helena Island held an annual exhibition of the work of
black students, accompanied probably by singing contests. The exhibition
of 1878 was held in a packed church, with persons who came from as far
as Savannah having to be turned away. No white visitors attended that year,
though apparently they had in the past. Mrs. Towne noted the enthusiasm of
the blacks for the event, and felt guilty because to her it was quite tiring.[27]

Throughout the South African Americans organized and held "industrial
fairs" exhibiting, among other things, their skill as artisans and craftsmen.
One at Pine Bluff, Arkansas, toward the close of the 19th century, was judged
by Mifflin Gibbs a complete success. A feature attraction of some such fairs
was the "drill and marital bearing" of participating black militia companies.
"The colored citizens took quiet pride and much interest in these companies
and were saddened when many were commanded by the State authorities to
disband."

The directors of the World's Exposition at New Orleans in 1884 invited
African Americans to furnish "exhibits of their productions from farm, shop
and home." Former United States Senator Blanche K. Bruce of Mississippi,
an African American, was appointed chief director for "The Department of
Colored Exhibits." Mifflin Gibbs, as honorary commissioner for the state of
Arkansas, was in good position to view the whole proceedings. On "Emancipation Day" or "colored people's day" the blacks exhibited their best in farm
products, livestock, sewing, cooking, and so on. A good many whites attended. To show them the evidence of the African Americans' advancement,
Gibbs thought a worthy achievement in itself, and the exhibits stimulated
pride among members of the race. Some fellow blacks did not entirely agree
with him, however, deeming the "appointment of a particular day . . . [for their
exhibits] derogatory to their claim of recognition, and equality of citizenship." This reminded Gibbs of another black who had cried: "how long, O'
Lord, are we to bear these discriminations?" "For sometime longer," Gibbs
believed, yet "all things considered, we are making progress."[28]

Singing festivals in which individuals and groups vied for recognition
and prizes were held in many southern black communities. The enthusiasm
for the annual festival on St. Helena Island led Rossa Cooley to wonder if it
were not true that the "love of singing" was the factor which had carried the
blacks "through all their experiences without bitterness." Blacks were more
sensitive to musical effects than whites, Nathaniel Shaler concluded after
hearing a black musical competition. A black was hardly to be found who
did not "enjoy the songs of his people," and those who could not read a note
of music rendered some of the most effective performances Shaler had ever
heard. Studies of this aspect of African American life might prove beneficial

to the whole nation, Shaler suggested, considering "how large a place music has in our life."[29]

At Christmas, Arthur Bradley said, "the Negro had it all to himself," making a big time of it. In rural Virginia as the holiday approached blacks abandoned their employers for the "social joys so dear to the Ethiopian breast." "'Cake walks' and frolics and preachings filled the cabins with sound and merriment; whiskey . . . flowed freely, and stimulated with . . . its fires the merry antics of the coloured revelers." On St. Helena Island Christmas was always the best of times. An old inhabitant told Rossa Colley that "We has Christmas Eve, Christmas Eve's Eve and Christmas, Christmas Adam and Christmas Madam!'" Ex-students of Penn School returned for the holiday, and the air was filled with spirituals and carols. At the school itself the "Christmas story" was generally re-enacted. Grits and potatoes were brought for the poor. After the program the blacks engaged in "merry antics", similar to those described by Bradley in Virginia.[30]

The romantic relationships between black boys and girls and men and women were selfdom observed by outsiders, but Ernst Von Hesse-Wartegg was an exception. The meeting of black couples and their efforts at courting appeared to him somewhat strange. Men concentrated great efforts on pleasing their sweethearts. Everyone seemed to flirt. The blacks were apparently at their best when they capered and shook as they danced a cotillion in the local ballroom. Julian Ralph probably would have found the scene primitive and immoral, to Hesse-Wartegg it was "a precious, cheerful sight," a welcome relief from the African Americans' otherwise "monotonous life."[31]

When things got too dull a black could always, it seemed, go to a wedding or a funeral. Whites, whether outsiders or natives, took more interest in funerals than in weddings, but Iza Duffus Hardy did attend a wedding held in a laundry at Orlando, Florida. The numerous guests formed a circle around the young couple, "both as black as one could imagine." The bride, about fourteen, but seeming a little older, was dressed in "white muslin, with an enormous wreath, that made her look top-heavy, especially as her black face was modestly inclined on one side, turned away from the bridegroom, until it nearly rested on her shoulder." The groom, who wore a "beautiful brown velvet coat, white gloves much too large for him, kept his left hand, with fingers outstretched, laid upon his heart." He had a "sheepish appearance and the bride was inclined to giggle." The only peculiarity which Iza observed in the ceremony was the omission of "baptismal names." The important questions were put simply; "O man, wilt thou have this woman? And 'O woman, wilt thou have this man?" "Once the service was over, 'the black as a coal' minister called for the 'salute' to the bride." "Thereupon ensued a general kissing match."[32]

A northern teacher in the South attended not only the wedding for one of her students but also the reception following. The student was a "slight, graceful mulatto girl" who wore a white cotton dress, a muslin veil, and carried a "wreath of coarse artificial flowers" that was ugly yet "looked picturesque enough contrasted with the black suit and blacker face of the bridegroom." He was an older man possessing a "kind face." Completing the wedding party were "two giggling, self-conscious bridesmaids . . . and two groomsmen." Following the outdoor ceremony a reception or supper was held in a "little back room" of cakes, biscuits, and fried chicken. Although everything was clean, the disorder did not encourage the teacher's appetite. After supper the festivities continued by moonlight. In one of the ring games a couple "walked all around a circle and all joined in a song that seemed to say:

> Lonesome without you,
> Lonesome, lonesome
> Lonesome without you,
> Lonesome, lonesome

Accompanying the singing were rhythmical motions of the feet and body, as one might expect from "a tropical race," but "no signs of excess of any kind." Though "all very humble, and poor and crude," "yet there was a rude poetry in the scene, softened as it was by the mild Southern moonlight."[33]

Mary Allan-Olney attended funeral services for "Brother Wash" Turpin, a Virginia black. Turpin was eulogized as "a man of God" who loved his church and worked for it. The eulogy was said amid foot-stomping, hand-clapping, shouts, and cries of "Thank God?" A white man who said he was looking for turkeys and "didn't know Brother Wash was there" had shot "Brother Wash" through the heart. The preacher admonished the audience that "how Brother Wash died is God's business, not yours," "and when Brother Wash fell, the angel took up his soul, and he flew away with it, till he came to the gate of heaven." After a sermon of an hour and a half, the minister called for an offering for "Brother Wash's widow," saying that it was the duty of the church to help her "so long as she remains a widow indeed, but no longer." This service convinced Miss Allan-Olney that "true religion was almost unknown among blacks, who were to be the dominant race in the South", and deepened her feeling that were she a southern woman her eyes would be dimmed and her cheeks "furrowed with weeping, for the desolation of my country."[34]

That there were segregated cemeteries often shocked outsiders. The general reaction was summed up by William Russell (after visiting Arlington Cemetery, where blacks were buried a half mile away from whites.) "Even in death the white and black are divided." Before attending a black burial in Virginia Susan Showers learned that "some peculiar customs" were connected with black funerals and interments. One of the strange customs she alleged was to bury the deceased and defer the funeral until later, even as much as a year later, thus allowing ample time for mourners to gather from distant places, suitable clothing to be prepared, and the preacher to select the most appropriate words. In the cemetery which Susan Showers visited some of the graves were marked with a wooden slat, some with a stake only, and many not at all. A goodly number were "decorated with bits of broken glass and china and old bottles." This practice represented the survival of "an old heathen custom that missionaries had found in Africa."

At the burial to which Susan Showers went a large crowd of sympathetic but curious blacks of all ages was present. "The ignorant everywhere have a morbid curiosity about . . . the last long sleep; and in the plantation Negro this . . . reaches an abnormal development," partly because of his "quick sympathy" and partly because of "the atmosphere of superstition in which he lives." The ceremony began with the singing of a doleful and depressing hymn. After many stanzas and the traditional "earth to earth" the formal interment came to an end, to be followed, however, by loud "How yo' feel?" and "Mighty po'ly thankee!" greetings. Despite the bereaved family, and all the ingredients for sorrow, Susan Showers sensed, as Mary Allan-Olney had, that these activities were in a way a source of entertainment.[35]

Secret and benevolent organizations or lodges often assisted African American families to pay funeral expenses. In Farmville, Du Bois reported that the lodges were second in influence only to the churches. (On account of their secret nature, outsiders, especially whites, however, could know little about them.) Besides helping with funeral costs, the groups provided funds for relief in case of sickness. The money came from small, regular contributions by members. The organizations were made more attractive "by a ritual, ceremonies, officers, often regalia, and various social features." On the whole they had been "peculiarly successful," Du Bois thought, especially when one remembered that they were conducted by people untrained in business methods.[36]

Booker T. Washington had pledged at Atlanta in 1895 that "in all things social" blacks and whites could remain as separate as the fingers on the hand. For the most part, they remained so throughout the first quarter of the twentieth century. At the same time they were supposed to work together for mutual economic advancement. If this formula proved successful, there should be improvements in the African Americans' social condition corresponding to their economic advancement. The observers' reports permit a long look at health and housing, and glances at lighter matters such as dress and recreation in the age of Booker T. Washington.

Among diseases, which weighed especially upon blacks the most conspicuous, probably, was tuberculosis. Its prevalence was highlighted in a study
conducted by Thomas Jesse Jones with the assistance of various associates
including African American physicians. Jones discovered that the black death
rate from the disease was far above that in any other American ethnic group.
He rejected "racial characteristics" as a reason because "the extent to which
the racial element enters into the cause of tuberculosis has not yet been determined." A more plausible explanation was poor, unsanitary living conditions
in both city and country. Jones visited in rural Virginia a typical black cabin
of two rooms in which twelve of thirteen children born since the Civil War
had died in childhood.

Illiteracy was an important factor in the African American's ill-health, far
more serious than most people realized. Jones had known an ignorant black
man, since dead, who infected his wife and nine children with tuberculosis.
Though seven of the children were unable to walk, the consumptive mother,
herself "at the brink of the grave," continued to wash for white people, and
her two sons worked in barber shops.

Jones emphasized also "the economic disadvantages of the race assumed
proportions which totally eclipse any racial disposition," and develop "an
environment" which contributed much to the increase of mortality from con-
sumption. The majority of tuberculosis cases of all races were in the laboring
and servant classes, and over 80 per cent of African Americans belonged to
those classes.

The outlook for the African America consumptive was not promising.
The only public efforts in Virginia were an outdoor department at "the State
Insane Asylum for Negroes (Petersburg) and a few free dispensaries. Jones
blamed the states and cities and African American physicians for the failure.
(Very little was being done for the southern white consumptive either.) Jones
called upon African American doctors numbering more than one thousand,
the black ministers, the colleges, and governmental authorities to move immediately to provide hospital and sanatorium facilities for African Americans. White and black alike must realize that the untreated African American
consumptive was a danger to the nation.[37]

The poverty of medical services at Pulaski County, Georgia, was brought
home to Ray Stannard Baker by his finding that a boy shot in the head during one of the frequent fracases at black parties had laid in a cabin in critical
condition for some time. Just the night before, his father said, the family
"done thought he was acrossin de ribbah." Apparently the only treatment
administered had been prayer.[38]

In the mining area of Jefferson County, Alabama, the state of the African
Americans' health was far from enviable. The "camp physician" reported that

disease and intemperance had incapacitated many women for motherhood. If children were born, the infant mortality rate was as high as fifty per cent, caused chiefly by "neglect" and "ignorant management." Recent recruits to the mines, especially those coming directly from the farm, were usually robust, but immorality soon pulled them down also. The physician saw little hope for improvement in physical condition in the absence of a corresponding lifting of morals.[39]

A study of syphilis among African Americans in the hospitals of Washington, D.C., was undertaken in 1914 by Henry H. Hazen, a dermatologist. That blacks suffered syphilis at a greater frequency than whites, Hazen found, could not be denied. Among African American professional and business people syphilis was not more prevalent, in his opinion, than among whites. It was the poorer class, much more numerous, and dwelling under conditions that could "breed neither good morals nor good health," who crowded the hospitals and dispensaries and were responsible for the syphilitic stigma attached to the race. Hazen asserted that African Americans sprang "from a southern race, and as such his sexual appetite is strong; all of his environments stimulate this appetite, and as a general rule his emotional type of religion certainly does not decrease it." Both white and black physicians testified that virginity was "very rare" among black girls of the poorer class, as rare as continence "among white men." Though the ratio of illegitimate births was no higher among the African American population of Washington than in European cities, Hazen understood that sexual promiscuity was a serious problem in the black schools, 'social clubs' having been formed in them for the sole object of sexual indulgence. The result had been syphilis infection among children, an occurrence rare among whites, though "by no means unknown."

The prophylaxis of syphilis in African Americans was especially difficult, Hazen said, "for it is impossible to persuade the poor variety . . . that sexual gratification is wrong, even when he is in the actively infectious stage." Lectures on sex hygiene were unlikely to have the slightest effect. As possible remedies Hazen suggested circumcision "for the purpose of avoiding . . . irritation which increases the sexual appetite;" artificial prophylactics; improvement of black living conditions; curtailing the use of cocaine and alcohol; and a strict curfew. While African Americans sought treatment "just as faithfully" as white patients, the seriousness of the situation among them increased the urgency of preventive measures.[40]

To sum up, the factors which lay at the root of the African Americans' physical ills were poverty, ignorance, absence of sanitation, and poor diet. Booker T. Washington had inaugurated a "Negro Health Week" to inspire blacks to guard their health and develop sanitary practices which would strengthen the race. But the evidence shows by the end of the World War that he had largely failed—the black undertaker still had more than his share of business.

The evidence suggests that African American victims of mental disease suffered just as grievously as those struck by physical ailments though their deaths may not have been as early or as numerous. Just prior to the First World War insanity was "on the increase in the colored race," (James Bryce had said the same thing thirty years before.) According to a psychiatrist, Aarah B. Evarts, who was assigned to the wards for black females at the Government Hospital for the Insane, Washington, D.C., and there examined the mental condition of a number of southern black women, an increase in African American insanity was inevitable, Dr. Evarts felt, considering that the blacks were being called upon to make an adjustment (presumably that from slavery to freedom) "much harder . . . when we consider the factors to be used in the problem, than any other race has yet been called upon to attempt."

The disorder especially interesting to Dr. Evarts because of its prevalence among African Americans was dementia precox, "a deteriorating psychosis" which was "protean in its manifestations, every case being a case by itself." The psychosis as existing in the African race differed "in no essentials" from that among whites, but African Americans "because of the vicissitudes" of their history were "peculiarly prone to this form of mental trouble." Among "the colored females" admitted by the Government Hospital for the Insane thirty-seven cases out of every one hundred were dementia precox.

African American victims of dementia precox, unlike whites, were able to carry on their daily tasks long after being stricken by the disease. Among them Doctor Evarts quite often found "a strain of heredity" though the record was "necessarily short, being invariably lost in the darkness of fore de war." In the African American the "two great exciting causes" of dementia precox were worry and emotional shock. These were not uncommon among whites, but the sources of the disturbances differed. African American patients were generally most concerned over the waywardness of a child, or the growing difficulty of making ends meet, or neglect by a lazy husband. Instances of shock were the sudden insanity of a brother and the sudden death of a relative. One patient exhibited a deep catatonic stupor following the institution of divorce proceedings in which she was named as correspondent.

Among African American precox patients sexual perversions appeared much less frequently than among whites. Evarts thought the reason was that sexual instincts among blacks were "peculiarly unrestrained," and that, despite the "moderation" which they were learning, their desires were "usually fully satisfied with no feeling of having done wrong."

Contrary to reports from Jamaica, the catatonic type of precox was very pronounced in southern blacks. "Its three cardinal symptoms, resistance, negativism, and mutism" were found "in so extreme a degree that it seems impossible they could grow deeper." In the end, Evarts concluded, dementia precox was dementia precox, whether in black or white, though it was aggravated in African Americans by their being "an already primitive race."[41]

Substantial improvements in African American housing were found in the Tidewater area of Virginia by Carl Kelsey, who went south from Pennsylvania in 1902 to study the Negro farmer. The old-one-room cabins were out of fashion and had largely given way to comfortable structures of several rooms. In these "white-washed" homes stoves had supplanted fire places. Yard fences were often neat and in good repair. No other rural district that Kelsey saw in the South would compare with this one.[42]

On St. Helena Island, "most prosperous of the Negro districts" of the Sea Islands, the condition was considerably worse than in Virginia, and perhaps more typical. The cabins basically of one room often partitioned into two, were roughly constructed and seldom painted, though sometimes whitewashed. Fences were rare, and damage by livestock was evident. "Outbuildings" were few and "privies" almost unknown. Wells were "shallow," six feet or so in depth, and usually open, though some had pumps.[43]

African American living conditions left an unfavorable impression upon Clifton Johnson, of Hadley, Massachusetts. He was inclined to blame African Americans alone for their unwholesome surroundings. Johnson, who wrote travel accounts for a living, made his most extensive southern trip from St. Augustine to Virginia during 1903–1904. The dirt and dilapidation by which one could always tell a "nigger's place" testified to the poverty and lack of pride general among the blacks. "They simply exist." Yet a dog was always in evidence around their living quarters. A "poor nigger" would generally have two, "a desperately poor nigger" half a dozen. Hounds and coon dogs were preferred, but "any sort of cur" was acceptable.[44]

The black tenements of St. Louis were just as bad, if not worse, than the cabins of the rural South, according to Paul Adam. Located mostly on the right bank of the Mississippi, they were constructed of brick with the iron ladders, which served as fire escapes hanging outside. Within a long staircase from the lobby to upstairs apartments which consisted usually of "two stinking rooms decorated with political posters" and containing a tiny, broken stove, a wooden table, a suspended oil lamp, two or three chairs, an iron bed, and a zinc pot with its base on a tripod. These "hovels" rented for $10.50 a month. Even more unfortunate than their occupants were the blacks living in the basements of stores and warehouses. One of these buildings would be occupied by ten or twenty persons, each sleeping only on a straw mattress, and separated by parallel walls or partitions.[45]

Dilapidated housing, consisting of "dim" and "discomfortable" "shanties," was seen at Charleston and Washington by Henry James in 1906. Most of the African American homes in Atlanta that Ray Stannard Baker visited just after the 1906 riot offered hospitality that would have "done credit to a society woman" but were poor in quality and the rooms "squalid." Baker left "impressed by the tragic punishment meted out to ignorance and weakness by our complex society." In rural Georgia the primitive conditions were not pleasant to contemplate. Albert Bushnell Hart found the housing for blacks to be poor and crude whether in urban tenement or rural cabins. The worst was "on the land of the least progressive and humane planters."[46]

African America housing was not always poor, Sir Harry H. Johnston thought. The worst he saw was in the rural areas of Virginia where Kelsey had found the best African American dwellings in the South. In the forests of Alabama blacks occupied "picturesque" log huts with clay chimneys and ample, comfortable, clean beds inside. Other homes were of "gray planks, the roof of gray shingles, with glass windows, green shutters, and green verandah rails." Petroleum lamps might permit the reading of books on agriculture and the ever-present Bible. Very much worse off were the dwellers in Washington tenements that were "grotesque survivals of the life of the 'forties' and 'fifties." These blacks, lived "in a condition of ramshackle poverty—perhaps one may say dirt," should be stimulated either to improve their quarters or to move away to the country where they could be "as untidy as they like." At Savannah Mildred Cram saw signs of improvement in 1918. Although the black masses still lived in squalid homes, rows and rows of neat frame and brick houses had in part replaced the old cabins of one or two rooms.[47]

The urban blacks were not dressed richly, but their rural counterpart was in many instances hardly dressed at all. Such was the impression of the French author, Paul Adam. Half-naked black children were commonly seen walking around, and ragged men with straw hats worked in the fields. Adam was amazed that even under these circumstances African Americans managed to grin, and to laugh "stupidly." Raggedness was also the rule at Charleston and Washington when Henry James reviewed the American scene in 1906. The ragged blacks, despite their "tatters" were "portentous." The dress of African Americans, especially in Atlanta, was better, however, than Ray Stannard Baker had expected to see, "having in mind, perhaps, the tattered country specimens of the penny postal cards." Similarly, Sir Harry Johnston found African American men all over the South, "from the artisan to the college professors," as well dressed as the average white American. The clothes of Booker T. Washington and his sons were appropriate and of good cut. Sir

Harry hoped that Washington had no "frockcoats" or silk hats, for they became few white men and never look "other than ugly and inappropriate on a person of dark complexion." The black women at Tuskegee dressed richly but not tastefully. Among two hundred, who attended a party at the Institute, a portion of the darker ones came dressed in snowy white or cream color "which simply made them unendurably grotesque." The few who wore brown, dark blue, "greenish blue" or "gray-green" looked "exceedingly nice."[48]

William Archer, Scottish critic and journalist who came to the United States in 1908 specifically to study the race problem, saw African American children in the typical half-naked state at Long Key, Florida. The black children were playing with two Orientals in a scene that appeared to Archer "like kings in exile among a rabble of savages." Later Archer met an African American "philanthropist" wearing a diamond pin in his shirt and displaying a mouth full of gold. Ragged black masses were still seen near Eura, Virginia, and at Charleston, Jacksonville, and Key West when American troops were embarking for Europe in 1917. But at Savannah an African American chauffeur, "ridiculously proud," pointed out well-dressed black women in white shoes and "pickanninnies in sailor suits and socks, riding Kiddy-Kars along the sidewalks." Mildred Cram at first thought this scene less picturesque than that of ragged, poverty-stricken blacks, but later admitted that to demand picturesqueness at the price of "eternal raggedness and poverty" was wrong.[49]

Fishing, singing and dancing, "Nigger Day," and "cakewalks" continued as popular leisure time activities for southern blacks. Of these, the "cakewalk' seemed least likely to endure. When Mrs. Tweedie saw it at New Orleans in 1901 only the dance survived, the cake no longer being rewarded as a prize. Her effort to learn the origin of the term "cakewalk" met with little positive success. Most could only say that the whole affair had originated in slave days and that the expression, 'He takes the cake,' originated from the awarding of a cake to the best performers. A slightly different version of the "cakewalk" was still a favorite amusement among southern blacks' children at birthday parties when Timothy Williams visited the region in 1903. As of old, a cake was placed upon the table as a prize, while the couples walked around the house, in through the door, around the table, and out again. As the procession moved on; one of the "old folks" presented flags to various couples. The marching continued until a gun was discharged outside; then the couple with a flag that happened to be nearest the table was considered the takers of the cake.[50]

"Ring games" remained popular, too, especially among African American children. One of the favorites was "Hop like de rabbit ho!" As Williams saw it, one player entered a circle made by the others and chose a partner. In a "queer embrace" they clasped shoulders and jumped around. Meanwhile those in the ring clapped their hands and beat their feet singing:

> Hop like de rabbit, ho!
> Hop like de rabbit, ho boy!
> De rabbit skip.
> De rabbit hop.
> De rabbit eat my turnip top!
> Hop like de rabbit, ho!
> Hop like de rabbit, ho boy!

Particularly since "the conditions of their life" were not such as to acquaint black children "with the sports usually enjoyed by other children," Williams was much impressed with their ability to have fun with their own games. He was obviously unaware of African American participation, reported by other observers, in such sports as football and baseball.[51]

In the twentieth century African Americans added boxing to their list of sports while continuing baseball and football on a modest scale and largely ignoring croquet, which Du Bois had seen at Farmville, Virginia. Mrs. Tweedie witnessed an African American match in Louisiana. As among whites of the day, a couple of tin pails were turned upside down for the combatants to sit upon, old sacks being spread below as "carpets." The men took off their boots, one boxing barefooted, the other in socks. Each had a second, and the surrounding crowd betted on the result in amounts as much as ten dollars, which showed "how well off" they were. Mrs. Tweedie called the match an "amusing sight."[52]

Most southern cities barred blacks from public recreation facilities except as nurses to white children, but Memphis and a few other places had established separate parks for African Americans by 1917, when Julian Street toured the South. Street thought such establishments were commendable. By the beginning of the twentieth century the privilege of the galleries in white theaters was being increasingly denied to southern blacks. At the same time, however, separate theaters for African Americans began to appear in cities like New Orleans, Atlanta, and Jackson, Mississippi. The theater at New Orleans Ray Stannard Baker thought particularly "fine."[53]

Traditional forms of entertainment and recreation such as storytelling, lost much of their appeal as African Americans moved from farm to city and as more and more of the ex-slaves died. While old blacks lived, however, the old joys would not completely fade away. At Mound Bayou, Mississippi, mainly a black town, Sir Harry Johnston listened to the reminiscences of one of the patriarchs who was a son of the favorite slave of Joseph Davis, Jefferson Davis' brother. Sir Harry observed that the African American had a remarkable command of English and it was "like hearing the recital of a sequel to Uncle Tom's Cabin" to hear him tell how "a contraband copy" of Harriet Beecher Stowe's famous work had been smuggled into the slave quarters when he was a young man, and how the one or two educated slaves read it aloud to the others by "stealth."[54]

Near White Sulphur, Virginia, Louise Hale met an old, well-mannered, ex-slave who had belonged to "one of the very best families in Virginia." He spoke proudly of the fact that he and his kin had been owned throughout their bondage by one family and since emancipation had continued to work for them. Mildred Cram was not so successful in her bid to get a story from an ex-slave at Savannah. This woman, said to be 100 years old, was barely alive. She bowed to the white visitors, but protested her inability to tell of conditions 'befo' the wah' because she had a fever and was dying. Another black laughed and suggested that a quarter would loosen the old black woman's tongue. Mildred Cram gave the quarter, and the woman took it and "gazed at it fixedly like an ancient ape," but steadfastly refused to talk.[55]

As some of the old amusements declined, other traditional ones gained strength, adjusting their formats to the times. Fairs and festivals (bi-racial or black dominated) held as much excitement for the twentieth-century African American as for his predecessors. Increasingly literate and skilled, the blacks had more to offer at such events, and more of which to be proud. The Georgia-Carolina Fair at Augusta in the fall of 1906 saw an African American from Richmond County win first prize over many white exhibitors for the best bale of cotton raised. Such feats, Baker believed, had given the African American farmer a "genuine reputation for ability." Baker also attended the first state fair ever held by blacks in Georgia at Macon in 1906. It followed close behind the notorious Atlanta riot, yet was well attended by both blacks and whites. Largely the brainchild of Richard R. Wright, president of the Georgia State Industrial College at Savannah, the fair proved a complete success. The blacks raised $11,000 for it, spent only $7,000, and drew between 25, and 30,000 spectators.[56]

An opportunity to see Christmas through the eyes of African American children was afforded Timothy Williams during his sojourn in the South. He felt that there was something unique in the fact that their stockings were filled only "with an orange, an apple, a doll, or a stick of candy" rather than with lavish and expensive toys. Adults and children alike tended to stop all work and make Christmas a weeklong celebration.[57]

The emphasis on self-help programs in the age of Booker T. Washington led to increased activity among fraternal and benevolent societies. They remained second only to the church among African American social institutions, and in a few cases might even be considered more important. Carl

Kelsey noted on the Sea Islands in 1903 a rapid development of burial and sick benefit societies usually under such religious names as "Morning Star" or "Star of Bethlehem." Collecting weekly assessments of five to ten cents per person, some of them had been able to construct "good sized" lodge halls that often rivaled the church buildings and were used for fraternal and social purposes.[58]

At the mining camp in Jefferson County, Alabama, such secret organizations had become by 1907 the most prominent factor in the African Americans social life, outstripping the church. There were four different lodges in this camp alone, each having a female branch. The "best" men and women of the race belonged. Some southern white men regarded the secret orders with distrust, however, thinking their motives to be "offensive" rather than "defensive and progressive."

The northern physician who described the orders in Jefferson County attributed their popularity to their tendency to bolster "a racial pride, fostering the advancement of members of the race;" to the social activities; to the sick and death benefits; and, finally to the assurance of a grand funeral, the "brothers" and "sisters" being certain to 'turn out' on such an occasion. Another very important feature and probable attraction, resembling that of African American churches, was the opportunity for self-government. The chance to exercise governmental functions was even better than in the church, in that the lodges severely punished their members for disorderly and criminal conduct, imposing more discipline in fact than the state authorities did.

The female departments furnished important, though presumably rudimentary, nursing care for sick members, and provided young girls with instruction aimed at preventing their seduction by white men. These activities, like those of the male branch were giant forward steps for the race, the physician believed.[59]

African Americans' secret orders struck Albert Bushnell Hart as on the whole "a good thing." Besides their social, sick, and burial functions, many of them gave training in public speaking and experience in "common action." They served as a source of employment, even publishing newspapers, and they were soundly and honestly managed.[60]

In spite of the generally poor housing in which African Americans lived, the ragged dress, and the deplorable conditions of health, the increased social activity, as shown in fairs and exhibits, and social institutions, like lodges, undoubtedly did much to confirm Booker Washington's belief that the race could make "progress," although separated from the mainstream of American life. Others no doubt continued to ask, could there really be "progress" alongside oppression?

The fact that social conditions had not measurably improved for African Americans after the first world war produced a degree of bitterness among some black intellectuals, but it did not appear among the Missouri and Alabama blacks who Walter George saw and liked in 1920. They were unfailingly cheerful, greeting the slightest courtesy or consideration with a smile and not appearing "to worry over social standing, material success, or career; instead they seemed "content to work, to marry, and to teach their pickaninnies how to sing 'Josua fit the battle of Jericho,'" Gilbert Chesterton was also struck by the "charming and astonishing cheerfulnesss" among blacks. "My sense of pathos was appealed to much more by the Red Indians." Similarly, the African Americans encountered by Prossinagg, mostly servants, were well-mannered, cheerful, and courteous.[61]

Harold Spender, an English journalist who visited Georgia and Tennessee in 1923, had expected to see a region that was "still in a sort of backwater" and African Americans in a wretched state. Instead he found a courageous and self-confident South and "a happy Negro", happier than the blacks of the North, "where he was alternately cuddled and cursed, corseted and cuffed."[62]

Among the more intelligent blacks some had changed their manners since 1898, Andre Siegfried granted. But he thought the number to be small. Only a small elite showed any sign of bitterness, or any desire to agitate against discrimination. The masses, still humble, "docile, passive," accepted "their subjugation without a murmur." Their attitude was "that of parasites, gravitating around the whites, whom they considered their patrons. The title 'Boss', which they often use for . . . whites, reflects their instinctive recognition of their ethnic position." Siegfried did note, however, that most blacks had come to detest the "poor whites" and showed them little deference.[63]

Class antagonisms were increasing within African American circles in certain cities. At Charleston, Richmond, and other places Africans from the West Indies whose ancestors had always been free did not mix with the descendants of slaves. Also blacks of light complexion tended to set themselves apart from their darker brothers and sisters. Siefried actually visited African American churches where the best pews were reserved "for the palest of the faithful." Considering the oppressed condition of the race as a whole, African Americans could, he thought, ill afford such divisions.[64]

Amenability was not characteristic of southern blacks in the experience of black Pan-Africanists Amy and Marcus Garvey. She felt that they were disinclined "to take orders from their own." He went even further, calling the African American "the most stubborn individual to discipline," reluctant to carry out an order given by "a superior" of his own race because he felt himself the equal or superior of any other person of African descent. For this attitude Garvey blamed a "complex inferiority," which the African Americans "environments" had forced upon them.[65]

Rossa Cooley and her associates, the Gordons observed, had spent much of their lives "testing" the African American's "capacity for social development." On St. Helena Island the job had been done well. While the Gordons were not personally attracted to blacks, they granted them "a gesture, a sense of grace which . . . is almost aristocratic." Furthermore, blacks greeted one with "straight and candid eyes; there is no artificiality in them."

Slowly but surely African Americans were also acquiring an admirable racial pride. According to Rossa Cooley this had been difficult to accomplish on St. Helena Island (as it undoubtedly was elsewhere). The most noticeable progress, she told the Gordons, was among the black children. When she first made black dolls for them, none would take one, preferring the white, golden haired dolls. By degrees, however, the children came to associate the black dolls with themselves, and demand for them outstripped the supply. The psychological implications of Rossa Cooley's experience, one which African American parents have constantly faced, have been studied by Professor Kenneth Clark in his famous "Doll Tests."[66]

Increasing pride among blacks was also testified to by Lance Jones. Some had denounced it as arrogance, but the British educator saw it as "legitimate," pointing out that the African American had "traveled far since the days of slavery." His banks, businesses, farms, homes, artists, scientists, and educators, were ample grounds for self-praise.

The old-line "good nigger" of the South, the type George, Chesterton, Spender, and most other observers saw or thought they saw, was not prominent among the blacks observed by Professor Tannenbaum. Instead, he encountered in the region "a newer type of negro." This person, educated for leadership and occupying positions of responsibility, had "achieved a cultural outlook" sharply differentiating him from "the type of negro who served as a slave." Also unlike most other observers, Tannenbaum detected bitterness among post-war southern blacks, particularly educated ones. He attributed it in part "to the craving for distinction" on the part of intelligent blacks. They resented a system which equated them with the lowest members of their own race and placed them below the "least reputable white man." Tannenbaum recognized, and urged fellow whites to recognize, that in a world which was not static marked changes in African American attitudes were inevitable.[67]

NOTES

1. Hardy, *Oranges and Alligators*, 102, 104, 111–112.

2. Du Bois, United States Department of Labor *Bulletin*, III, No. 14, pp. 23, 37–38. Du Bois, *Atlantic Monthly*, LXXXIII, 101–102.

3. Barrows, *Atlantic Monthly*, LXVII, 808–809, Nelson, *Harper's Weekly*, XXXVI, 654: Albert Tissandier, *Six Mois Aux E'tats-Unis* (Paris: Libraire de L'Academic de Me'decine, 1886), 27–28.

4. Bryce, *The American Commonwealth*, II, 523: Lombroso, *North American Review*, CLXV, No. 493, p. 648.

5. Towne, Letters and Diary, 276, 281–282, 287.

6. Cooley, School Acres, 98.

7. Barrows, "What the Southern Negro is doing for himself,"808–809.

8. Campbell, *The Southern Highlander*, 211.

9. Brown, *My Southern Home*, 189–190.

10. Sutter, *American Notes*, 1881; Wamer, *On Horseback*, 112; Hesse-Wartegg, *Mississippi-Fahrten*, 212–213, 251, 268–269.

11. Brown, *My Southern Home*, 168–170.

12. Allan-Olney, *The New Virginians*, I, 225.

13. Hesse-Wartegg, *Mississippi-Fahrten*, 255–256.

14. Cowan, *A New Invasion of the South*, 33–34: Freeman, *Some Impressions of the United States*, 149.

15. Wyman, *New England Magazine*, IV 524.

16. Bradley, *Other Days*, p. 396.

17. Warner, *On Horseback*, 145–146.

18. Buttersworth, *Zig-Zag Journeys on the Mississippi*, 190, 193.

19. Bradley, *Sketches from Old Virginia*, 259. Bradley, *Other Days*, 395.

20. Hesse-Wartegg, *Mississippi Fahrten*, 268–269.

21. Ralph, *Harper's Weekly*, XXXVII, 39.

22. Brown, *My Southern Home*, 167–168: Wyman, *New England Magazine*, IV, 523.

23. Ibid.

24. Bassett, *Lippincott's Magazine*, XXVIII, 208.

25. Campbell, *White and Black*, 376.

26. Du Bois, United States Department of Labor, *Bulletin*, III, No. 14, p. 37.

27. Towne, *Letters and Diary*, 286.

28. Gibbs, *Shadow and Light*, 196–200, 206–209.

29. Cooley, *School Acres*, 141.

30. Bradley, *Sketches from Old Virginia*, 263. *Cooley, School Acres*, 74–75, 142.

31. Hesse-Wartegg, *Mississippi-Fahrten*, 269–270.

32. Hardy, *Oranges and Alligators*, 92–97.

33. Susan Showers, [pseudo.], "A Weddin 'and a Buryin' in the Black Belt," *New England Magazine*, SVIII (June, 1898), 478–480.

34. Allan-Olney, *The New Virginians*, II, 252–262.

35. Showers, *New England Magazine*, XVIII, 480–481: Russell, *Hesperothen* I, 89. Showers, *New England Magazine*, XVIII, 481–483.

36. Du Bois, United States Department of Labor, *Bulletin*, III, No. 14, pp. 35–36.

37. Thomas Jesse Jones, "Tuberculosis among the Negroes, Transactions, 2nd Annual Meeting of the National Aviation for the Study and Prevention of Tuberculosis (Washington, D.C., May 16–18, 1906, II, 97–106.

38. Baker, *Following the Color Line*, 41–42, 88.

39. A Camp Physician (pseudo.), *Independent*, LXIII, 790–791.

40. H. H. Hazen, "Syphilis in the American Negro," *Journal of the American Medical Association*, LXIII (August, 1914, 463–465. Henry Honeymoon Hazon (b. 1879), a native of New Germantown, New Jersey, taught at Johns Hopkins (1910–1912) and Harvard (1911–1925) inventor and visiting dermatologist at Germantown University Hospital, Freedom's Hospital and Columbia Hospital for women in Washington, D.C. He was also a special consultant to the Venereal Disease Division of the U. S. Public Health Service in 1918–1921 and 1924. *Who's Who in American Medicine*, 1925 (New York: Who's Who Publishing Co., 1925) 663.

41. Arrah B. Evants, "Dementia Precox in the Colored Race," *Psychological Review*, I (1913–1914) 394–398, 403, Evants, a native of Dodge Center, Minnesota received M.D. and C.M. degrees from Hamline University. She practiced medicine in Washington, D.C. (1912–1913), before becoming head of the female division of Rochester (Minn.) State Hospital. *Who's Who in America*, 1925, p. 471.

42. Carl Kelsey, *The Negro Farmer* (Chicago: Jennings and Pye, 1903), 34, 39. Kelsey was born in 1870 at Grinnell, Iowa, attended Iowa College, Andover Theological Seminary, and the Universities of Gottingen and Berlin, and received a Ph.D. from the University of Pennsylvania in 1903. Beginning his career as a high school teacher, he became a social worker and eventually a professor of sociology at the University of Pennsylvania. *Who's Who in America*, 1920–1921, p. 1570.

43. TBA

44. Clifton Johnson, *Highways and Byways of the South* (new York: The MacMillon Co., 1904) title page, 333–334. Johnson was born in 1885 and died in 1940. Rupert B. Vance in Clark, ed., *Travels in the New South*, II, 57–60.

45. Adam, *Vues D'Amerique,* 151–152, 154.

46. Henry James, *The American Scene* (New York: Harper and Brothers Publishers, 1907), 360–361, 384–385. James (1843–1916), one of the foremost names in American literature, was born in New York, educated in France and Switzerland and at Harvard Law School, and lived most of his adult life in England. He began his literacy career as a contributor to periodicals just after Appomattox. Baker, *Following the Color Line*, 28, 62, 100. Albert Bushnell Hart, *The Southern South* (New York: D. Appleton and Co., 1910), 115–116. Hart, long-time professor of history at Harvard, was born in 1854 at Clarksville, Pennsylvania, and graduated from Harvard in 1880. He was the author of a number of works on such diverse subjects as the formation of the union, slavery and abolition, and foreign policy, editor of *The American Nations series*, 28 vols., 1904–1918), and an officer in both the American Historical Association and the American Political Science Association. *Who's Who in America*, 1910–1911, p. 854; *Harper's Encyclopeida of United States History* (4 vols., 1901–1915; New York: Harper and Brothers, 1915), IV, 200.

47. Sir Harry Johnston, *The Negro in the New World* (London: Methuen and Co., Ltd., 1910), 422, 425–426, 473–474. Johnston (b. 1858) explored Portuguese West Africa and the River Congo, 1882–1883), commanded the scientific expedition of the Royal Society to Mt. Kilimanjaro, 1884, and was British Consul-General for Tunis and Uganda. He wrote works on colonization, slavery, and diplomacy, Sir Harry's

Southern trip (1908) was confined mainly to Alabama and Virginia. *Who's Who* 1902, p. 705. Mildred Cram, *Old Seaport Tours of the South* (New York: Dodd, Mead and Co., 197), 350–351. Mrs. Cram of New York was apparently born in the South, but was taken from the region as am infant in 1916, she, and her husband Allen, returned for their first real look at her native land. Clark, ed., *Travels in the New South*, II, 31.

48. Adams, *Vues D"Amerique*, 151–152, 154. James, *The American Scene*, 360–361, 384–385. Baker, *Following the Color Line*, 28, 62, 100. Johnston, *The Negro in the New World*, 413–414.

49. William Archer, *Through Afro-America: An English Reading of the Race Problem* (London: Chapman and Hall, Ltd., 1910), 174, 183. Archer (1856–1924) was trained as a lawyer but became a writer for the Edinburgh *Evening News*, then a dramatic critic for London newspapers. He was a lover of travel, languages, literature, and adventure. *Dictionary of National Biography*, 1922–1930, pp, 22–23; Cram, *Old Seaport Towns of the South*, 82, 125, 153–154, 192, 350–351.

50. Mrs. Alec Tweedie, *America As I Saw It* (New York: The Macmillan Co., 1913), 357–358, 360–361. Mrs. Tweedie received her education at Queen's College, London, and in Germany. She served on several committees of the International Council of women, which met in London in 1899. She had also been active in the Paris Exhibition of 1890. A constant contributor to London newspapers and magazines, she wrote plays and travel accounts. She was in the South in 1900–1901, 1904, and 1912. *Who's Who*, 1902, p. 1303. Timothy Shaler Williams, "The Sports of Negro Children," *Saint Nicholes*, XXX (September, 1913), 1004. Williams (1862–1930), was born in Ithaca, New York and educated at Cornell University. Then he worked for a newspaper and was a private secretary to governor 1889–1894) before serving as secretary-treasurer, vice president, president and director of the Brooklyn Rapid Transit System (1895–1923). *Who's Who in America*, I, 1355.

51. Williams, Ibid

52. Tweedie, *America As I Saw It*, 363.

53. Julian Street, *American Adventure* (New York: The Century Co., 1917), 545. Street (b. 1879) was principally a writer of magazine articles and novels. He visited the whole South in 1917. *Who's Who in America*, 1910–1911, p. 1857.

54. Johnston, *The Negro in the New World*, 442–443.

55. Louis Closser Hale, *We Discover the Old Dominion* (New York: Dodd, Mead and Co., 1916), 194–195. Mrs. Hale (1872–1933) made her stage debut at Detroit in 1895. Among her novels was Motor Car Divorce (1906). Who's Was Who in America, I, 502.

56. R. R. Wright, while a student in a Freedmen's Bureau school in Atlanta, inspired John Greenleaf Whittier's famous poem, "Black Boy of Atlanta." One Sunday General Oliver O. Howard, head of the Freedmen Bureau, addressed the pupils. When he asked for a message to take back to the people of the North, young Wright stood up quickly and said: "Tell 'em massa, we is rising." A famous but neglected name in African American history, Wright studied at Atlanta and Harvard Universities, travelled in Europe, and served in the Spanish-American War; Baker, *Following the Color Line*, 92.

57. Williams, *Saint Nicholes*, XXX, 1007.

58. Kelsey, *The Negro Farmer*, 42.

59. A Camp Physician (pseudo.), *Independent*, LXXXX, 791.

60. Hart, *The Southern South*, 118–119.

61. George, *Hail Columbia!*, 185–187; Chesterton, *What I saw in America*, 154.

62. arold Spender, "A Glimpse at America,: *Fortnightly Review*, CXIX (April, 1923), 576–578. Spender (b. 1864) was educated at Oxford University and lectured for the Oxford University Extension Delegacy, 1889–1892. His journalist career included work with the London Echo and the Manchester *Guardian*. Among his publications were the *Story of the Home Rule Session* (1893) and *Herbert Henry Asquith* (1915). *Who's Who*, 1922, p. 2525.

63. Siegfried, *America Comes of Age*, 100–101

64. Ibid

65. Garvey, *Garvey and Garveyism*, 85.

66. Gordon, *On Wandering Wheels*, 273–274.

67. Jones, *The Jeanes Teacher in the United States*, 123; Tannerbaum, *Darker Phases of the South*, 10–13.

Chapter Six

Manners and Morals

Most African Americans in the late nineteenth century lacked the material and physical comforts enjoyed by the bulk of the Euro-American population, but still managed to display an unusual cheerfulness, or so a majority of outside observers thought. William Saunders summed up his impression by declaring that "there are no people in America as happy as the genuine blacks." They could always be counted upon for a "cheerful laugh" or a "pleasant melody." In the end even "the worst of the blacks are not worse than the worst of the whites."[1]

A courteous, polite African American was seen one Sunday on his way to church by Mary Allan-Olney. But blacks in general could sometimes make themselves obnoxious to Miss Allan-Olney by an unthinking lack of courtesy and ignorance of the "social graces," reminding her,

> of a dog, who, when dripping with rain,
> will rush in and nestle close to his master
> or mistress; or he will, just after being
> caressed, turn around and begin a vigorous
> scratching and biting, quite unconscious
> that his behavior is offensive, and that
> you wish him a hundred miles off.

Miss Allan-Olney, like many other observers, liked the old blacks best. "They are all thieves, of course, but they are civil and respectful in their manners."[2]

Southern blacks were "a good sort of people," quite obliging, and always eager to serve, in the experience of Sir George Campbell. He had not seen the like among white or black at the North.[3]

119

The "better class" blacks "who had been domestic slaves in Baltimore families seemed to retain all their old affectionate obsequiousness of manner, George Sala observed. A similar though more refined attitude existed among the intelligent blacks in Washington. Lillie Wyman and William Langdon noted the cheerful attitude of African Americans of the "better class." In southern Louisiana, Hesse-Wartegg, came in contact with a good many amiable blacks, especially among the old black "mammies." Those that George Barbour came to know in South Florida were a "strange set of beings" known for uproarious laughter, "wonderful jokes," and picturesque anatomies.[4]

The great majority of African Americans, clergyman Henry Field found, were industrious and amenable. Similarly Samuel Barrows saw in the African American a new sense of self-respect and a pride in race that were winning the admiration of even his white neighbors. Julian Ralph also felt the blacks were making great social progress. They managed to remain "eternally happy, even against fate . . . their faults are so open and so very human, and their virtues are so human and admirable."[5]

A downright sentimental view was voiced by Henry Nelson. He saw the blacks as "a simple-minded people" who, from the lowest class all the way up to the top layer, represented by Frederick Douglass, had a touching confidence, a child-like faith, in "the superior race." Quite properly, Nelson felt, there was no attempt to intrude into the white circle. The "upper layer' blacks did tend to assume a "patronizing superiority" toward their less successful brethren, which was to be expected. A kinder, more loyal, gentle, and intelligent group than the blacks, Nelson concluded, could scarcely be found. It was all proof of what had been done for the African by contact with American civilization, "even when the contact was of the slave with the master."[6]

While it was true that many African Americans were cheerful and courteous, moral and law-abiding, it was misleading to attribute these wholesome characteristics to the whole race, for a good many others, as several observers learned, were immoral, and some were even criminals.

The African race, Mary Allan-Olney believed, possessed a tendency to petty thievery and lying. T hat the African Americans would steal was an almost universally accepted maxim. In North Carolina A. L. Bassett wondered how the blacks managed to keep constant fires in winter although they bought no wood. He soon discovered that the wood they used came from his and his neighbor's woodpiles. Yet these people were great church-goers, Methodists and Baptists. Such "licensed immorality" practiced in the "most, open, unblushing manner" frightened Bassett. Sir George Campbell heard and believed a good deal about chicken-stealing and "such things," but seemed to regard it as a minor matter since the race as a whole was "a good sort of people."[7]

Aboard a steamer bound for New Orleans to the sugar country Hesse-Wart-egg noted a white man and a French-speaking black woman outside a cabin, both appearing black in the dark. Watching from a distance, he witnessed race relations in their most intimate and oldest form. Such intercourse did not help to improve the African American's "base sexual" morality, which together with their "loquacity" was their poorest characteristic. Young black women were preyed upon by both black and white men, so much so that African American historian William Wells brown thought institutions to save them "ought to be established in every large city."

Another interracial aspect of African American immorality came to Brown's attention at Huntsville, Alabama, where "unprincipled store-keep-ers, some of them northern men," had "established the custom of giving the country Negroes, who came to buy, as much whiskey as they wished to drink." This was done in a special back room. Once drunk, the blacks were "induced to purchase all sorts of useless and expensive goods." Brown was not disposed, however, to blame all African American immorality on Euro-Americans. He placed a good deal of the fault on the black church, and he also saw shortcomings within individual blacks themselves.[8]

African American railroad workers in South Florida were prone to use what George Barbour called the most "shocking profanity and disgustingly vile language." Their simplest remarks were "interlaided with a number of oaths and foul words that is positively startling." Barbour attributed the prac-tice partially to "association with low whites, and to a desire to 'talk as big as the white folks.'"

Almost all African Americans, Barbour found, were prone to slip into the woods for a little gambling after pay-day. "The darkey is a most inveterate gambler, the equal of the Chinaman or Indian in this vice. . . . The darkey will gamble all he has earned by months of hard labor, and all he can steal." The baser aspects of African American character were conspicuous in the urban areas of the lower South, according to Presbyterian clergyman Henry Field. One saw blacks lazy and shiftless to a high degree, idling about the streets. Yet even there the great majority was industrious and amenable. In Baltimore George Sala met "shiftless and generally dejected Negroes of both sexes, who appeared to be just the kind of waifs and strays who would stand in a mill-pond longer than they ought to," but he also encountered a "better" class of blacks here who were more refined.[9]

Lillie Wyman was interested in the marital situation among southern blacks and found much to deplore. Especially "among the lower blacks," there were many cases of men deserting wives and children, and of women "false to their conjugal obligations, even if according to their abilities they observe their maternal duties." The huddling together of all ages and both sexes in cabins of one or two rooms was partly responsible for the poor moral conditions, and the influence of whites was as an important factor. "Those persons who speculate upon the undesirability of having this country occupied by a mixed race overlook the fact that a mixed race already occupies a large portion of it." She had observed the "great dangers" to which young black girls were exposed, and had seen the results. Yet in spite of the general conditions, "the better class of the colored people" were trying "to establish a higher standard in ethics.[10]

Arthur Bradley, who had a keener insight than most into the changes taking place among African Americans, saw a decline in black morals based upon the migration of young blacks from farm to mine and factory. Younger blacks of the "lower class" bore much of the responsibility for the race's immorality, William Langdon thought. Wholly wanting in character, they were insolent "in language, and in conduct." Langdon himself had seen a "vulgar Negro boy" insult a white girl, and blacks force whites from the sidewalk. Julian Ralph visited a place in New Orleans where young black deckhands threw away their earnings. The "Coonie dance-house," as it was called, "suggested a place in the heart of Africa at a savage merry making." The African American couples did a "Virginia reel" in a "primitive" and vulgar manner. No other place in Christendom could present such "a spectacle of low and almost absent morality."[11]

Even Du Bois asserted that "the moral tone of the Negroes" left room for "great betterment." To be sure, the "idlers and loafers" he saw at Farmville, Virginia were a smaller element than the respected class of blacks, but they were re-enforced by the "lazy, shiftless and dissolute of the country around." Du Bois had earlier praised "the industrial situation in Farmville" but he now blamed it in part for the immorality because steady employment not menial was difficult to find.

Returning after an absence of ten years to the site of his old school near Alexandria, Tennessee—the school building itself had been torn down to make way for a slightly better one—Du Bois discovered here also a deterioration in moral tone. One of his former students, who had an illegitimate child and no prospect of marriage was dead of a "broken heart"; two others, now escapees from prison, had been convicted of stealing wheat; and another was rocking one baby and expecting a second, though still unmarried.

The African American scholar was saddened by the sight. He had had high hopes that these young people with "their weak wings" would fight the "barriers of caste" and reap a good youth, and a good life. As he rode back to Nashville in the "Jim Crow" railroad car, he fell to musing. He might have asked himself how he had expected the young blacks of rural Tennessee to crash the barriers of caste, when he, a Harvard-trained professor at Atlanta University, could not break them himself. Perhaps he did![12]

The African Americans' progress in morality far outweighed their immoral acts, Samuel Barrows believed. Unlike some other observers, he felt it was in the new generation of "African Americans" that a "progressive spirit" existed.[13]

In the matter of crime and punishment the outside observer had an opportunity to witness and react to one of the most critical areas of African American life and southern race relations. The importance of the subject is demonstrated by the large number of observers' comments on it. Almost universally they testified to, and deplored, the African Americans' proneness to petty theft, most of which went unpunished. Crimes of a more serious nature often drew heavy penalties.

African Americans had "brought from slavery times a sort of childish want of respect for property in certain things," Sir George Campbell admitted. But he was inclined to think that petty thievery which resembled a child's "taking a spoonful of jam" was a "misconduct" rather than a crime. Sir George placed blacks above most other races in that they were "not much given to violent, and . . . vicious crimes" (He was probably unaware of the rather large number of homicides attributed yearly to them). A much harder justice seemed to be dealt to the blacks than to whites. African Americans were disproportionately represented in the prison population, a fact which Sir George attributed, probably correctly, to harder justice and to the absence of blacks on juries. He detected also "a strictness in penal management," as far as blacks were concerned, a strictness which needed watching considering "how much of the administration of justice is now in the hands of whites." The most shocking thing to him was the continued existence of lynching, particularly in cases of alleged assault by blacks on white women. "The blacks are popularly said to be prone to that kind of crime; with what justice I cannot say."[14]

It was rare for an African American to be convicted, according to Mary Allan-Olney, unless he or she had "done something very bad—either arson, horse-stealing, or murder." She was afraid of a group of black convicts put to work on a canal near her farm house. They were "ugly even for Negroes"; partly because of their striped uniforms with baggy, ill-fitting trousers. Under cover of the noise of a convict prayer-meeting, nine of them escaped. The escape alarmed the whole countryside, blacks even more than whites. Ultimately all were captured, except two, a few being shot. "Some scalawags [sic] and carpetbaggers," she noted indignantly, tried to arouse sympathy for the convicts, "pretending they were cruelly treated." On the contrary, whatever they got was no more than they deserved, and they were actually plump and shone with "good nourishment and good health." "As to the crowding, it is as natural to niggers to crowd together as it is to pigs or fowls." Among the blacks themselves Mary Allan-Olney noted a tendency, which she censured, to regard the convicts with "awe," presumably as persons who had accomplished something big.[15]

As a rule African American men went armed, Barbour discovered in Florida. Razors were their "characteristic and especially favorite weapon," but they also liked revolvers. "Give the ordinary Negro a cheap, shiny watch, a revolver, and a cane, and he is 'happy as a lord.'" These proclivities meant that the blacks "would be a terribly dangerous element in society, were it not for their well-known fear of firearms, and their naturally peaceful disposition." How blacks could be fond of revolvers yet afraid of firearms, and armed with razors yet peacefully disposed, Barbour did not explain.[16]

African Americans were prone to violence regardless of location, judging from the reports of Cowan. On the *Robert E. Lee* between Vicksburg and New Orleans he saw an African American knifed by a fellow deckhand. It was not altogether unusual or unexpected, he learned. But to Cowan it was dismaying.[17]

The well known fact that an African American was in particular danger when involved in a crime against a white woman was brought forcibly home to the Edinburgh engineer, Archibald Sutter. While he was in Atlanta a black man accused of murdering the wife of a physician there was caught and burned to death by a mob. Sutter recalled the cries of the dying "murderer:" "'Hang me—hang me on de gum-tree. Save me, massah!'" Do not burn me! The cries went on until the end. A different view of the whole question of African American crime and punishment was taken by William Langdon. He noted that white girls, and even older women, had been insulted on southern streets by young blacks against whom no action was taken. He had also seen white policemen afraid to arrest black thieves for fear of rescue by an African American mob or cries of police brutality. These young blacks were, moreover, the same class of blacks clamoring for political freedom.[18]

In Mississippi and South Georgia observers reported relentless pursuits of African American criminals rather than laxity on the part of police authorities. According to Jonathan Baxter Harrison, when black prisoners hired out to a Mississippi "republican official" [sic] escaped, the employer and guards "chased them with dogs, using a pack of hounds to follow by the scent. . . . I expressed my disgust." Bourget witnessed the search for a mulatto, once the servant of Bourget's host, a southern "Colonel, as a member of the search party refused to shoot the black, and the Black man passed up an opportunity to fire on him. When two other whites wounded the black suspect, the "Colonel" attended his wounds and gave him a cigar and whiskey in prison. Bourget understood that the "Colonel" was the prisoner's father, but the caste system in the South precluded his trying to prevent the execution.[19]

Like Sir George Campbell, Du Bois emphasized the minor character of most offenses by African Americans. At Farmville, Virginia, the misbehaving black could best be described as a "semi-criminal," for his "depredations" were "generally petty and annoying rather than dangerous." Partly this was because most of the worst criminals had moved on to the North, and it was true that "the problem of Negro crime . . . is best studied and solved" in towns the size of Farmville.[20]

From a study of the rising homicide rate in the United States, "the founder of the science of criminology," Cesare Lombroso, concluded that it was the African American population which kept homicide from being "almost as rare" in the United States as in "the most civilized countries of Europe." Professor Lombroso recognized that in the South much prejudice against African Americans persisted; that they faced severe racial discrimination; and that they were careless about concealing crimes and more prone than whites to confess them whether guilty or not. Lombroso also thought that a warm climate was "prone to engender violence." Yet the African Americans' tendency to crime arose mainly from "natural," i.e., inherent, causes; they had "latent within him the primitive instincts of the savage." Lacking the sentiment of pity, he regarded "homicide as a mere incident and as glorious in case it is the outcome of revenge." The "abolition of slavery had produced a ferment in the minds of the colored people" and an exposure to social problems with which they could not cope. This ferment and exposure adversely affected morals and helped increase criminality.[21]

Conclusions quite different from those of Lombroso, and probably more accurate, were reached by the American sociologist, Frances Alice Kellor, in a study of the African American that took her as far South as Alabama. Though many black criminals were "vicious and depraved," the majority were merely inept thieves and perpetrators of simple violence. African Americans usually failed at crimes requiring reason, skill, and cunning. That black criminality was "out of proportion to the population, the proportion being greater than among the foreign whites," was to be explained not by the African American's physical and mental make-up but by a number of geographical, topographical, dietary, social, economic, and political factors. The southern climate, for example, did not permit year-round agricultural labor, wherefore the African American went to the city and there turned to crime when unable to find work. Poor diet caused illness, restlessness, weak family ties, and hence immorality and crime. African Americans who were educated expected opportunities often not actually available, and crime might result from their disillusion.

The African American criminal received stiff penalties. Whipping and solitary confinement were likely to be added to convict labor. (The continuing use of the whipping-post by itself in punishment of minor crimes was noted by Sir George Campbell and William Wells Brown in Virginia.) Miss Kellor did not doubt that racial discrimination played a large part in the penalties meted out, as well as in the total African American criminal record. The substitution of black-dominated justice would not be likely, however, to improve the situation greatly. Black justices were less fair than white ones, she had observed, and often "unwisely chosen." Black churches, the race's most important social institutions, did not restrain crime, and their failure left little reason to expect success from elsewhere within the African American Community. In the end one could expect to diminish the African American's criminality only by altering the complete fabric of southern society.[22]

Most observers agreed that Booker T. Washington possessed a social character worthy of emulation by all African Americans. Even some of his most vociferous white opponents would admit that such was true. Washington himself stressed good character as a key to African American advancement. However, not all blacks could live up to the high standards advocated by Washington. They might lapse into gross immorality, or become involved in crime, even ending up in a latter day kind of slavery—southern imprisonment.

African Americans in Mississippi had begun by 1901 to show marked degeneracys in character, if Mrs. Alec Tweedie was right. Assuming for themselves the titles of "ladies" and "gentlemen," they looked upon their white employers as mere "men" and "women." They had become notorious liars while maintaining their well-known proclivities to petty theft and gambling. In the end, though, they still reminded Mrs. Tweedie of children, and one could of course, always forgive a child.[23]

Southern blacks were a "vast imperfectly assimilated mass of barbarism veneered" according to Charles Francis Adams, who came South in 1902 to address the New England Society of Charleston. He came waving the flag of reconciliation rather than the "bloody shirt." Even the most advanced African Americans, Adams concluded, would if left alone without the influences of southern whites deteriorate and steadily gravitate towards the "normal African conditions." Even with white influence they had made little progress, and were in fact, causing degeneration in white manners and morals, particularly in South Carolina. In this respect, Adams concluded, it was the whites of the South who were the disadvantaged race.[24]

A French diplomat, Paul D'Estournelles de Constant, who was first in the South in 1902, took a view of African American social character more favorable than that of Adams. He encountered servants in hotels, private homes, and on trains that were polite, exact, and honest, which led him to conclude that African Americans monopolized these qualities. The same high character was manifest at Tuskegee in none other than Booker Washington himself. D'Estournelles de Constant could not, however, grant southern blacks equality with those of Latin America, especially Cuba. The superior character of the Cuban Negro, he believed, stemmed from the fact that the Spaniards had treated Africans well while those in the South had been "sentenced . . . without appeal." The Americans, D'Estournelles de Constant felt, had lowered the dignity of their blacks, thereby producing degradation.[25]

Carl Kelsey saw vast improvements in African American manners and morals in Tidewater, Virginia. Both races testified to a decline in illegitimacy. The whites, Kelsey learned, were assisting the blacks by arresting and fining men of both colors for seducing black girls. Another strong factor making for improved morals was the example of the alumni of Hampton Institute, "who in their homes, their schools and daily life, have stood for better things."

Outside Tidewater, Virginia, Kelsey found the moral situation far from satisfactory. On the Sea Islands there had been a decided retrogression. In the rest of the South sexual immorality was widespread, among both children and adults, and the African American family was in shambles. Marriages and divorces were affected without sanction of law, so that women were "married" to one man today, another tomorrow, and children often knew little of their fathers. Many who did know them came to resent their "great abuse," meaning presumably their proneness to promiscuity and desertion. White laxity in enforcing the legal codes, and white assumptions that there were "different" moral standards for African Americans, were chiefly to blame, Kelsey concluded. Despite "obvious progress," he saw a long, hard road ahead before the black masses of the South overcame this unsavory condition.[26]

Harvard's German-born psychologist, Hugo Munsterberg, whether young or old, saw the great masses of African Americans as lazy, dishonest, and sensual. The "unrestrained sensuality of the Negro," he believed, "had led him time after time to attempt criminal aggressions on white women, and so contributed infinitely to the misery of his situation." He regretted that "the best members of the Negro race" had to suffer for the immorality of the masses.

In comparing the African and the American Indian, Professor Munsterberg found a great contrast. The Indian was "proud, self-contained, selfish and revengeful, passionate and courageous, keen and inventive." The African on the contrary was "subservient, yielding, almost childishly good natured, lazy, and sensual, without energy or ambition, outwardly apt to learn, but without any spirit of invention or intellectual independence." Yet he warned against speaking of millions of blacks "as if they were of one type."[27]

The character of urban blacks, particularly in and around New Orleans, was found wanting by Jules Huret, a French journalist, who visited Louisiana

and Alabama in 1903–1904. City blacks were "less polite" than the plantation ones. Many had become as rude as the whites. Even the waiters, porters,
and shoeshine boys irritated Huret by their "seductive" smiles. The fact that
they smiled when reproached or insulted convinced him that the blacks were
insincere. For his part, Huret preferred the "philosophical Uncle Tom" and
the "adolescent Booker Washington" of the rural South to the city black.[28]

Another Frenchman, author Paul Adam, lashed out at African American
immorality in St. Louis. Whole African American families including children regularly got drunk, and when intoxicated became "lewd fools." At a
smoke-filled black St. Louis night club "Devils and Jezebels" did a square
dance amid the "odor of unclean underwear." Frenzy overtook them and
they "moved around like animals," abandoning most of their clothes, even
falling to the floor "like monkeys in a zoo," transformed in less than an hour
from " so-called civilized beings" into beasts. Besides being immoral, Adam
found African Americans negligent, lazy, cowardly, forgetful of the past, and
disdainful of the future. In a word, blacks were little more than "swine" and
"erotical maniacs."

Henry James, like Charles Francis Adams, saw the mass of African Americans as imposing upon the whites of the South. Whether at Washington,
Richmond, or Charleston, blacks with their careless attitude could not help
but get "intensely 'on the nerves' of the South." The African race, unable to
progress itself, was a burden to southern advancement.[29]

The problem of African Americans in the South was, according to Ray
Stannard Baker, really that of the so-called "worthless Negro," the African
American "without training or education." Unlike Professor Munsterberg,
Baker thought the worthless, a very small part of the "8,000,000" African
Americans, had given "a bad name" to the entire black race. They would
often, for example, sing in bliss:

> I doan has to work so had'd
> I's got a gal in a white man's ya'd;
> Ebery night 'bout half pas' eight
> I goes 'round to the white man's gate;
> She brings me butter and she bring me la'd—
> I doan has to work so ha'd.

One could find the "worthless" African Americans' children on the streets of
cities like Atlanta, "shooting craps, stealing, learning to drink."[30]

A pseudonymous northern doctor employed in a mining camp saw gross
immorality among African American coal-mining families near Birmingham.
In 1907 he agreed heartily with the opinion of other observers that the move
from farm to industry had adversely affected African American behavior.

Drunkenness, gambling, profanity, vulgarism, and the use of cocaine were very common in the mining camp, "especially on the regular monthly paydays and on Saturday afternoons and Sundays." Women as well as men engaged in those activities. The marital tie was regarded here, as elsewhere among the blacks, very lightly. The physician was aware that a "better" class of African Americans shunned the mines because of their injury to moral character. He was also inclined to blame the tolerance of white employers and police, who did not take the interest in the morals of their laborers that he had observed among plantation owners and foremen.[31]

Even an avowed sympathizer with African Americans like Albert Bushnell Hart found little to applaud in the social position of the masses of the race. A minority of a million or two, a large proportion of them mulattoes, measured up to white standards of character and ability. But the great majority, "eight or nine millions of average Negroes," were ignorant with a "child's fondness for fun, freedom from care for the morrow;" and were partakers of liquor, cocaine, and morphine. Among the "cotton hands" drugs were even more widely used than liquor. Hart could only regret a condition which so "intensely" troubled "friends and well-wishers" of the race, especially as it appeared to stem from natural and historical factors rather than environment.[32]

The principal of Penn School at St. Helena Island saw none of the retrogression in morals and manners among African Americans alleged by so many outside observers, however. Even as late as 1908, Rossa Cooley was impressed by the courtesy and respect blacks showed each other and to white persons, never failing to say "'How is you, sister?'" or "'Howdy ma'm?!'" As to their moral state, white women could drive at night over any part of St. Helena Island and feel safer than in Savannah or New York. This proved to her that the African American was naturally "gentle."[33]

The distinction between good and bad character among blacks was seen as one of generations, rather than of class, by Edward Hungerford, a New York journalist, who was in the South from 1909 to 1913. His view was, of course, by no means unique. At Charleston Hungerford noticed that the older blacks touched or removed their hats in the presence of white persons and would step into the gutter to permit a Caucasian to pass on the streets. They were products of a generation which thought more of good manners than of attending desegregated schools or riding in integrated railroad cars. But the young blacks affected by "fifty years" of the Fifteenth Amendment had become insolent and immoral. Hungerford was saddened by the fact that so few of the older blacks, and so many of the younger, occupied the cities of the South.[34]

There was actually more myth than reality in discussions of African American morals, according to Professor George E. Howard, who was in the

South in 1917. He denounced as a "false dogma" the notion of "inborn" moral deficiencies. The assertion that lust was a racial instinct "uncontrollable and ineradicable" in the African American represented a "sinister lesson taught by the novels, the dramas, the essays, the newspapers, and the political demagogues that have shaped public opinion in the South." Howard also attacked the myth that the African American was particularly prone to the crime of rape. On the contrary, the white men of the South were "far more guilty," of rape than the black men, "because the relative helplessness of Negro women" had exposed them to Caucasian lust in a greater degree than was the case with white women and black men.[35]

Even if African Americans were not particularly prone to rape or any other crime, they were nevertheless responsible for a disproportionate number of major crimes committed in the South, and constituted a disproportionate number of the inhabitants of southern jails and prisons. At the same time the absence of African American lawmen, especially among county sheriffs and deputies, an absence directly connected with the loss of the ballot, meant that African Americans accused of crime were dealt with entirely by whites. This arrangement contributed to the appearance, and probably to the reality, of a very high crime rate among African Americans.

In the Highlands region, where the small African American population was congregated mainly in "urban and industrial centers" such as Knoxville, John Campbell observed that the rate of homicide was "commonly high," and that almost all were by blacks.[36]

At New Orleans Mrs. Alec Tweedie visited the African American sections of the prison. She saw about thirty inmates, the youngest a "nice looking boy of fifteen," awaiting trial for murder; "niggers shoot or stick one another on the slightest provocation, and consider the successful man in such a squabble quite a hero." In general, the blacks seemed "to value human life as they would that of a dog."[37]

Du Bois, an African American apologist in many matters, recognized in the early 1900's, that crime was rampant among the blacks. Two overriding reasons accounted for "a distinct criminal class. First, it had been inevitable that when the emancipated 'human particles' were suddenly "thrown broadcast on the sea of life" some would "swim, some sink and some hang suspended, to be forced up or down by the chance currents of a busy, hurrying world." "The appearance . . . of the Negro criminal was a phenomenon to be awaited, and while it causes anxiety, it should not occasion surprise." Secondly, the ending of the antebellum police system, which had been primarily designed to control slaves, had removed much of the restraint upon criminal tendencies.

Du Bois also perceived a "minor" factor in African American criminality, which he ought probably to have regarded as major. The courts had been used in many parts of the South "as a means of re-enslaving the blacks,," for "when the Negroes were freed . . . the whole South was convinced of the impossibility of free Negro labor." African Americans accordingly tended to look upon courts as "instruments of injustice and oppression, and upon those convicted in them as martyrs and victims." Certainly the punishments meted out, whatever the justice of the convictions, were hardly conducive to rehabilitation of the convict or prevention of further crime. Du Bois often saw black boys, some no more than twelve years old, working in chains on the streets of Atlanta, directly in front of the schools, in company with older and hardened criminals. An "indiscriminate mingling of men, women, and children made the chain-gangs perfect schools of crime and dubachery."[38]

After seeing African American criminals at New Orleans, Atlanta, and Columbia, South Carolina, Thomas Young was told by white southerners that many blacks committed capital crimes simply to gain notoriety. Unable to verify this thesis, Young concluded that it was mainly a specious justification for lynching.[39]

The principal cause of lynching in the South, Professor Munsterberg believed, was attacks by black men on white women. Much as he deplored the "unrestrained sensuality" that drove the black men to this crime, he still believed that the lyncher was legally a murderer and that the better classes of southern whites shared this opinion. Professor Kelsey thought that the prevalence of black assaults upon white women was grossly exaggerated, that they were in fact few and occurred chiefly in those regions where white and black met as competitors "for ordinary labor."[40]

The use of cocaine, and the ready availability of weapons, contributed heavily to urban black crime, Ray Stannard Baker discovered at Atlanta. Blacks under the influence of cocaine were particularly noted for offenses against women. "The low class of Negroes and whites" could readily purchase revolvers and knives for "criminal purposes" in the pawnshops of African Americans. Even in the rural South, Baker observed the frequency of crime among African Americans under the influence of cocaine and liquor. One could hardly expect an African American party to end without fighting, often shooting, and death. Inasmuch as many of the areas where these "all too familiar" incidents occurred were already "dry" by law, Baker had no simple, concrete solution to offer. The "better-class" of African Americans did not condone the criminality of their race. In fact the two kinds of people they feared most were their own criminals and those whites who hated blacks.

Baker was told that half-illiterate, half-drunken white men were known to attack educated blacks on the slightest of provocation and with little fear of punishment. On the other hand, Baker listened to a trial in Fulton County, Georgia, in which a white boy's complaint that a "nigger" had "insulted" him resulted in the black's being fined $3.75 and admonished by the judge that he "mustn't insult white people." An "intelligent and prosperous" African American tradesman at Montgomery told William Archer a similar story somewhat in reverse. In this case a black worker's charges that he had been struck by his employer for "impudence" were dismissed by the recorder, the African American being told to be thankful that he wasn't killed and warned not to appear in the court with such charges again unless he wished to be sent to the prison farm. After hearing this story, Archer agreed that there was little justice for the African American in the South.[41]

Evidently punishment did not effectively deter blacks from crime, according to a mining camp physician who wrote of Jefferson County, Alabama. He had seen African American convicts gambling under the very eyes of their guards. The guards may have thought, as the doctor did, that the African American's love for gambling was insatiable, or they perhaps did not regard gambling as a crime.[42]

Albert Bushnell Hart accepted that African Americans furnished more than their proportion of criminals as a fact. The lowest element in the population might be expected to contain the "lowest and most criminal members;" the reverse would have been cause for shock. As basic causes of African American crime Hart saw liquor, lack of home influence on children, contacts with immoral whites, and the "brutalizing" effects of southern penal systems. The laxity of the courts when perpetrators and victims were African Americans, or when whites interceded for blacks, and their severity on other occasions, was also damaging, Hart believed. The assertion, which he had heard, that graduates of Hampton and Tuskegee were among the top black criminals, was "absolutely without foundation." On the record African Americans were not drawn to crimes requiring previous organization and preparations, such as one would expect the educated group to commit, and most African American criminals were of the lowest type, some "undoubtedly maniacs."[43]

White sheriffs in several southern towns of heavy black population told Sir Harry Johnston that little if any black crime existed in their bailiwicks. Johnston himself took a tolerant view of African American life, but he knew that crimes by blacks against blacks were unhappily "very frequent" in most southern areas, though proportionately fewer, perhaps, than among Italian settlers. Much of the crime, Sir Harry felt, stemmed from the younger blacks in which education had "awakened a keener appetite for pleasure." The "excessive dullness of their lives" had turned many to immorality and crime. It was incumbent upon the churches to do more in the area of social activity.[44]

The plight of African American convicts, grievous to some, won little sympathy from Mildred Cram. On a train from Baltimore to Annapolis she saw two black prisoners shackled to a deputy sheriff. That they were "shoved, pushed, pulled, and jostled" by their guards elicited little pity from Mrs. Cram, whose concern was rather for the safety of the deputy. The "black wretches," were big enough to strangle him "with one hand," but they proved to be "dumb and docile, staring constantly at the floor, apparently lacking the aesthetic sense even to turn and look at the passing landscape."[45]

Spurred by tales from local blacks, Julian Street attended a session of the police court in Richmond. It was filled with African American prisoners and spectators, all at the rear of the room. The prisoners, lodged in a steel cage, were brought one by one to face an elderly judge who peered over the top of his glasses "with a look of shrewd, merciless divination." The prisoners, mainly ragged men, constituted a "sad spectacle." The first black denied the charge that he had been drunk and attacked his wife, protesting that as long as one could "navigate" he should be considered sober. The judge shrugged aside his argument and fined him ten dollars. Observing "if it ain't worth ten dollars to get drunk, it ain't worth nothing at all." This mockery of justice continued all day, each of the accused being summarily found guilty and fined. At last an African American whose trousers were supported by a safety pin faced the bar. The judge, suspecting that he was not a local black, asked: "You ain't a Richmond nigger?" The prisoner confessed that he was a North Carolinian, a confession which netted him six months in jail. The blacks in the court roared with laughter as they did each time the judge meted out his justice and his colloquy. Street, too, found the whole affair amusing, but the serious implications of the mockery were not lost upon him. Proceedings such as those in the police court in Richmond were, no doubt, common in the early part of the century and perhaps would have lead one to agree with Paul Adam's pronouncement, from New Orleans, that "the Negro question in getting worse."[46]

Morality among all classes of blacks, George thought was improving by 1920. He based his optimism primarily on the degree of racial pride demonstrated by the repugnance which African Americans now felt toward relations between black girls and white men.[47]

Many poor, ignorant "field" blacks were observed by Beulah Amidon Ratlif, a northern bride honeymooning with in-laws at Drew, Mississippi. These blacks lived in a row of cabins across the railroad tracks from the main plantation house. It was not unusual, Mrs. Ratliff discovered, for a man more or less legally married to one woman, to "live with" another at the same time. Since the arrangement was acceptable to the plantation owners as long as there was no violence, the northern guest did not feel called upon to condemn it.[48]

Gambling among African American deckhands appalled John T. Faris as he rode south on the Tennessee River in 1920. Many gambled away all their earnings. One who did not, when asked why, replied that he had a wife and child waiting for food and shoes, and in any case had "no use for these niggahs' triflin' ways!" Faris regretted that more did not possess this sober attitude.[49]

Alcohol, Chesterton found, had "a very exceptionally destructive effect upon Negroes" and provoked "the passions that are the particular temptation of the race," leading to "appalling outrages" which were followed "by appalling popular vengeance." Apparently Chesterton felt that without liquor there would not have been attacks by black men on white women, and no subsequent lynching. What Chesterton took to be "appalling outrages" Tannenbaum thought were largely the products of imagination and emotion. "Fear and expectancy" more than African American immorality accounted for most of the reports of black attacks on white women. He cited an incident in which a white girl who accidentally encountered a black man on a lonely rural road screamed, and the man ran. In the excitement that followed what had actually happened was soon obscured, and the black man became another of those hunted for a crime of passion.[50]

Whites, Siegfried felt, were responsible for most of the immorality in the South, usually with African American victims. He was aware that many lower class black women did not resist "the whims of the white man," but it would have availed them little if they had. Even "the best class of colored women" was subjected to "insulting advances" by white men "in the streets and shops," and their husbands defended them at the risk of their lives. What African American immorality there was, he seemed to suggest, paled in comparison with that of whites; and the majority of blacks were, in any case, too passive to violate moral standards wholesale.[51]

An African American who went so far as to commit a crime had, in most cases, to take his chances with an all-white administration of justice, from the arresting officer to the chain gang guard. The swarming of whites in pursuit of a black accused of having killed a white man in Mississippi was vividly narrated by the northern bride Beulah Ratliff. The suspect was a local black. "It seems that negro criminals, instead of leaving the country, almost always go "'back home,' trusting their friends to hide them." (A contention which Albert Bushnell Hart vigorously disputed.) Virtually the whole country congregated at the Fitzhugh Plantation to assist in capturing the black man. This "nigger chase" gave Mrs. Ratliff a "higher education in the practical aspects of the race question," an experience that proved most wearing and upsetting.[52]

When Marcus Garvey's wife, Amy, visited Baton Rouge shortly after her husband was imprisoned she found the people "tense and nervous" in consequence of a lynching the previous night. In an effort to relieve the anxiety she preached a sermon, even though preaching was not her vocation. Mrs. Garvey viewed lynching as a "practical demonstration of racial hysteria; it is actuated through fear, a guilty conscience or a retributive foreboding."[53]

Lynching of African Americans after 1918 continued to be associated most commonly with attacks upon white women. This was true of a majority of the twelve recorded in 1929. It is doubtful that Arnaldo Cipolla actually saw a lynching, but he believed that blacks had been "barbarically lynched" for alleged attacks on white women when "their intentions were only to be nice and courteous." Professor Tannenbaum entertained a like opinion.

An instance of punishment reminiscent of the days of bondage was reported by Beulah Ratliff from a plantation in the Yazoo Delta of Mississippi. One of the female black servants had stabbed in the thigh another black woman involved in adultery with the assailant's husband. The victim, not seriously wounded, brought the matter to the attention of the plantation owner, only to find herself whipped by him with the admonition. "I don't want to hear another word out of you!" The black woman promised to say no more. According to Mrs. Ratliff, the episode bore out the owner's "reputation for unusual fairness to his negroes."

In southern prisons, which were segregated, the population was predominantly black while the management was all-white. Those in charge had, Tannenbaum found, "certain notions of discipline and control of the colored prisoner which came from experience outside the prison walls. But the white prisoners do not escape the mood and the temper of the treatment of the colored generates—and too they suffer with their darker fellows." At one institution, an officer "with club in hand," described the black inmates as happy and willing to sing lustily for a quarter. What Tannenbaum actually heard, instead of lusty happiness, was "the strains of 'Nearer, my God to Thee,'" rendered by a group of death-row blacks with "a pathos and a sadness in the tones, a melodious and passionate self-surrender that melted and softened the greatest of all fears—the fear of death." Other black prisoners locked in a cage sang in "mellow" voices which were "passionate" and "tearful," not joyous. Professor Tannenbaum (once jailed himself for pro-labor activities) gave the blacks what he "could for little things [presumably small purchases] and they sang for me." They had paid him back "the only way they could."

In the federal penitentiary at Atlanta, conditions seem to have been vastly better than in state institutions. Within a few months after Marcus Garvey was placed there he had secured a position as "Head Cleaner" and was permitted to move freely "around the buildings for inspection of the work." In addition, "he wore his own clothes, attended movies, and ball games . . . Other prisoners did . . . chores for him and treated him as nicely as he did them."

NOTES

1. Saunders, *Through the Light Continent*, 78–80.
2. Allan-Olney, *The New Virginians*, I, 4–5, 228–229, II, 40–41.
3. Campbell, *White and Black*, 327, 329.
4. Sala, America Revisited, 165; Wyman, New England Magazine, IV, 529–530; Langdon, *Political Science Quarterly*, VI, 35–38; Hesse-Wartegg, *Mississippi-Fahrten*, 256, 269–270. Barbour, *Florida for Tourists*, 233–235.
5. Barrows, *Atlantic Monthly*, LXVII, 615; [Ralph, *Harper's Weekly*, XXXVII, 38–39.]
6. Nelson, *Harper's Weekly*, XXXVI, 654.
7. Allan-Olney, *The New Virginians*, I, 4–5; Bassett, *Lippincott's Magazine*, XXVIII, 207; O'Rell, *Jonathan and His Continent*, 282–283; Campbell, *White and Black*, 327–329.
8. Hesse-Wartegg, *Mississippi-Fahrten*, 256; Brown, *My Southern Home*, 169–170, 218.
9. Barbour, *Florida for Tourists*, 233–235; Fields, *Bright Skies and Dark Shadows*, 165.
10. Wyman, *New England Magazine*, IV, 529–530.
11. Bradley, *Other Days*, 329; Langdon, *Political Science Quarterly*, VI, 35–38; Ralph, *Harper's Weekly*, XXXVII, 38–39.
12. Du Bois, *United States Department of Labor Bulletin*, III, No. 14, pp.22–23; Du Bois, *Atlantic Monthly*, LXXXIII, 102–104.
13. Barrows, *Atlantic Monthly*, LXVII, 815.
14. Campbell, *White and Black*, 169–171.
15. Allan-Onley, *The New Virginians*, II, 114–119.
16. Barbour, *Florida for Tourists*, 238.
17. Cowan, *A New Invasion of the South*, 53.
18. Sutter, *American Notes*, 62–63; Langdon, *Political Science Quarterly*, VI, 39.
19. Harrison, "Studies in the South," *Atlantic Monthly*, LI, 93; Bourget, Outre-Mer, 396–401.
20. Du Bois, United States Department of Labor, *Bulletin*, III, No. 14, p. 23.
21. Cesare Lombroso, "Why Homicide Has Increased in the United States," Part 1, *North American Review*, CLXV (December, 1897), 647–648, Lombroso (1836–1909), an Italian Jew, became widely known through his investigations of the abnormal human being, and spent much time in minute measurements of criminal types. He looked on criminality as marking a reversion to an earlier type and as largely the product of nervous disease. Lombroso does not seem to have gone any further South than Virginia.

22. Frances A. Kellor, "The Criminal Negro," *Arena*, XXV (January-June, 1901), 60–68, 190–197, 308–316, 314–422, 419–428. Miss Kellor, born in 1973 at Columbus, Ohio, received her education at the University of Chicago, the New York School of Philanthropy, and Cornell Law School. She served as general director of the Inter-Municipal Research Committee and was a member of the New York State Immigration Commission. At the time of her year-long study of black criminals she was on the faculty of the University of Chicago. Who's Who in America, 1910–1911, p. 1056.

23. Tweedie, *America As I Saw It*, 357, 361–362, 364.

24. Charles Francis Adams, *Studies, Military and Diplomatic, 1775–1865* (New York: The MacMillan Co., 1911), 230–231, Charles Francis Adams, brother of Brooks and Henry, was a Union officer throughout the Civil War, a railroad executive and student of railroads, an overseer of Harvard, president of the Massachusetts Historical Society, and the author and editor of various historical works. *Dictionary of American Biography*, I, 48–52.

25. Paul H. B. D'Estournelles de Constant, *America and Her Problems* (New York: The Macmillan Co., 1915), 364–366. Paul Henri Benjamin Baron D'Estournelles de Constant (1852–1924), diplomat, member of the French Parliament, co-winner of the Nobel Peace Prize in 1909, was in the South in 1902, 1907 and 1911. *Colliers Encyclopedia*, IX, 1963 ed., 330–331.

26. Kelsey, *The Negro Farmer*, 33–35, 39, 61–62, 65–66.

27. Hugo Munsterberg, *The Americans* (trans. by Edwin Holt; New York: McClure, Phillips, and Co., 1904), 167–168, 171–172, 179. Professor Munsterberg (1863–1916), born at Danzig, studied philosophy, natural sciences, and medicine at Leipzig and Heidelberg, taking both the Ph.D. and M.D. degrees. He taught at the University of Freiburg before coming to this country and to Harvard. He served as and director of the Psychological Laboratory at Harvard (1908–1916). It is not quite clear when Munsterberg visited the South, but the best guess is 1903. *Wer ist't*, 1905, p. 587; *Who's Who in America*, 1912, p. 1514; Rupert Vance in Clark, ed., *Travels in the New South*, II, 74.

28. Jules Huret, *En Amarique: De New York La Nouvelle-Orleans* (Nuevieme Mille: Paris: bibliotheque-Charpentier, 1904), 357–358. Huret was born in 1864 in the Boulogne-sur-Mer district of France, educated in private grammar schools in the district, and chose a career in journalism that eventually led him to the Paris *Figaro*, which he later edited. *Qui Etes-Vous*? 1908 (Paris: Librarie ch. Delagrave, 1908), 246.

29. Adam, Vues D'Amerique, 150–162; James, *The American Scene*, 360–363, 383.

30. Baker, *Following the Color Line*, 52–60.

31. A Camp Physician (pseudo.), *Independent*, LXIII (October, 1907), 790.

32. Hart, *The Southern South*, 104–105, 109.

33. Rossa B. Cooley, "Aunt Jane and Her People: The Real Negroes of the Sea Islands," *Outlook*, XC (October, 1908), 425–426.

34. E. Hungerford, *The Personality of American Cities* (1913), 140. Hungerford (b.1975) was born in Dexter, Nw York. After graduation from Syracuse University,

he became a journalist in upstate New York. At the time of his Southern trip he was an advertising manager for Wells-Fargo and Co. He wrote at least two works on railroads. *Who's Who in America*, 1920–1921, p. 1438.

35. George Elliott Howard, "The Social Cost of Southern Race Prejudice," *American Journal of Sociology*, XXII (March, 1917), 588–589. Howard (1849–1928), born at Saratoga, New York, was an academician mainly associated with the University of Nebraska, where he became professor of history, political science, and sociology. Howard wrote *The Preliminaries of the American Revolution* (1905) in the original American nation series. *Who Was Who in America*, I, 593.

36. Campbell, *The Southern Highlanders*, 115.

37. Tweedie, *America As I Saw It*, 357.

38. Du Bois, *Annals*, XVIII, 132–134. Similar descriptions and views of the chain-gang system appear in Young, *The American Cotton Industry*, 79, and Hart, *The Southern South*, 190.

39. Young, *The American Cotton Industry*, 104.

40. Munsterberg, *The Americans*, 32–33; Kelsey, *The Negro Farmer*, 17.

41. Baker, *Following the Color Line*, 8–10, 47; Archer, *Through Afro-America*, 95–97.

42. A Camp Physician (psued.), *The Independent*, LXIII, 790.

43. Hart, *The Southern South*, 189–190, 192, 199–201.

44. Johnston, *The Negro in the New World*, 446–448.

45. Cram, *Old Seaport Towns of the South*, 36–37.

46. Street, *American Adventures*, 244–247; Adam, *Vues D"Amerique*, 282–283.

47. George, *Hail Columbia!*, 191.

48. Beulah Amidon Ratliff, "In the Delta: The Story of a Man-hunt," *Atlantic Monthly*, CXXV (April, 1920, 460–461.

49. Faris, *Seeing the Sunny South*, 204–205.

50. Tannenbaum, *Darker Phases of the South*, 36.

51. Siegfried, *America Comes of Age*, 100.

52. Ratliff, *Atlantic Monthly*, CXXV, 456–460.

53. Garvey, *Garvey and Garveyism*, 93, 157.

Chapter Seven

Political Participation

The specter of African American political domination supposedly has long haunted southern whites. The reaction against black participation in the political life of the South that arose during the critical post-Civil War period is, in some places, still with us. Although the outside observers do not afford systematic information on the African American in politics, it is interesting to learn whether they viewed blacks as ill-equipped, corrupt, tobacco-chewing, and whiskey-drinking lawmakers and vote sellers or as constructive black citizens and statesmen.

Since the Civil War Virginia blacks had, as far as Arthur Bradley could see by 1877, always voted "peacefully, and always for the Republicans." Bradley never knew anyone in the state who even attempted to influence his servants or laborers. The blacks voted in a bloc both locally and nationally, their unanimity arising "from a fear lest their late masters, stung by their loss, should oppress them."[1]

Conditions surrounding black voting in South Carolina were not quiet as peaceful as those depicted by Bradley in Virginia. Prior to the elections. of 1878 Joseph Hayne Rainey, a black member of Congress from South Carolina, told President Rutherford B. Hayes in Washington that whites were resorting to intimidation and violence in Sumter and other counties to prevent blacks from organizing for the elections. Hayes assessed the situation as a division due to color. Substantially all the whites were Democrats and all the blacks were Republicans. Yet there was really "no political principle in dispute between them. The whites have the intelligence, the property, and the courage which make power. The negroes are for the most part ignorant, poor, and timid." The "whites must be divided among themselves before a better state of things will prevail."

On St. Helena Island, where blacks were an overwhelming majority, Laura Towne observed that the elections of 1878 passed without incident. The people voted "steadily and silently without the usual play and laughter. The result on this island was nine hundred and eighteen votes, only nine of them Democratic and only one of the nine a colored man's vote." The total was much smaller than in the elections of 1876, showing "that here Democracy does not gain ground." The one distressing thing to African Americans was the defeat for re-election of Robert Smalls, a Civil War hero and a black member of Congress. Though beaten by a mob at Gillisonville during the campaign, Smalls remained cheerful, even in defeat. He told Mrs. Towne that the cheating in the last election was "the best thing that could have happened for the Republican Party, for it is so barefaced and open that it cannot be denied." She told Sir George Campbell that. no considerable number of blacks had gone over to the Democrats, and attributed the loss of the election entirely to "fraud and intimidation." That wholesale cheating had characterized the balloting was confirmed by Campbell, who was in South Carolina at the time.[2]

The political situation in Virginia, at least in the Petersburg congressional district, Campbell found much better for African Americans than it was in South Carolina. The black majority in the district had elected a Republican to Congress and some blacks to the state assembly. Here, as elsewhere, the blacks had great faith in General Ulysses Grant "as the man who gave them their freedom," and they went to the "poll as his supporters."[3]

Reprisals against blacks trying to exercise the suffrage in South Carolina had become so great by 1880 that author Edward Hogan felt they had no choice but to emigrate if they were to enjoy any political rights. While Hogan could not condone the violence, he thought critics at the North should realize that the white South Carolinians were a minority in a state where the African American was "at his worst as a man" and where the law placed him "on the platform of equality." Although voting regularly for the Republicans, African Americans knew very little, and cared even less, about the principles of the Republican Party. They were extremely susceptible to demagoguism, especially on the part of the black preachers who had become powerful political influences in several of the more populous congressional districts. Where the influence of the preachers failed, that of African American women could be counted upon for they were "intense Republicans, and almost fanatical in urging the men to vote that ticket in spite of all obstacles." Indeed, it was due largely to the women and the preachers that blacks "so steadfastly, and despite personal danger and every species of persecution, adhere to the fortunes of the Republican Party."[4]

African American allegiance to the Republican Party was also viewed unsympathetically by the Dutch journalist, Charles Boissevain. He saw the blacks enslaved to the Republicans, as they once had been to the southern planters. The Republicans used them to keep "control of the rich . . . patronage" in the South. The blacks themselves had no real understanding of the ballot. They simply acted as their Republican leaders told them to because they knew the Republicans had put an end to slavery. The "Negro's lack of fitness for the exercise of the ballot" could, Boissevain conceded, "be the basis for a movement for amending the Constitution," but he went on to say that those who used "deceit at the polls" to deny the African American the suffrage earned the "confidence of no one."[5]

African Americans in Mississippi, southern Alabama, and Louisiana were "not permitted to vote without illegal interference, or if they are allowed to vote, their vote is not fully registered and returned," newspaperman Jonathan Baxter Harrison concluded after a tour of all the South except Florida in the winter of 1881–1882. He drew his conclusion not from seeing elections but from what "leading citizens," themselves Democrats, told him. Harrison himself was convinced,

> that from this time forward it would be
> better for all the interests of the Southern
> people, better for the white race,
> that all men who are citizens of the United
> States, not insane persons or criminals,
> should enjoy and exercise the right of suffrage
> in the Southern States . . . We shall be
> obliged, I think, to include the negroes
> in the great experiment of democracy.

Nevertheless, though he saw "colored men as intelligent in regard to political matters as the average of the operatives in a New England factory town," most black voters were "entirely incapable of forming opinions or judgments of their own in regard to political principles, doctrines or activities." As far as he could judge, blacks would vote "for anything or any man" bearing the Republican label.[6]

Blacks had not asked to be deposited in the South, said T. Thomas Fortune, and would not leave it. Thus, they should have their political rights. In any case, "the corruption of the ballot by white men of the South is more pernicious than the misuse of it by black men." (Obviously he felt that such blacks as the one William Wells Brown reported as having sold his vote for a few pounds of sugar were rare). Whites had made a mockery of the equal citizenship guarantees of the Constitution, and blacks were at their mercy. Yet Fortune had confidence that a "bond of union between the white people and the negroes" could solve southern problems.[7]

The "fecundity" of African Americans coupled with their possession of the franchise, posed social as well as political problems for the South, William Aubrey believed. Even in 1888 the number of "illiterate" black voters was "appalling." Until education could do its job, Aubrey felt that the necessity "to earn their own living" would have to suffice as a check upon the growth of black families. Boissevain, who was equally concerned about an over-abundance of southern blacks, thought immigration of foreigners the best answer.[8]

"The overwhelmingly large proportion of the Southern negroes" seemed to William Langdon to be "utterly lacking in any moral preparation for the political responsibilities demanded of them. The "better type of negroes" were not hindered or objected to as voters and participated freely in elections. Another class of blacks were "inert," "un-ambitious," and totally indifferent. But a third class, "ignorant, turbulent, and offensive," were the source of all the political agitation in the South. These would-be voters, spurred on by "unscrupulous politicians," sought to "impose negro equality on the South" or to "set up again the negro rule of the past." They deserved to be crushed by the combined weight of southerners and northerners of good-will.[9]

African American officeholders served in all branches of government in the post-Reconstruction period, though their numbers were steadily diminishing. Some were elected, others appointed. President Rutherford Hayes noted in his diary for March 16, 1877, that southern Republicans were threatening to go over to the Democrats, and that the bar of the District of Columbia was "in a state of mind," because of the nomination of Frederick Douglass, "the most distinguished and able Colored man in the Nation," to be marshal for the District. Disturbed by this outcry, Hayes saw himself "damned if he did and damned if he didn't." The "ultra–Republicans: opposed his liberal policy towards the "late Rebels," while "extremists of the other wing" opposed any honor bestowed upon the African American. The President consoled himself that he was "right in both cases."[10]

Of the remaining African Americans in the Congress in the late 1870s one of the most distinguished was Joseph Hayne Rainey of South Carolina. When the Enrollment Committee of the House of Representatives met in June, 1878, President Hayes found Rainey the only member who was sober. Even the clerks were drunk. It was through the efforts of Rainey that attention was secured to the pending Civil Service Bill involving appropriations of around eighteen million dollars.

African American politics and politicians were acutely interesting to Laura Towne, an older abolitionist. She thought well of the Civil War hero and ex-Congressman, Robert Smalls of South Carolina, but came to be disappointed in Frederick Douglass, not so much as a politician, but as a race leader. She felt that Douglass' apology to his old master—she does not say for what—was a "surrender."[11]

Robert Smalls won also the admiration of Sir George Campbell. A "robust" man and "very popular with the blacks," Smalls was not supported by any political organization, locally or nationally, though he ran on the Republican ticket. This lack of support did not trouble him, but he was disturbed by "the want of justices" in the South, where the whites had sworn never to convict a Klansman. Yet Smalls did not think conditions so unfavorable that African Americans should migrate to Liberia, as had been proposed by some others.

The African American state legislators in Virginia and South Carolina, principally from the Petersburg area and the Beaufort district were mostly adequate to their jobs, in Campbell's opinion. One of the South Carolinians was illiterate, but, as Robert Smalls explained, "a good Christian." A justice of the peace at Columbia was "a pure Negro and notable character," a "pleasant" person who held his own, Campbell understood, as a justice. Educated in the North, he had traveled to Europe and Africa. He owed his position to a Democratic governor, Wade Hampton, and praised Hampton as willing to appoint "black men when they really are educated and fit." Campbell praised a black postmaster in South Carolina "said to be the best specimen of his class in this part of the country; in fact . . . the only man appointed by the Republicans who is not hopelessly corrupt." He reminded Campbell of the more educated East Indians in Calcutta. Quite dissatisfied with the position of his race in the United States, this black man was a supporter of the "Liberia idea." In North Carolina a good opportunity to elect blacks to federal and state offices was weakened by divisions among the blacks, two of them running in some instances against a white man.[12]

The work and character of African American officeholders in South Carolina and Virginia were not matched in Louisiana, if the observations of George Sala and Ernst Von Hesse-Wartegg were correct. The blacks whom Sala saw in the Louisiana Senate and House in 1879–1880 were still "in an infantile condition, and great allowances must in fairness be made for [them]." "As regards to parliamentary procedure, the colored members are very often . . . superior to their white colleagues. . . . They are continually rising to what they term 'pints of order'." But "when they address themselves to set speech-making, they usually gabble a quantity of intolerable verbiage." Hesse-Wartegg was so amused to see African American lawmakers, once "the last, now . . . the first." "Sambo the black, sweaty . . . grinning slave . . . sits in the old, high position . . . of his former master!" Many had "just learned to read and write, when they became powerful." Dressed in dirty shirts and stained coats, the black legislators indulged in verbosity punctuated with "shallow, pompous phraseology and made a mockery of parliamentary procedure. Smoking, tobacco chewing, eating, and sleeping were common during the debates. Blacks had "established themselves excellently as workers in the field;" but "in the house of Representatives of a million people, whose capital city is an international city," they played" a right dismal role."

African Americans in Arkansas, especially around Little Rock, apparently shared to a considerable degree in political processes as late as 1879–1880, Hesse-Wartegg regretted, however, that the blacks in the "Back Country" were not being allowed any political participation.[13]

The African American editor, Thomas Fortune, knew of "municipalities in the South today, where capable colored men are regularly voted into responsible positions by the best white men of their cities." In Washington also he had visited the offices of ex-Senator Blanche K. Bruce of Mississippi, then the Register of the United States Treasury, and witnessed "marks of respect shown to . . . Bruce by the white ladies and gentlemen in his department." Fortune characterized Bruce as "a gentleman by instinct, a diplomat by nature, and a scholar," and implied that a good many whites would agree.[14]

Mifflin Gibbs, an African American who held a number of appointive political offices in Arkansas, was an ardent supporter of presidents Grant, Hayes and Arthur. He had been one of those who had seen, during Reconstruction, "the inutility of depending on physical force to extract justice and lawful methods from an unwilling constituency." Prior to the presidential campaign of 1884, he attended at New Orleans a meeting of leading black Republicans including T. Thomas Fortune of New York, N. W. Cuney and Emmett Scott of Texas, W. A. Pledger of Georgia, and P. B. S. Pinchback, former lieutenant governor and acting governor of Louisiana. Among matters discussed was "the charge that Negro delegations (and voters) were marketable commodity . . . ever at the beck of the highest purchaser in the political market." In Gibbs' view, which was apparently that of the majority of blacks, "such a sweeping charge is most injust."[15]

That the African American politician was on the side of honest government was also the view of a correspondent of the *New York Daily Tribune* in the South to cover the Republican State Convention at Columbia, South Carolina in 1890. E.H. Deas, African American delegate from Darlington, urged the Convention to support Judge A.C. Haskell of Columbia for governor. Deas' speech was the "sensation of the day." The convention, he believed, must seize the splendid opportunity to show the people that the Republicans of South Carolina "had some regard for decency and good government and some detestation of 'Tillmanism'." Deas "wanted decency or wanted nothing. All of the trouble in the State came from the rule of illiterate whites and he did not want that to go on any longer.[16]

NOTES

1. Bradley, *Other Days*, 392.

2. Towne, *Diary and Letters*, 289, 292–293. See also *Dictionary of American Biography*, XVII, 224–225 and *Biographical Directory of the American Congress* (Washington: GPO, 1961, P. 1611 for biographical sketches of Robert Smalls.

3. Campbell, *White and Black*, 282. *Ibid.*, 331, 341.

4. Hogan, *International Review*, VIII, 111–112.

5. Handlin, ed., *This Was America*, 339–343.

6. [Jonathan Baxter Harrison], "Studies in the South," *Atlantic Monthly*, L (July, 1882), 103, 110, 198. Harrison (1835–1907), journalist and author, was especially interested in American social character and life. For the Indian Rights Association he wrote *The Latest Studies on Indian Reservations* (1887).

7. Fortune, *Black and White*, 116, 139, 142–143.

8. Aubrey, *Fortnightly Review*, XLIII, 861.

9. Langdon, *Political Science Quarterly, VI, 34–42.*

10. Hayes, *Diary and Letters*, III, 427, 488.

11. Towne, *Diary and Letters*, 271; Campbell, *White and Black*, 341–342.

12. Campbell, *White and Black*, 299, 327, 330, 342.

13. Sala, *America Revisited*, 190; Hesse-Wartegg, *Mississippi-Fahrten*, 184–185.

14. Fortune, *Black and White*, 181–182.

15. Gibbs, *Shadow and Light*, 174, 185, 190–191, 210–211.

16. *New York Daily Tribune*, September 20, 1890, p. 5.

Epilogue

In this study the observers who toured the South and wrote about it were mainly novelists, theologians, politicians, diplomats, professional economists, historians, sociologists, lawyers, and journalists. There were, to be sure, outsiders of little means or education in the South during this period, but their impressions seldom appeared in print. Our picture of the South and southern blacks thus comes from a rather select class of travelers, a class which might be expected, moreover, to have formed preconceptions and prejudices about the region and its people before arriving there. A good many were sure to be strongly influenced by contemporary scholarship, especially as to race. Indeed, several had contributed to such scholarship themselves.

Preconceived notions help to explain how some of the visitors felt themselves equipped after only a short stay in the region to comment authoritatively upon the South and its problems. Such notions may also help to explain how intellectuals of international stature, such as Professor Hugo Münsterberg and Lord James Bryce, could arrive at unscientific and contradictory assessments, while other observers, such as Sir Harry Johnston and Ernest Von Hesse-Wartegg, seemed to stretch the truth in an opposite direction in conveying their admiration of many African Americans traits. Considering their social and economic status, and their preconceptions, what impressions of African American life do we get from travelers who roamed the South in the half century following the close of Reconstruction? How did their impressions differ from those of native southerners? What significance does it all have?

Ethnic studies dating as far back as the fifteenth century appear to have affected the outsiders' comments on the African American physical appearance. Observers in the nineteenth century, especially, looked at blacks and, in most cases, immediately saw a mental if not a physical inferior, a being closer to beast than to man. Later observers tended much more to refrain from comment on the African American physiology. The explanation lay probably in the fact that the presence of a few Africans in Europe and the circulation of earlier travel reports, had made the African and African American less of a novelty by 1929 than he had been in 1877; in a disposition to assume that physical and mental differences between black and white were simply to be taken for granted; and perhaps in an increasing awareness that advances in scientific inquiry were demonstrating the fallacy of the bestial theory. Outsiders continued to give especial attention to the mulatto and other "mixed" African Americans. While many were unwilling to grant mulattoes full status as human beings, almost all believed that the whiter the mulattoes the greater their intelligence and the more "beautiful" their physical features. This class of blacks was also considered the most successful in all walks of life. Even the few observers like Albert Bushnell Hart and Edward Atkinson who completely rejected the bestial theory of African physiology and all associated with it, appear to have overlooked or de-emphasized the obvious point that the success of the mulatto might better be attributed to the special privileges accorded them on account of their heritage than to their physiology.

The gravest challenge that had faced the newly emancipated blacks had been the need to make a living. The testimony of outsiders confirms that: the challenge was, up to a point, successfully met, for African American economic activities after 1877 belied antebellum fears or contentions that black labor must always be slave labor. But observers differed widely about how free post-Reconstruction black labor actually was and how greatly it furthered the southern economy. Since most blacks remained tillers of the soil, and many even continued to work under rules and authority reminiscent of slavery, some outsiders saw little difference between the African American's labor as slave and as free person, and thought that the greater the white supervision the more successful the black's labor. Such observers as Matthew Hammond reported the worst farming in the South as being done by independent African American farmers and saw them as retarding the South rather than advancing it. The large class of black tenant farmers and sharecroppers scarcely improved the profession, although most viewers agreed that it was the tenant system itself rather than the color of the tenants that impeded southern agriculture.

The urban blacks who came under the eyes of outsiders were working mainly as domestic and personal servants (waiters, domestics, porters, shoeshine boys, etc.), factory hands, or skilled craftsmen. The craftsmen were almost invariably adjudged competent and successful, but they were a small group. In the tobacco factories, African Americans worked well and sang even better. But in the mines, the flour mills, and particularly the textile mills, their performances were not, on the whole, satisfactory. The work of African American servants was represented as generally poor and marred by proneness to petty thievery. African Americans in other service occupations, such as waiters and bellhops, were not much better thought of as a rule, though the ever smiling Pullman porter was a delight to all except the Prince of Sweden.

The African American professional class, principally preachers and teachers might, in some instances, receive less pay than farmers or factory workers, but the travelers attributed to them a greater degree of independence. Only a few seem to have used this independence, such as it was, to agitate for civil rights. That blacks operated successful businesses, especially after 1900, and showed a disposition to acquire property, was attested to almost universally. A number of energetic blacks even managed to amass a small fortune and to deposit funds in African American owned savings institutions. But the general picture presented by the travelers shows that this class was extremely small. The masses of blacks remained in manual or menial occupations in which they were fair-to-good workers at best and made fair-to-poor wages which they were often accused of squandering on liquor and luxuries.

The political rights which the Fourteenth and Fifthteenth Amendments seemed to guarantee to African Americans were being lost even before 1877. Varying degrees of intimidation, ranging from economic pressure to violence of the ku-klux-klan type, drove scores of African Americans from the ballot box and, subsequently, from the legislative assemblies.

Prior to 1900, however, enough African Americans remained on the voter rolls and held offices to provide outsiders with opportunities to observe them as participants in political processes. In the main black legislators were looked upon disapprovingly, but other blacks were thought to perform creditably in such capacities as justice of the peace or county school superintendent. Some travelers judged that African Americans cast ballots wisely, others that they were ill-fitted, educationally, for the franchise, and blindly loyal to the Republican Party. By 1900 the bulk of southern blacks had been forced from office and from the polls. Visitors to the South who commented on the situation for the most part disapproved of disenfranchisement and rejected southern justifications of it.

Efforts to educate the southern black after the Civil War attracted wide attention. Many doubted whether such an "inferior race" could learn. Others thought black education feasible, and the Freedmen's Bureau and northern missionary groups plunged energetically into the task. Not only grammar schools but also normal schools, colleges, and universities were established for blacks at many places throughout the South, and visitors to the region were curious to see the work of these institutions. Their assessments of African American educability often depended, it would seem, not upon what they actually saw in the schools—most did not see enough to make a judgment—but rather upon preconceptions derived from contemporary ethnology and psychology, and upon what they were told by teachers and others. The general verdict was that African American capacity was not equal to that of whites, even though mulattoes and other "mixed bloods" might closely approach the white level.

African American teachers were considered to be not far removed, intellectually, from their pupils, although at least one observer granted that those trained in northern colleges tried to imitate the methods employed there, and others praised the efforts of teachers who had graduated from black schools. Few commented on the fact that many teachers in black schools of the nineteenth century were not northern whites, nor did they attempt to compare the relative success of whites and of blacks in training black pupils.

The physical plants and instructional equipment of elementary and secondary schools for southern blacks were judged to be uniformly poor, even poorer than those for rural whites. Academicians like Albert Bushnell Hart and Lance Jones viewed these factors as retarding learning, but others seemed to suggest that facilities and equipment made no particular difference because, as Abbie Brooks put it, ideas could not reach the heads of African Americans even if propelled with the force of bullets.

Unlike the lower schools, some black colleges, particularly Tuskegee and Hampton, possessed adequate plants and equipment. For this reason, and because of the work of such teachers as Carver at Tuskegee and Du Bois at Atlanta, some observers saw significant advances in African American higher education. Others, while approving what Hampton and Tuskegee did, felt that their efforts affected only a few, and that the majority of blacks remained largely ignorant owing to lack of ability to learn. William Wells Brown was almost alone in contending that it might be too early to make a reliable judgment of the results of African American education, and consequently of African American capacity.

The housing, dress, and health of southern blacks appeared deplorably had to almost all of the travelers. The more judicious saw a clear relationship between these things and the economic, political, and social oppression of African Americans, but a number of observers blamed the poor social condition of the rural masses on laziness, uncleanliness, proneness to disease, and "racial characteristics."

To the older blacks, particularly those born in bondage, almost all observers attributed a gentle manner involving "proper" deference to white people and even courtesy to members of their own race. This traditional "nigger" or "darky" was universally admired. It was mainly the younger class of blacks, those born since slavery, who lacked "proper" manners and were immoral or even criminal. Immorality or criminality among these blacks was attributed, in the outsiders' view, to a number of factors. Freedom had cast tremendous responsibilities upon "underdeveloped minds," and had paved the way for additional leisure time activities. The church, the African American's most important social institution, might well have been expected to provide some of those activities, but did not. Mary Allan-Olney and William Langdon seemed to suggest that enfranchisement and civil rights legislation were responsible in some instances for African American misbehavior. These gave the youth an idea that they were as "good as white folk." Inherent defects, such as a bestial or savage nature, were also conjured up as causes of immorality and crime, particularly sexual assaults and murder.

Contemporary ethnological and psychological studies, and the tales of southern whites, probably led outsiders to exaggerate immorality and crime among African Americans. With respect to crime, however, the disproportionate number of blacks in southern prisons would suggest either that the race furnished a disproportionate number of criminals or that convictions of blacks were disproportionately large. Perhaps both explanations were true. Such was the belief of scholars like Albert Bushnell Hart and Francis Kellor who took racial discrimination into account.

The black church in the South, to reiterate, was the most important of African American social institutions. It afforded the blacks an opportunity to exercise independent leadership, indeed to develop politically, when such privileges were denied them elsewhere. Most of all, the black church was a tool for survival—the one place where the blacks could preach, pray, sing or shout about their daily oppression and frustration. Black church buildings were reported to be generally poorly constructed, poorly lighted, poorly ventilated, and poorly heated; though occasionally, as at Farmville, Virginia, they might rival the better white churches. And one observer, William Wells Brown deplored the tendency to build fashionable churches from the earnings of servants and laborers.

Few outsiders approved of African American preaching and the emotional outbursts of the congregation. The preachers, largely illiterate, were accused of distorting theology in their simple, fiery sermons. The shouts of the congregations were deemed nothing short of fanatical, and even the revered Negro spirituals were criticized by a few as akin to savage mumblings only vaguely resembling music. The outsiders did recognize, however, that the church was by far the most important institution the southern blacks possessed, and that religion, whether practiced in a Baptist church or a voodoo house, thoroughly affected them.

A review of African American life in the post-emancipation South as reported by the outside observers suggests first that the masses of southern blacks did not make the social and economic progress that many had expected of them. Politically, their position deteriorated after Reconstruction. A great reduction in African American illiteracy by the early 1900s constituted one real and much applauded advance. Yet, despite the significant work of institutions like Atlanta, Fisk, Hampton and Tuskegee, at the time of the Great Depression not more than ten percent of African Americans had any college education, let alone the social and economic status associated with a college degree.[1]

It is instructive and important to notice the obvious similarities between the impressions of southern blacks recorded by outsiders and those generally attributed to southern whites. If the latter, at least in the late nineteenth and early twentieth centuries, viewed African Americans as bestial, so did many non-southern observers. If southern whites believed blacks to be generally lazy, fun-loving (whether in telling a story or performing a singing duet with a dog), religiously fanatical, ignorant, filthy and immoral, so did large numbers of outsiders.

How then do we evaluate these outsider views of southern blacks? First, it should be noted that beginning in slavery African Americans have not always shown themselves to whites, natives or outsiders, as they were. "I have one face for the white man to see—one face that I know is me." This two facedness, some psychologists and other scholars believe resulted from three centuries of slavery and oppression which so conditioned the African Americans' personality that, in a sense, they remained enslaved psychologically and physically even after emancipation. Thus whatever potential capacities for industriousness and intellect which they may have had were largely obscured. In the post-emancipation South, these blacks extended the Sambo image of slavery times into the Uncle Tom characters who acted and reacted as they were supposed to, or thought they were supposed to, in the presence of whites. An internalization of behavior designed to meet white expectations, some scholars argued, left the real personality often submerged, or, in some cases, lost.

Other studies, however, suggest that African Americans learned in bondage that survival required that they submerge their real selves and present a persona expected by and acceptable to whites. Thus their two facedness was a ruse to deceive whites and to exist, sometimes with favors for being "the good nigger." Yet there was always numbers of blacks who demonstrated assertiveness, ingenuity, and even rebellion. Particularly in the post-emancipation era independence, responsibility and achievement—agency—was shown throughout the South in parallel social and economic institutions that extended beyond the church.

While, observers whose eyes and ears were cloudy or closed by contemporary ethnology or racial prejudice could not hope to see the real southern blacks. Others also may have missed seeing them if they were subjected to the ruses African Americans often played on whites. Only those outsiders who went beyond prejudgments and who had some understanding of African American history and culture could observe and report judiciously upon the lives of African Americans in the post-emancipation South. Within the limitations inherent in eye-witness accounts, this latter group provides us with valuable insights into black life in this crucial period of United States history.

NOTE

1. *New York Times*, October 27, 1921, p. 1.

Bibliography

WORKS BY OUTSIDE OBSERVERS

Biographical sketches of authors, and in some cases comments upon their works, can be found at the point where they have first been used in this study.

Adams, Paul Auguste Marie. *Vues D'Amerique*. 8th ed. Paris: Societe D'Editions Litteraries et Artistiques, 1906.

Adams, Charles Francis. *Studies, Military and Diplomatic, 1775–1865*. New York: The Macmillan Co., 1911.

Adams, William Edwin. *Our American Cousins: Being Personal Impressions of the People and Institutions of the Untied States*. London: Walter Scott, 1883

Allen-Olney, Mary. *The New Virginians*. 2 Vols. Edinburgh: William Blackwood and Sons, 1880.

Archer, William. *Through Afro-America: An English Reading of the Race Problem*. London: Chapman and Hall, Ltd., 1910.

Atkinson, Edward. The Negro a Beast," *North American Review*, CLXXI (August, 1905), 202–215.

Aubert, Georges. *Les Nouvelles Ameriques*. Paris: Pres L'Odeon, 1901.

Aubrey, W. H. S. "Social Problems in America," *The Fortnightly Review*, XLIII (1888), 843–861.

Baker, Ray Stannard. *Following the Color Line: American Negro Citizenship in the Progressive Era*. New York: Harper and Row Publishers, 1964.

Barbour, George M. *Florida for Tourists, Invalids, and Settlers*. New York: D. Appleton and Co., 1882.

Barrows, Samuel J. "What the Southern Negro Is Doing for Himself," *Atlantic Monthly*, LXVII (June, 1891), 805–815.

Bassett, A. L. "Going to Housekeeping in North Carolina," *Lippincott's Magazine*, XXVIII (August, 1881), 206–208.

Baumgarten, Johannes, compl. *Amerika: Eine ethnographische Rundreise durch den Kontinent und die Antillen.* Stuttgart: Rieger'sche Verlagabuchhandlung, 1882.

Beadle, Charles, *A Trip to the United States in 1887.* London: J.S. Virture and Co., Ltd., 1887.

Beacher, Mrs. H. W. *Letters from Florida.* New York: D. Appleton and Co., 1879.

Bennett, John "Revival Sermon at Little St. John's," *Atlantic Monthly*, XCVIII (August, 1906), 256–268.

Bourget, Paul. *Outre-Mer: Impressions of America*, London: T. Fisher Unwin, 1895.

Bradley, Arthur Granville. *Sketches from Old Virginia.* London: Macmillan and Co., Ltd., 1897.

Bradley, Arthur Granville. *Other Days: Recollections of Rural England and Old Virginia, 1860–1880.* London: Constable and Co., Ltd., 1913.

Brooks, Abbie M. *Petals Plucked from Sunny Climes.* Nashville: Southern Methodist Publishing House, 1880.

Brown, William Wells. *My Southern Home: or, The South and its People.* Boston: A. G. Brown and Co., Publishers, 1880.

Bryce, James. *The American Commonwealth.* Vol. II: The Party System—Public opinion—Illustrations and Reflections—Social Institutions. Revised ed. New York: The Macmillan Co., 1918.

Butterworth, Hezekiah. *Zig-zag Journeys on the Mississippi: From Chicago to the Islands of Discovery.* Boston: Estes and Lauriat, 1892.

"A Camp Physician," pseud. "The Alabama Mining Camp," *Independent*, LXIII (October, 1907), 790–791.

Campbell, Sir George. *White and Black: The Outcome of a Visit to the United States.* New York: R. Worthington, 1879.

Campbell, John C. *The Southern Highlander and His Homeland.* New York: The Russell Sage Foundation, 1921.

Campbell, John Kerr. *Through the United States and Canada: Being a Record of Holiday Rambles and Experiences.* London: S. W. Partridge and Co., 1886.

Chesnutt, Charles W. *The Conjure Woman.* Boston: Houghton-Mifflin Co., 1899.

Chesterton, Gilbert K. *What I Saw in America.* New York: Dodd, Mead and Co., 1922.

Cipolla, Arnaldo. *Nortre America y los Nortre Americanos.* Translated into Spanish by Ramon Mondira. Santiago, Chile: Editorial Nascimento, 1929.

Clowes, W. Laird. *Black America: Study of the Ex-Slave and His Late Master.* London: Cassell and Co., Ltd., 1891.

Cooley, Rossa B. "Aunt Jane and Her People: The Real Negroes of the Sea Islands," *Outlook*, XC (October 1908), 424–432.

Cooley, Rossa B. "America's Sea Islands," *Outlook*, CXXXI (April, 1919), 739–740.

Cooley, Rossa B. *School Acres: An Adventure in Rural Education.* New Haven: Yale University Press, 1930.

Cowan, John F. *A New Invasion of the South, Being a Narrative of the expedition of the seventy-first infantry, National Guard through the Southern states to New Orleans.* New York: Board of Officers Seventy-first Infantry, 1881.

Cram, Mildred. *Old Seaport Towns of the South*. New York: Dodd, Mead and Co., 1917.

D'Estournelles De Constant, Paul H. B. *America and Her Problems*. New York: The Macmillan Co., 1915.

D'Haussonville, Gabriel Paul Le Vicomte. *A Travers, Les E'tats-Unis: Notes et Impressions*. Paris: Ancienne Maison Michel Le'vy Freres, 1883.

Du Bois, W. E. Burghardt. "The Negroes of Farmville, Virginia: A Social Study," *Bulletin*, U. S. Department of Labor, Vol., III, No. 14.

Du Bois, W. E. Burghardt. "A Negro Schoolmaster in the New South," *Atlantic Monthly*, LXXXIII (January, 1899), 99–104.

Du Bois, W. E. Burghardt. The Relation of the Negroes to the whites in the South," *Annals of the American Academy of Social and Political Science*, IVIII (July, 1901), 121–140.

Du Bois, W. E. Burghardt. "The Opening of the Library," *The Independent*, LIV (April, 1902), 809–810.

Du Bois, W. E. Burghardt. *Dusk of Dawn: An Essay Toward an Autobiography of Race Concept*. New York: Harcourt, Brace and World Co., 1940.

Du Bois, W. E. Burghardt. *Autobiography*. New York: International Publishers, 1968.

Dyke, Charles Bartlett. "Theology versus Thrift in the Black Belt," *Popular Science Monthly*, LX (February, 1902), 360–364.

Evarts, Arrah B. "Dementia Precox in the Colored Race," *Psychoanalytic Review*, I (1913–1914), 388–403.

Faris, John T. *Seeing the Sunny South*. Philadelphia: J. B. Lippincott and Co., 1921.

Field, Henry M. *Bright Skies and Dark Shadows*. New York: Charles Scribner's Sons, 1890.

"Find Them, 'Slogan of Dentists' Meet." *Pittsburgh Courier*, July 19, 1924.

Fortune, T. Thomas. *Black and White: Land, Labor, and Politics in the South*. New York: Fords, Howard, and Mulbert, 1884.

Freeman, Edward A. *Some Impressions of the United States*. London: Longmans, Green and Co., 1901.

Garvey, Amy Jacques. *Garvey and Garveyism*. Kingston, Jamaica: Amy J. Garvey, 1963.

George, W. L. *Hail Columbia: Random Impressions of a Conservative English Radical*. New York: Harper and Brothers Publishers, 1921.

Gibbs, Mifflin Winstar. *Shadow and Light: An Autobiography*. Washington, D. C.; The author, 1902.

Gordon, Jan and Cora Gordon. *On Wandering Wheels*, New York: Dodd, Mead and Co., 1928.

Hale, Louise Closser. *We Discover the Old Dominion*. New York: Dodd, Mead and Company, Publishers, 1916.

Hammond, M. B. "The Southern Farmer and the Cotton Question," *Political Science Quarterly*, XII (September, 1897), 450–475.

"Harding Says Negro Must Have Equality in Political Life." New York *Times*, October 27, 1921.

Hardy, Iza Duffus. *Oranges and Alligators: Sketches of South Florida Life*. London: Ward and Downey, 1886.

[Harrison, Jonathan Baxter]. "Studies in the South," *Atlantic Monthly*, L (July, 1882), 103, 110, 198.

Hart, Albert Busnell. *The Southern South*. New York: D. Appleton and Co., 1910.

Hazen, H. H. "Syphilis in the American Negro," *Journal of the American Medical Association*, LXIII (August, 1914), 463–466.

Hearn, Lafcadio. *Miscellanies*. Vol., I. London: William Heinemann, Ltd., 1924.

Hesse-Wartegg, Ernst Von. *Mississippi-Fahrten: Reisebilder aus dem amerikanischen sudden (1879–1880)*. Leipzig. Carl Reissner, 1881.

Hogan, Edward. "South Carolina To-day," *International Review*, VIII (February, 1880), 116.

Hole, Samuel Reynolds. *A Little Tour in America*. London: Edward Arnold, Publishers, 1895.

Holmes, George K. "The Peeps of the South," *Annals of the American Academy of Social and Political Science*, IV (1893), 265–274.

Howard, George Elliott. "The Social Cost of Southern Race Prejudice," *American Journal of Sociology*, XXII (March, 1917), 577–593.

Hungerford, Edward. *The Personality of American Cities*. n. p.: n. p., 1913.

Huret, Jules. *En Amerique: De New York A La Nouvelle-Orleans*. Neuvieme Mille. Paris: Bibliothe'que-Charpentier, 1904.

James, Henry. *The American Scene*. New York: Harper and Brothers, Publishers, 1907.

Johnson, Clifton. *Highways and Byways of the Mississippi Valley*. New York: The Macmillan Co., 1906.

Johnston, Sir Harry H. *The Negro in the New World*. London: Methuen and Co., Ltd., 1910.

Jones, Lance G. E. *The Jeanes Teacher in the United States, 1908–1933: An Account of Twenty-Five Years' Experience in the Supervision of Negro Rural Schools*. Chapel Hill: The University of North Carolina Press, 1937.

Jones, Thomas Jesse. *Educational Adaptations: Report of Ten Years' Work of the Phelps-Stokes Fund, 1910–1920*. New York: Phelps-Stokes Fund, 1920.

Jones, Thomas Jesse. "Tuberculosis Among the Negroes," *Transactions of the Second Annual Meeting of the National Association for the Study and Prevention of Tuberculosis* (Washington, D. C., 1906), II, 97–113.

Kellor, Frances A. "The Criminal Negro," *Arena*, XXV (January-June, 1901), 59–68, 190–197, 308–316, 419–428.

Kelsey, Carl. *The Negro Farmer*. Chicago: Jennings and Pye, 1903.

Langdon, William Chauncy. "The Case of the Negro," *Political Science Quarterly*, VI (March, 1891), 29–42.

Lombroso, Cesare. "Why Homicide Has Increased in the United States," Part I, *North American Review*, CLXV (December, 1897), 641–648.

Martí, José. *Martí on the U.S.A.* Selected and translated by Luis A. Baralt. Carbondale, Illinois: Southern Illinois University Press, 1966.

Muirhead, James Fullarton. *America The Land of Contrasts*. London: John Lane, 1898.

Münsterberg, Hugo. *The Americans*. Translated by Edwin Holt. New York: McClure, Phillips, and Co., 1904.

Nelson, Henry Loomis. "The Washington Negro," *Harper's Weekly* XXXVI (July, 1892), 654.

O'Rell, Max, and Jack Allyn. Jonathan *and His Continent: Rambles through American Society*. Translated by Madame Paul Blouet. New York: Cassell and Co., Ltd., 1889.

Pairpont, Alfred J. *Rambles in America, Past and Present*. Boston: Alfred Mudge and Con, Printers, 1891.

Prossinagg, Ernst. *Das Antlitz Amerikas: Drei Jahre diplomatischen Mission in der U.S.A.* Wien: Amaltheaverlag, 1931.

Ralph, Julian. "The Plantation Negro," *Harper's Weekly*, XXXVII (January, 1893), 38–39.

Ratliff, Beulah Amidon. "In The Delta: The Story of a Manhunt," *Atlantic Monthly*, CXXV (April, 1920), 456–460.

"Republicans Earnest in the South: Determined to Defeat Tillman in South Carolina." *New York Daily Tribune*, September 20, 1890.

Russell, William Howard. *Hesperothen: Notes from the West*. Vol., I. London: Sampson Low, Marston, Searle, and Rivington, 1882.

Sala, George Augustus. *America Revisited*. New York: I. K. Funk and Co., 1880.

Saunders, William. *Through the Light Continent*. 2nd ed. London: Cassell, Petter, and Galpin, 1879.

Shaler, N. S. "The Future of the Negro in the Southern States," *Popular Science Monthly*, LVII (June, 1900), 147–156.

Showers, Susan. Pseud. "A Weddin' and a Buryin' in the Black Belt," *New England Magazine*, XVIII (June, 1898), 478–483.

Siegfried, André. *America Comes of Age: A French Analysis*. Translated by H. H. and Doris Heming. New York: Harcourt, Brace and Co., 1927.

Smith, William. *A Yorkshireman's Trip to the United States and Canada*. London: Longmans, Green, and Co., 1892.

Soulsby, L. H. M. *The America I Saw in 1916–1918*. London: Longmans, Green and Co., 1920.

"Southern Schools Turn Out Over 1,000 Graduates," *Pittsburgh Courier*, June 7, 1924.

Spender, Harold, "A Glimpse at America," *Fortnightly Review*, CXIX (April, 1923), 576–578.

Street, Julian. *American Adventures*. New York: The Century Co., 1917.

Sutter, Archibald. *American Notes, 1881*. Edinburgh: William Blackwood and Cons, 1882.

Tannenbaum, Frank. *Darker Phases of the South*. New York: G. P. Putnam's Sons, 1924.

"The American Colour Problem." *London Times,* July 21, 1910.

Tissandier, Albert, *Six Mois aux E'tats-Unis*. Paris: Libraire de L'Acade'mie de Me'decine, 1886.

Tweedie, Mrs. Alec. *America as I Saw It*. New York: The Macmillan Co., 1913.

Ware, Edward T. "Higher Education of Negroes in the United States," *Annals of the American Academy of Social and Political Science*, XLIX (September, 1913, 209–218.

Warner, Charles Dudley. *On Horseback: A Tour in Virginia, North Carolina, and Tennessee*. Boston: Houghton, Mifflin and Co., 1889.

Willey, D. Allan. "The Negro and the Soil," *Arena*, XXIII (May, 1900), 553–560.

William, Prince of Sweden. "America from a Pullman Car," *Living Age*, CCCXXXV (November, 1928), 200–201.

Williams, Timothy Shaler. "The Sports of Negro Children," *Saint Nicholas*, XXX (September, 1903), 1004–1007.

Wyman, Lillie B. Chace. Colored Churches and Schools in the South," *New England Magazine*, III (February, 1891), 785–796.

Wyman, Lillie B. Chace. "Southern Study," *New England Magazine*, IV (June, 1891), 521–531.

Young, Thomas M. *The American Cotton Industry: A Study of Work and Workers, Contributed to the Manchaster Guradian*. London: Methuen and Co., 1902.

OTHER SOURCES

Boas, Franz, "Human Faculty as Determined by Race," American Association for the Advancement of Science, *Proceedings of Forty-Third Annual Meeting* (Brooklyn, New York, 1894), 311–327.

Brinton, Daniel G. *Races and Peoples: Lectures on the Science of Ethnography*. New York: N.D.C. Hodges, Publishers, 1890.

Calloway, Thomas J. "The President at Atlanta and Tuskegee," *Harper's Weekly*, XLII (December, 1898), 1299–1300.

Ferguson, George Oscar. "The Psychology of the Negro: An Experimental Study," *Archives of Psychology*, V (1916), 8.

Galton, Grancis. "The Comparative Worth of Different Races," *Library of the World' Best Literature*, Vo., XV (ed.) Charles Dudley Warner. New York: J.A. Hull and Co., 1896, pp. 6177–6184.

Handlin, Oscar (ed.). *This Was America*. Cambridge: Harvard University Press, 1949.

Holland, Rupert Sargent (ed.). Letters *and Diary of Laura M. Towne: Written From the Sea Islands of South Carolina, 1862–1884*. Cambridge, Mass.: Riverside Press, 1912. For a biographical sketch of Mrs. Towne, see above, p. 40, n. 3.

LeBon, Gustave. *The Psychology of Peoples*. 2nd ed. Ne York: G.E. Stechert and Co., 1912.

Tinker, Edward Larocque. *Lafcadio Hearn's American Days*. New York: Dodd, Mead and Co., 1925.

U.S. Bureau of the Census. *Negro Population*, 1790–1915. Washington: Government Printing Office, 1918.

U.S. Bureau of the Census. *Negroes in the United States*, 1920–1932. Washington: Government Printing Office.

Williams, Charles Richard (ed.). *Diary and Letters of Rutherford Birchard Hayes, Nineteenth President of the United States*, Vol. III, Columbus, Ohio: The Ohio State Archaeological and Historical Society, 1924.

SECONDARY WORKS

Anna T. Jeanes Foundation. *The Negro Rural School Fund*. New York: The Anna T. Jeanes Foundation, 1907.

Clark, Thomas D. (ed.). *Travels in the New South, a Bibliography*. 2 vols. Norman, Oklahoma: The University of Oklahoma Press, 1962. Indispensable for travel books on the South.

Colliers Encyclopedia. Vols. II an IX. New York: Crowell-Collier Publishing Co., 1963.

Dictionary of American Biography. 20 vols. New York: Charles Scribner, 1936.

Dictionary of National Biography, 22 vols.; 5 Supplements. London: Smith, Elder and Co.; Oxford University Press, 1908–1949.

Dictionary of American Scholars, 1942. Lancaster, Pennsylvania: The Science Press Printing Co., 1942.

Dollard, John, *Caste and Class in Southern Town*. 3rd ed. New York: Alfred A. Knopf, 1964.

Du Bois, W. E. B., ed., *The Negro Church*. Lanham, MD: Rowman and Littlefield, (originally published 1903) 2003

Dutcher, G.M., et al. (eds.). *A Guide to Historical Literature*. New York: The Macmillan Co., 1931.

Encyclopedia Americana. 25 vols. New York: Encyclopedia Americana Corporation, 1963.

Encyclopedia Brittanica, 24 vols. Chicago: William Benton Publishers, 1965.

Frazier, E. Franklin. *The Negro Family in the United States*. Chicago: The University of Chicago Press, 1939.

Frazier, E. Franklin. *The Negro Family in the United States*. 2nd. ed. New York: Macmillan, 1957.

Frazier, E. Franklin. *The Negro Church in America*. New York: Schocken Books, 1963.

Furneaux, Robert. *The First War Correspondent, William Howard Russell of the Times*. 2nd. ed. London: Cassell and Co., Ltd., 1945.

Greene, John C. *The Death of Adam: Evolution and Its Impact on Western Thought*. New York: Mentor Books, 1961.

Haller, Mark Hughlin. *American Eugenics: Heredity and Social Thought*, 1870–1930. Ann Arbor: University Microfilms, Inc., 1957.

Haller, Mark Hughlin. *Eugenics*. New Brunswick: Rutgers University Press, 1963.

Harper's Encyclopedia of United States History. 4 vols. New York: Harper and Brothers, 1901–1915.

Hornsby, Alton, Jr., ed., *In the Cage: Eyewitness Accounts of the Freed Negroes in Southern Society, 1877–1929*. Chicago: Quadrangle, 1971.

Hornsby, Alton, Jr., ed., *A Companion to African American History*. Malden, MA: Blackwell, 2005, 2008.

Lincoln, C. Eric and Lawrence H. Mamiya. *The Black Church in the African American Experience*. Durham, NC: Duke University Press, 1990. Please also note their extensive bibliography.

Logan, Rayford W. *The Negro in American Life and Thought: The Nadir, 1877–1901*. New York: The Dial Press, Inc., 1954.

Mays, Benjamin E. and Joseph Nicholson. *The Negro's Church*. New York: Russell and Russell, reissue 1969.

National Cyclopedia of American Biography. 8 vols. New York: James T. White and Co., 1930.

Qui Etes-Vours? 1908. Paris: Libraire ch. Delagrave, 1908.

Robert, Joseph Clark. *The Tobacco Kingdom: Plantation, Market, and Factory in Virginia and North Carolina, 1800–1860*. 1937; reprint, Gloucester, Mass.: Peter Smith, 1965.

Rose, Willie Lee. *Rehearsal for Reconstruction: The Port Royal Experiment*. Indianapolis: Bobbs-Merrill, 1964.

Rudwick, Elliott M. *W.E.B. DuBois: A Study in Minority Group Leadership*. Philadelphia: University of Pennsylvania Press, 1959.

Silberman, Charles E. *Crisis in Black and White*. New York: Random House, 1964.

The National Cyclopedia of the Colored Race. Montgomery, Alabama: National Publishing Co., Inc., 1919.

Tilley, Nannie May. *The Bright-Tobacco Industry, 1860–1929*. Chapel Hill: The University of North Carolina Press, 1948.

Tindall, George B. *The Emergence of the New South, 1913–1945*. Baton Rouge: The Louisiana State University Press, 1967.

Wer ist's? Leipzig: H.A. Ludwig Degener, 1905, 1908.

Who Was Who in America, Historical Volume, Chicago: A.W. Marquis, Co., 1963.

Who Was Who in America. 2 vols. Chicago: A.N. Marquis Co., 1966.

Who's Who. Vols. II-IV. London: A. and C. Black, 1902–1904.

Who's Who in America. Vols. I-XIV. Chicago: A.N. Marquis Co., 1905–1920.

Who's Who in American Medicine, 1925. New York: Who's Who Publications, Inc., 1925.

Williamson, Joel. *After Slavery: The Negro in South Carolina During Reconstruction, 1861–1877*. Chapel Hill: The University of North Carolina Press, 1965.

Index

Adams, Charles, 126
African Americans: alleged traits of,
    5–7, 8n11; beauty perceived by, 13;
    cheerfulness of, 119–20; Chinese
    servants compared with, 29; as
    distinct race, 14; divisions among,
    113; geographic distribution of, 44;
    in government, 139–40, 142–44;
    hidden selves of, 152; nature
    experienced by, 58; plantations
    owned by, 35, 37; progress expected
    of, 151–52; Republican Party
    supported by, 139–41; wealthy, 42;
    weapons carried by, 124, 131; white
    servants compared with, 30
agriculture, southern, 36–37; economic
    structure of, 19; education on, 37;
    factory and urban work vs., 23; in
    Progressive Era, 36; on Sea Islands,
    19–20, 44
alcohol, 96; immoral behavior caused
    by, 128–29, 134; at market day, 99;
    stereotypes related to, 93
Allan-Olney, Mary, 10, 13, 29, 54, 58,
    70, 102, 119, 123
American Indian, 12, 127
American Negro Religion, 52
appearance, physical: 19 century vs.
    20th century descriptions of, 15;

beauty in, 11–13; "bestial," 12–13;
    Du Bois' perception of, 13–14;
    ethnic studies' impact on perception
    of, 147; hair in, 12; health and
    clothing in, 150; novelty of, 15, 148;
    skin color in, 10–11
Archer, William, 80
Arkansas, politics in, 144
Atlanta, Georgia, wealthy African
    Americans in, 42
Atlanta Compromise address, 3, 76
Atlanta University, 27, 74–75;
    intellectual culture of, 80–81; white
    president of, 76

bank, 34
baptism, 58, 66
Baptist faith, 52
barber, 33
Barbour, George, 12, 26, 29, 121, 124
Barrows, Samuel, 27, 31, 94
baseball, diversity in, 99
basket name, 64
Bassett, A.L., 12, 29
beauty: African-Americans' perception
    of, 13; whites' perception of, 11–13
Bennett, John, 61–62
"Black Belt": churches in, 55; housing
    in, 93; schools in, 73

About The Author

Alton Hornsby, Jr. is the Fuller E. Callaway Professor of History at Morehouse College. He has been editor of *the Journal of Negro History* (1976–2001) and *the Papers of John and Lugenia Burns Hope.* His latest works include *A Short History of Black Atlanta, A Companion to African American History* (editor-in-chief), and *Black Power in Dixie: A Political History of African Americans in Atlanta*

www.ingramcontent.com/pod-product-compliance
Lightning Source LLC
Chambersburg PA
CBHW021818270326
41932CB00007B/244